ALL
ABOUT
REPAIRING
SMALL
APPLIANCES

ALL ABOUT REPAIRING SMALL APPLIANCES

by Michael Squeglia

Illustrated by Carl Bryant

HAWTHORN BOOKS, INC.
W. Clement Stone, Publisher
New York

It's nice, of course, to have a handyman
around the house, but it seems that he's
never there when the steam iron won't
steam or the toaster won't toast. So this
book is written for and dedicated to the
housewife who needs a repair manual on
hand for those all too many fix-it jobs—
especially those that occur among the
vast array of small electrical appliances.

Edited by the Staff of Vocational Horizons, Inc.

ALL ABOUT REPAIRING SMALL APPLIANCES

Library of Congress Catalog Card Number: 72-80942
ISBN: 0-8015-0156-3

4 5 6 7 8 9 10

Contents

LADY'S ELECTRIC SHAVERS

Section II: General Repair Procedures

PREFACE

Modern technology has surrounded the American household with a vast assortment of electrical appliances. These are the tools that today's men and women have grown to depend upon to help in performance of around-the-house chores. They have become expert in their use, but they too frequently lack instruction in what to do when any of these tools malfunctions.

The individual's patience and manual dexterity will aid in the effective use of this book. It deals directly with the most frequently encountered problems in small electrical appliances. It provides the practical "know-how" needed to restore operation to and to prolong the useful life of appliances, in easy-to-follow, step-by-step instructions. Each repair can mean substantial dollar savings. Equally important, this book will serve as a guide for determining when the services of professional repair technicans are required.

Line drawings are used abundantly throughout the book because they are usually better visual aids than photographs. The appliances used as models for illustrations were chosen because they incorporate the design features most often found in popular brands.

The repair procedures outlined in each *problem solver* are arranged in simple, short steps. Each *problem solver* should be read through completely to establish continuity before beginning adjustment or repair. Naturally, any appliance being worked on should be unplugged. Extreme care has been exercised to make sure that the person attempting repairs will encounter no danger of injury. All repairs are simple and easily made. Any complex repairs or those involving any possible risk clearly must be referred to the attention of a qualified repair technician.

In many instances the author suggests the use of common household tools and materials to accomplish the adjustment or repair of an appliance. A glossary is included to introduce and illustrate less familiar tools.

ALL
ABOUT
REPAIRING
SMALL
APPLIANCES

Section I

Repair Problems and
Their Solutions

-b
98

Problem Solver #1

APPLIANCE: Clothes Irons (Steam and Regular)

PROBLEM: Iron does not slide smoothly over cloth.

EXPLANATION: There are two conditions that most often cause an iron to snag and pull. One is caused by foreign material that has burned and hardened on the sole plate of the iron. The second is caused by small burrs (often difficult to see or feel) that have been scratched out of the soft aluminum sole plate.

TOOLS AND MATERIALS NEEDED:

   (a) a small block of wood or small empty plastic box

   (b) a piece of fine grit sandpaper or emery cloth

   (c) fine-texture steel wool pad or an abrasive type plastic cleaning pad

   (d) scouring cleanser powder (used for sinks, etc.)

SOLUTION: 1. Wrap sandpaper (or emery cloth) around the sanding block (wood or plastic box). (*Figure 1*)

   2. Hold iron in upright position and rub sanding block against the sole plate with a straight up and down movement. Keep the sanding block flat against the sole plate, and use only moderate pressure. (*Figure 2*)

   3. Continue to sand the sole plate until all burned-on residue and deep scratches have been removed. Be sure not to overlook any nicks along the edges of the sole plate.

   NOTE: Use a fresh piece of sandpaper as often as necessary.

   4. Sanding is properly completed when the sole plate takes on an even, dull appearance.

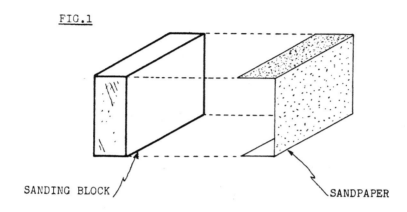

FIG.1

SANDING BLOCK

SANDPAPER

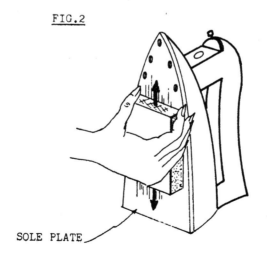

FIG.2

SOLE PLATE

5. Form steel wool into a pad and place it under the sanding block. (*Figure 3*)

6. Rub the steel wool in an up and down motion against the sole plate until a fine satin finish is obtained.

7. Thoroughly dampen a soft piece of cloth with water and fold it to form a pad the size of the sanding block and about ½ inch in thickness. Place the pad on the sanding block.

8. Sprinkle scouring cleanser on the damp pad and allow cleanser to absorb some of the moisture from the pad to form a thick paste.

9. Polish the sole plate with the cleanser paste until it takes on a bright sheen.

   CAUTION: If you are working on a steam iron, remove any cleanser paste that may have accumulated in the steam ports of the sole plate with the end of a paper clip or hairpin. (*Figure 4*)

10. Wipe the sole plate with a clean damp cloth to remove the scouring cleanser.

    CAUTION: To avoid damaging the sole plate of the iron, never allow sharp objects or hard, rough surfaces to come in contact with the sole plate. Always rest and store your iron on its heel.

<u>FIG.3</u>

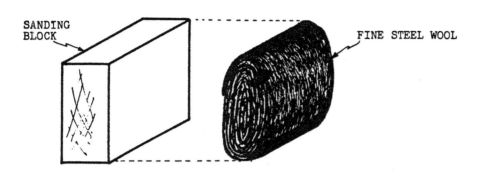

SANDING
BLOCK

FINE STEEL WOOL

<u>FIG.4</u>

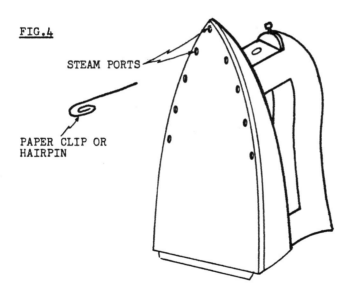

STEAM PORTS

PAPER CLIP OR
HAIRPIN

Problem Solver #2

APPLIANCE: Clothes Irons (Steam Only)

PROBLEM: Not enough steam comes from the iron.

EXPLANATION: Minerals contained in water form hard deposits in the steam chamber and steam ports and can clog the steam passages.

TOOLS AND MATERIALS NEEDED:

(a) a paper clip or hairpin

(b) liquid measuring cup

(c) ½ cup of white vinegar

SOLUTION: 1. Clean the steam ports located in the sole plate with a paper clip or a hairpin bent into shape as illustrated. (*Figure 1*) Wiggle paper clip or hairpin in the steam ports to loosen hardened mineral deposits.

2. Mix a cleaning solution consisting of ½ cup of white vinegar with ½ cup of water. Fill the iron with the vinegar-water solution. (*Figure 2*)

3. Set the fabric indicator dial to the "steam" setting and allow all of the cleaning solution to steam through the iron. Repeat cleaning with vinegar solution if necessary. (*Figure 3*)

NOTE: Iron may be used immediately after cleaning.

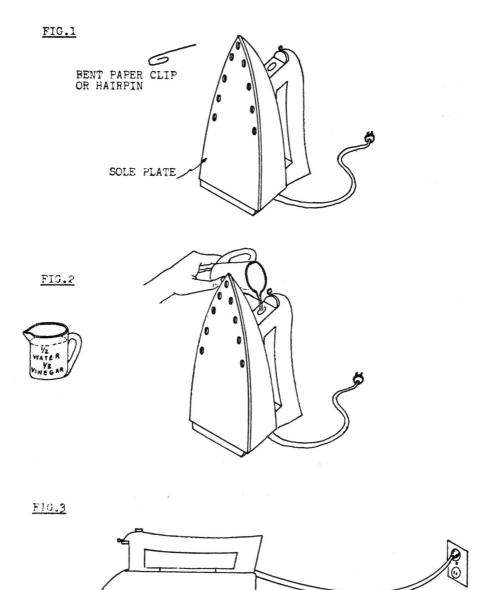

FIG.1

BENT PAPER CLIP
OR HAIRPIN

SOLE PLATE

FIG.2

½ WATER ½ VINEGAR

FIG.3

ALL STEAM PORTS OPEN

Problem Solver #3

APPLIANCE: Clothes Irons (Steam Only)

PROBLEM: Water and steam sputters out of steam ports during operation.

EXPLANATION: This condition is caused by an overheated iron. There are two reasons why an iron becomes overheated. The first may simply be an incorrect dial setting. The second may be caused when the thermostat, which automatically controls the temperature of the iron, does not function correctly.

TOOLS AND MATERIALS NEEDED:

(a) a small screwdriver (sewing machine type)

(b) a paper clip

(c) a pair of pliers

SOLUTION: 1. Make certain fabric indicator dial is set correctly to "steam" position.

2. If water and steam continue to sputter from steam ports with fabric dial correctly set to steam, the thermostat must be checked and adjusted.

CAUTION: Remove plug from electric outlet and allow iron to cool to room temperature before proceeding.

SPECIAL NOTE: *Figures 1 and 2* illustrate two of the more widely used types of steam irons. Moreover, they are designed so that the thermostat adjustment screw can be reached easily. The design of other types of irons requires a more complicated disassembly procedure and should therefore be taken to a qualified appliance repair shop for service.

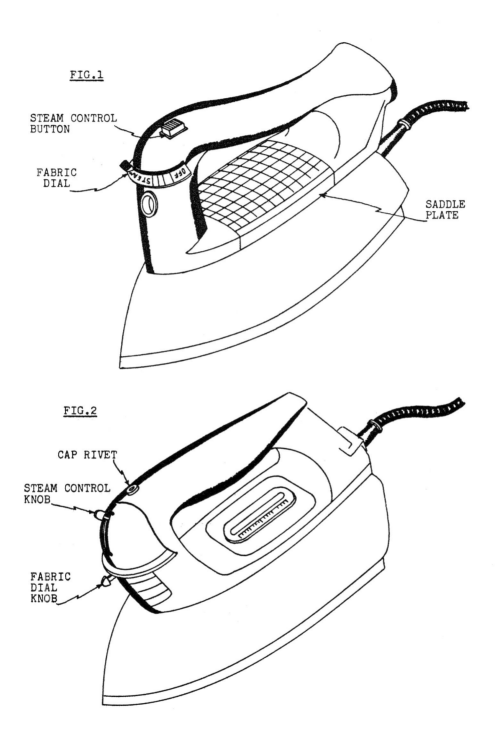

FIG.1

STEAM CONTROL
BUTTON

FABRIC
DIAL

SADDLE
PLATE

OFF

STEAM

FIG.2

CAP RIVET

STEAM CONTROL
KNOB

FABRIC
DIAL
KNOB

3. To reach the thermostat adjustment screw for the type of iron shown in *Figure 1,* gently pry the metal saddle plate off by grasping and lifting both sides with the fingertips. A stubborn saddle plate may be removed by carefully prying one side up with the blade of a screwdriver. (*Figure 3*)

   CAUTION: When using a screwdriver, take care not to pry against the plastic portion of the iron handle located directly below the saddle plate.

4. With saddle plate removed, locate the slotted thermostat adjustment screw. (*Figure 4*)

5. Insert screwdriver blade into the thermostat adjustment screw slot and give the adjustment screw a quarter turn in a clockwise direction.

6. Retest the steam operation of the iron. If the sputtering condition has been improved but some sputtering still exists, give the adjustment screw an additional quarter turn clockwise. Repeat the adjustment once more if necessary.

   NOTE: If adjustment does not correct the sputtering condition, it means that the thermostat is defective and must, therefore, be replaced. Refer such repairs to a qualified appliance service shop.

7. For the final test, shut the iron off and allow it to cool to room temperature. When the iron has thoroughly cooled, set the fabric dial to the lowest heat position (usually "synthetics"). Plug iron into wall receptacle. If iron heats up, adjustment is complete, and the malfunction has been corrected. However, if iron does *not* heat on lowest setting, it means that the thermostat did not respond to the adjustment and is, therefore, defective. Such a defective thermostat must be replaced.

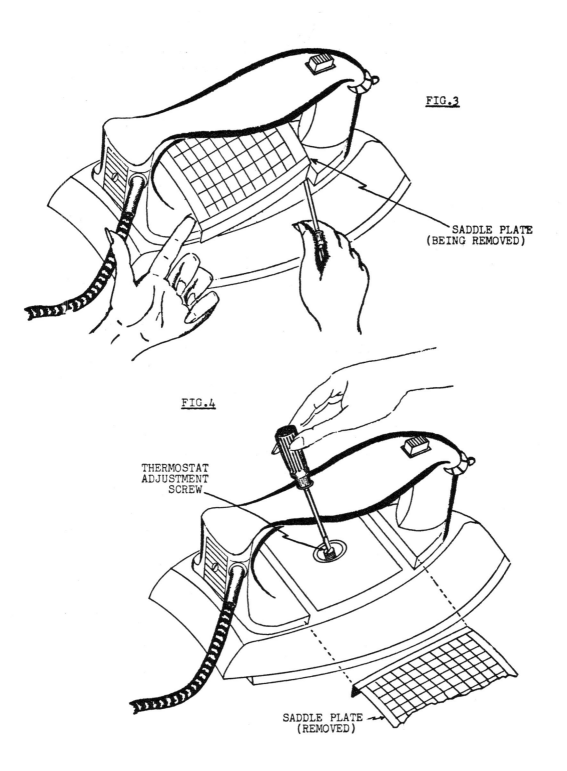

FIG.3

SADDLE PLATE
(BEING REMOVED)

FIG.4

THERMOSTAT
ADJUSTMENT
SCREW

SADDLE PLATE
(REMOVED)

8. To reach the thermostat adjustment screw for the type of iron shown in *Figure 2*, bend a paper clip as shown in *Figure 5*. Place the tip of the paper clip in the center of the plastic cap rivet located on the iron handle and press firmly down until the rivet is pushed clear through into the handle.

9. Grasp the front cap of the iron handle and pull it forward. Disconnect the steam control lever from the top of the valve shaft and remove the front cap. (*Figure 6*)

   CAUTION: Retrieve the cap rivet, which will be found in a little well directly below its position in the handle. Set it aside carefully so that it may be reinstalled after the thermostat adjustment has been completed.

10. Unscrew the valve nut (turn counter-clockwise) with pliers and remove it. Lift off the washer and the thermostat control cam. (*Figure 6*)

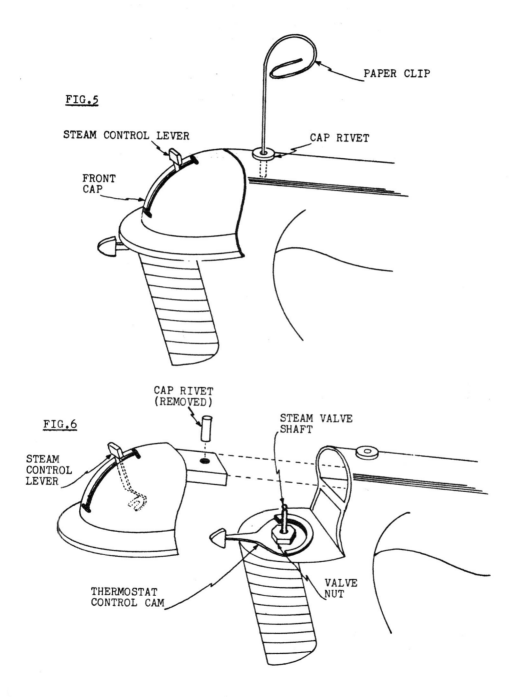

FIG.5

STEAM CONTROL LEVER

PAPER CLIP

CAP RIVET

FRONT
CAP

FIG.6

CAP RIVET
(REMOVED)

STEAM VALVE
SHAFT

STEAM
CONTROL
LEVER

THERMOSTAT
CONTROL CAM

VALVE
NUT

11. Locate the thermostat adjustment nut. (*Figure 7*) Grasp the adjustment nut with fingers and give it a half turn in a clockwise direction. If nut is stubborn, grasp nut with pliers to turn it. Use only moderate pressure.

12. Replace the thermostat control cam, washer, and valve nut. Tighten valve nut securely with pliers. (*Figure 6*) Connect the steam control lever to the top of the valve shaft and slide the front cap into place. Install the cam rivet. Press rivet firmly into place with the flat side of the pliers.

13. Retest the steam operation of the iron. Repeat thermostat adjustments if necessary (half clockwise turns at a time) until iron steams properly. If adjustments fail to correct sputtering condition, thermostat is defective and should be replaced by a qualified appliance technician.

14. For final test, allow iron to cool to room temperature. Then set fabric dial to the lowest heat position (synthetics). Plug the iron into the wall receptacle. If iron heats up, adjustment is complete and condition has been corrected. If, however, the iron does *not* heat on the lowest setting, it means that the thermostat did not respond to the adjustment and is, therefore, defective and must be replaced.

<u>FIG.7</u>   EXPLODED VIEW

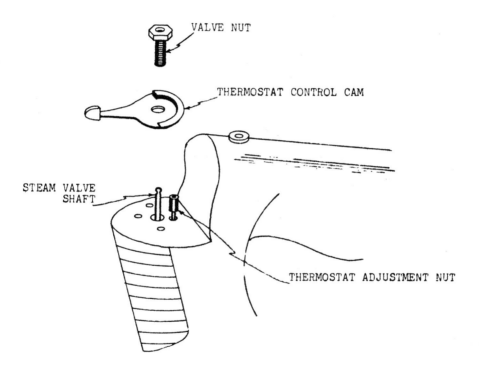

VALVE NUT

THERMOSTAT CONTROL CAM

STEAM VALVE
SHAFT

THERMOSTAT ADJUSTMENT NUT

Problem Solver #4

APPLIANCE: Clothes Irons (Steam and Regular)

PROBLEM: Iron does not heat.

EXPLANATION: Heat is produced in an iron by the effect of an electric current passing through an internal heating element wire. Anything that prevents the electric current from reaching the heating element wire or from passing completely through it will prevent the iron from heating. Most often, the flow of electricity is stopped either when a fuse is blown or when the wires in the iron line cord break due to the flexing, bending, and tugging strain that occurs during normal use.

TOOLS AND MATERIALS NEEDED:

(a) asbestos- and cloth-covered line cord (can be purchased completely assembled with plug and terminal connectors)

(b) a small screwdriver (sewing machine type)

(c) a pair of pliers

SOLUTION:
1. Make certain that the wall outlet has electric power. Plug a lamp or other appliance known to be in good working order into the outlet used for the iron. If lamp or other appliance also fails to operate, it can be assumed that a fuse has blown or that a circuit breaker has tripped "off," thus preventing electric power from reaching the wall outlet, or that the wall receptacle itself is faulty. Refer to Section II, General Repair Procedures, Fuses and Circuit Breakers, for further information about this condition. If, however, the lamp or other appliances operates, it means that the problem is in the iron.

2. Examine the line cord plug. Check the plug prongs for looseness. Test the condition of the line cord wires going into the plug by tugging firmly on the plug against the line cord. (*Figure 1*) If the plug prongs wiggle freely or if the plug seems to part from the line cord when pulled, the plug should be replaced. See Section II, General Repair Procedures, Plugs, for further information.

FIG.1

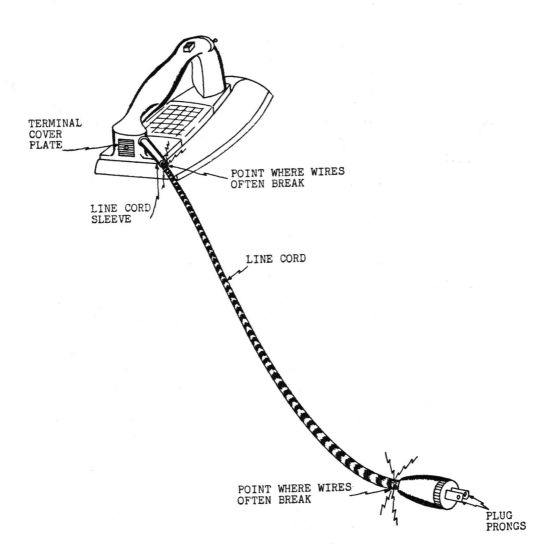

TERMINAL
COVER
PLATE

POINT WHERE WIRES
OFTEN BREAK

LINE CORD
SLEEVE

LINE CORD

POINT WHERE WIRES
OFTEN BREAK

PLUG
PRONGS

SPECIAL NOTE: While it is possible for wires to break anywhere along the length of the line cord, they are most apt to break at points where sharp bending occurs during use. These points are located where the line cord enters the plug and again where it enters the line cord sleeve. When you are uncertain about breakage or whenever the line cord shows outward signs of wear, such as fraying, replace the entire line cord as outlined in the steps that follow.

CAUTION: Remove line cord from wall outlet before working on iron.

3. Remove the terminal cover plate screw by turning it counter-clockwise with a small screwdriver. (*Figure 2*)

4. Insert the flat tip of the screwdriver along the edge of the terminal cover plate and *gently* pry it out. (*Figure 3*)

5. Examine the line cord wires going to the terminal posts. (*Figure 3*) If wires are attached with push-on connectors, simply grasp each connector with fingertips and pull upwards with a slight side-to-side motion and remove them. (*Figure 3*)

CAUTION: Use moderate pressure to avoid bending or otherwise damaging the terminal posts.

6. If wires are attached with terminal screws, loosen the two screws by giving them two full turns counter-clockwise. (*Figure 4*)

7. Remove the line cord wire ends.

NOTE AND CAUTION: If the line cord wire ends under the screws have U-shaped connectors, the wire ends will slip out from behind the terminal screws. If the line cord wires use circular eyelets (*Figure 4*) as connectors, the two terminal screws must be removed completely in order to disconnect the line cord wires. Take care not to drop the terminal screws into the iron if it becomes necessary to remove them. Refer to Section II, General Repair Procedures, Terminal and Wire Connectors, for further information.

8. Remove the line cord by prying the cord sleeve out of the recess in the handle. (*Figure 4*)

FIG.2

TERMINAL COVER
PLATE

TERMINAL
COVER
PLATE SCREW

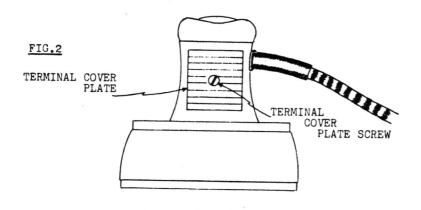

FIG.3

TERMINAL
COVER PLATE
SCREW

HANDLE RECESS

TERMINAL COVER
PLATE (REMOVED)

PUSH-ON
CONNECTORS

FIG.4

CORD SLEEVE

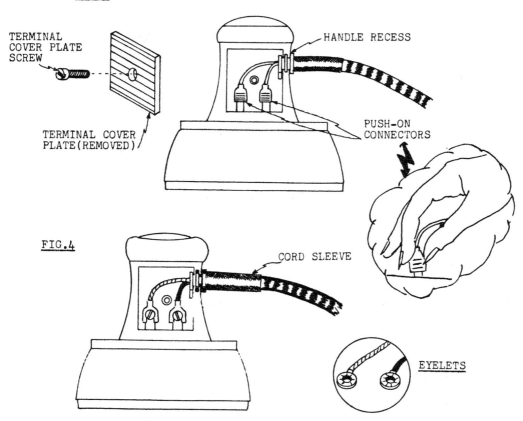

EYELETS

9. Cut the line cord as close to the metal cord stop as possible with a pair of heavy poultry or sewing shears and remove the cord stop. (*Figure 5*)

10. Slide the cord sleeve off the line cord.

    NOTE: Both the cord stop and cord sleeve must be reinstalled on the new replacement line cord.

11. Slip the terminal ends of the new line cord through the cord sleeve.

12. Widen the metal cord stop with a pair of pliers. Place it on the line cord (about ¾ of an inch above the wire ends). Clamp the cord stop securely to the line cord by squeezing it with a pair of pliers. (*Figure 6*)

13. Slide cord sleeve firmly against the cord stop.

14. Place cord sleeve into recess in handle and connect wire ends to terminal posts. Position wires so that no strain is placed on terminal posts and make certain that terminal posts *do not* touch each other.

15. Replace the terminal cover plate.

    SPECIAL NOTE: To extend the life of a line cord, never wrap the line cord around the handle of an iron for storage. Coil it loosely beside the iron.

FIG.5

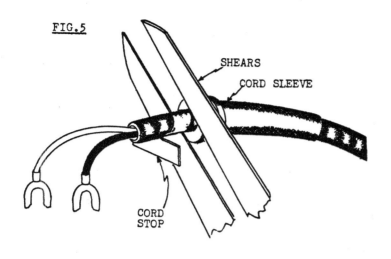

SHEARS

CORD SLEEVE

CORD
STOP

FIG.6

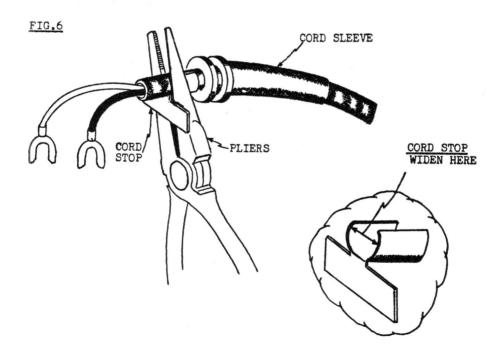

CORD SLEEVE

CORD
STOP

PLIERS

CORD STOP
WIDEN HERE

Problem Solver #5

APPLIANCE: Clothes Irons (Steam and Spray Type)

PROBLEM: **Iron does not spray water.**

EXPLANATION: There are two methods most commonly used by manufacturers to produce the water spray action in steam
and spray irons. One type operates as a simple hand
pump (similar to the hand pumps used to dispense
hand lotion, perfume, and cleaners from bottles). The
second type employs the pressure created by its own
steam system to produce the water spray action. The
hand pump can be identified in two ways:

A.   A single spray of water is produced when the
spray button is depressed and ceases when the
button reaches the bottom of its stroke.

B.   The small orifice in the spray nozzle that emits the
water spray is uncovered and visible.

The pressure spray iron is identified by the continuous
spray of water (and steam) emitted when the spray
button is held down. It is further identified by a sliding
cap that moves up and allows water to be sprayed from
the spray nozzle orifice when the spray button is depressed. It moves down to cover and close the water
spray orifice when the spray button is released.

The size of the water spray orifice in both spray systems
is extremely small. Therefore, when either kind fails
to produce a water spray, the orifice must be checked
for and cleared of any foreign particles that may have
clogged it.

TOOLS AND MATERIALS NEEDED:

(a) a single fine bristle (natural or nylon), at least
¾ of an inch long, removed from a clothes brush or
hairbrush

(b) a pair of eyebrow tweezers

SOLUTION: 1. Locate and identify the water spray orifice. (*Figures 1 and 2*)

FIG.1

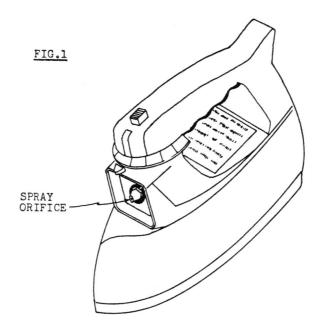

SPRAY
ORIFICE

FIG.2

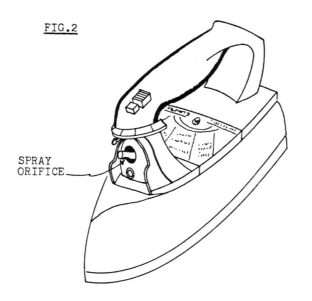

SPRAY
ORIFICE

2. To clear exposed orifice (*Figure 3*) hold brush bristle at one end with tweezers and insert other bristle end into orifice opening. Make certain that the thickness of the bristle is not larger than the orifice opening and that the bristle is stiff enough to exert pressure upon any foreign particle that may be stuck in the orifice. Bristle must pass through orifice opening.

3. To clear capped orifice (used in pressure systems), depress the spray button. This will raise the cap to expose the orifice. (*Figure 4*)

   NOTE: If cap does not rise to expose the orifice, the spray mechanism has a serious mechanical defect, and the iron should be taken to a qualified appliance repair shop.

4. Hold the spray button in the depressed position and insert the bristle end through the orifice.

5. Retest spray operation of iron. If spray operation has not been restored, iron should be taken to a qualified appliance service shop for further testing and repair.

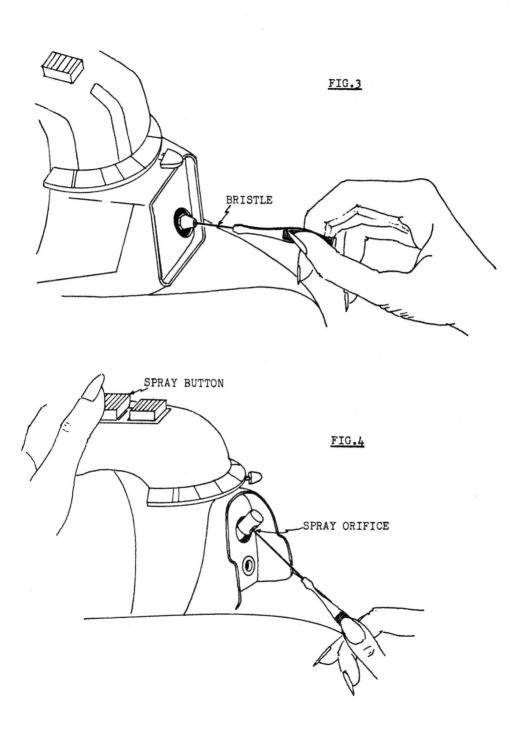

FIG.3

BRISTLE

SPRAY BUTTON

FIG.4

SPRAY ORIFICE

Problem Solver #6

APPLIANCE: Clothes Irons (Steam and Regular)

PROBLEM: **Iron does not shut off.**

EXPLANATION: When an iron continues to heat after the fabric indicator knob has been placed in the "off" position, it
means either that the thermostat needs adjustment or
that the electrical contact points of the thermostat are
stuck in a closed position. Jammed thermostat contact
points present a more serious problem, and in addition
to not shutting off, the iron will heat to extremely high
temperatures, often causing aluminum sole plates to
melt. When this condition is suspected, discontinue
using the iron to avoid permanently damaging the sole
plate, and have iron serviced by a qualified appliance
technician. In most cases, however, adjusting the
thermostat (when no evidence of extreme overheating
exists) will allow the iron to shut off when the fabric
indicator knob is set to the "off" position.

TOOLS AND MATERIALS NEEDED:

(a) a small screwdriver (sewing machine type)

(b) a paper clip

(c) a pair of pliers

SOLUTION: 1. Remove line cord plug from wall outlet and allow
iron to cool to room temperature.

SPECIAL NOTE: *Figures 1 and 2* represent two of the
more common kinds of irons. Moreover, they are designed so that only a minimum number of parts need
be removed to gain access to the thermostat adjustment screw (or nut).

2. Set the fabric indicator knob to the "off" position.

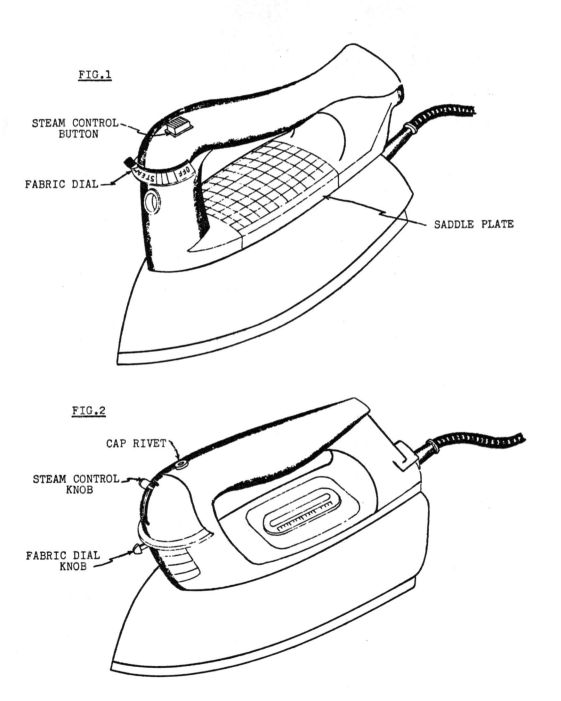

FIG.1

STEAM CONTROL
BUTTON

FABRIC DIAL

SADDLE PLATE

FIG.2

CAP RIVET

STEAM CONTROL
KNOB

FABRIC DIAL
KNOB

3. To reach the thermostat adjustment screw for the iron illustrated in *Figure 1*, gently pry the metal saddle plate off by grasping and lifting both sides with fingertips. A stubborn saddle plate may be removed by carefully prying one side up with the flat blade of a screwdriver.

4. With saddle plate removed, locate the slotted thermostat adjustment screw. (*Figure 3*)

5. Insert screwdriver blade into the thermostat adjustment screw slot and give the adjustment screw a quarter turn in a clockwise direction.

6. Plug the line cord into the wall outlet. Make sure fabric indicator knob is still set to the "off" position. Check to see whether or not iron heats up.

7. If iron does not heat in "off" position, adjustment has corrected the condition and no further adjustment is necessary. Replace the saddle plate.

8. If iron continues to heat in "off" position, remove the line cord from the wall outlet. When the iron has cooled to room temperature, give the thermostat adjustment screw an additional quarter turn clockwise.

9. Retest iron in "off" position. Repeat the adjustment once more if necessary.

FIG.3

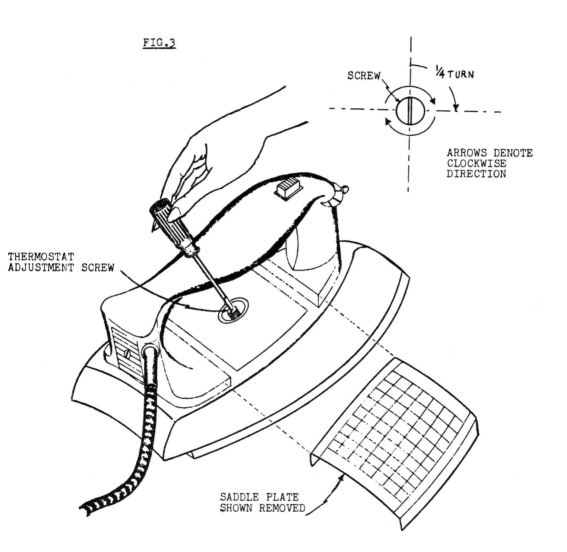

SCREW

¼ TURN

ARROWS DENOTE
CLOCKWISE
DIRECTION

THERMOSTAT
ADJUSTMENT SCREW

SADDLE PLATE
SHOWN REMOVED

10. If adjustments do not prevent the iron from heating in the "off" position, the indication is that the thermostat is stuck and will probably have to be replaced. Further testing and repairs should be performed by a qualified appliance technician.

11. To reach the thermostat adjustment nut for the iron shown in *Figure 2*, bend a paper clip as shown in *Figure 4*. Place the tip of the paper clip in the center of the plastic cap rivet located on the iron handle, and press firmly down until the rivet is pushed clear through into the handle.

12. Grasp the front cap of the iron handle and pull it forward slowly. Disconnect the steam control lever from the top of the valve shaft and remove the front cap. (*Figure 5*)

    CAUTION: Retrieve the cap rivet, which will be found in a little well directly below its position in the handle. Set it aside carefully so that it may be reinstalled after the thermostat adjustment is completed.

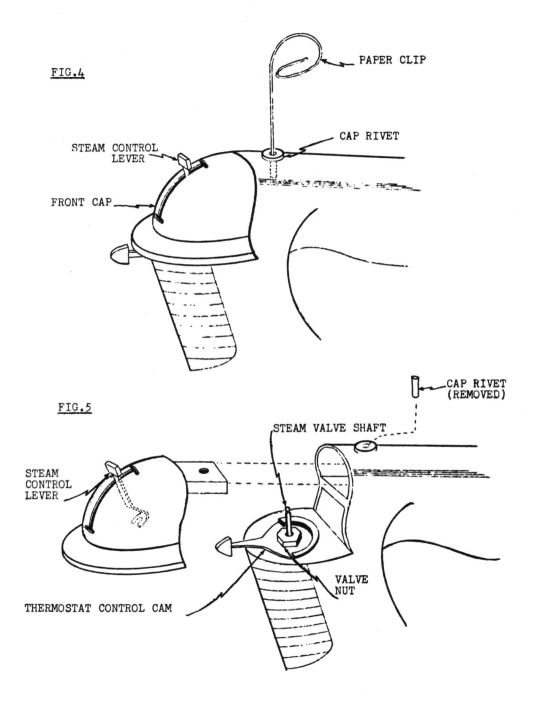

FIG.4

PAPER CLIP

CAP RIVET

STEAM CONTROL
LEVER

FRONT CAP

FIG.5

CAP RIVET
(REMOVED)

STEAM VALVE SHAFT

STEAM
CONTROL
LEVER

VALVE
NUT

THERMOSTAT CONTROL CAM

13. Unscrew the valve nut (turn counter-clockwise) with pliers and remove the nut. Lift off the washer and the thermostat control cam. (*Figure 6A*)

14. Locate the thermostat adjustment nut. (*Figure 6*) Grasp the adjustment nut with fingers and give it a half turn in a clockwise direction. If nut is stubborn, grasp nut with pliers to turn it. (*Figure 6B*) Use moderate pressure only.

15. Replace the thermostat control cam, washer, and valve nut. Tighten valve nut securely with pliers. Connect the steam control lever to the top of the valve shaft and slide the front cap into place. Install the cam rivet. Press rivet firmly into place with the flat portion of the pliers.

16. Retest iron on "off" position. If iron does not heat, adjustment has corrected condition. Repeat the adjustment if necessary.

    NOTE: If iron fails to respond to adjustments and continues to heat in the "off" position, have iron checked by qualified appliance technician.

FIG.6 EXPLODED VIEW

FIG.6A

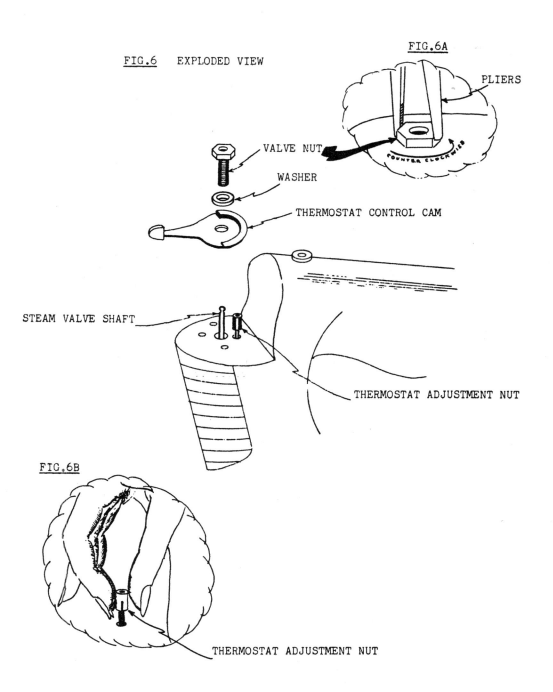

PLIERS

VALVE NUT

COUNTER CLOCKWISE

WASHER

THERMOSTAT CONTROL CAM

STEAM VALVE SHAFT

THERMOSTAT ADJUSTMENT NUT

FIG.6B

THERMOSTAT ADJUSTMENT NUT

Problem Solver #7

APPLIANCE: Clothes Irons (Steam and Regular)

PROBLEM: Iron burns cloth.

EXPLANATION: When this happens, it is obvious that the iron temperature is too hot for the material being pressed.
Excessive iron temperature may be caused by an incorrect setting of the fabric indicator knob or a malfunctioning thermostat.

TOOLS AND MATERIALS NEEDED:

    (a) a dial thermometer
        (used for candymaking and deep frying)

    (b) a small screwdriver (sewing machine type)

    (c) a paper clip

    (d) a pair of pliers

    (e) cooking oil

SOLUTION: 1. Make certain that the fabric indicator knob is
                 correctly set for fabric to be pressed.

                 NOTE: Modern fabrics contain a variety of synthetic
                 fibers. Identifying these fibers and knowing the correct
                 ironing temperature to use are important for their pro-
                 tection. Always follow the fabric or garment manufac-
                 turer's washing and ironing recommendations. When
                 the composition of the fabric is unknown or whenever
                 there is doubt concerning the correct ironing tempera-
                 ture to use, begin ironing with the fabric indicator
                 control knob set to the lowest heat position.

              2. If iron is correctly set for the fabric being ironed
                 but the iron still burns the fabric, the iron must
                 be checked to determine if the correct temperature
                 is being maintained by the thermostat.

              3. Set the fabric indicator knob to the lowest
                 "synthetics" position on the fabric dial.

              4. Plug the iron into wall outlet and allow iron to
                 heat for at least three minutes.

                 CAUTION: When testing steam irons, make certain wa-
                 ter has been removed and iron is completely dry.

5. Dip the end of the liquid thermometer (about two inches) into clean cooking oil. Turn the iron upside down and place the thermometer on the sole plate. (*Figure 1*) Hold thermometer steady so that good contact is made with the sole plate. The cooking oil will help to transfer the heat of the sole plate to the thermometer for a more accurate thermometer reading.

6. The thermometer should slow to a stop at a temerature between 220° and 280° F. If the thermometer reads above this range, it indicates that the iron thermostat is not working properly and is allowing the iron to overheat.

FIG.1

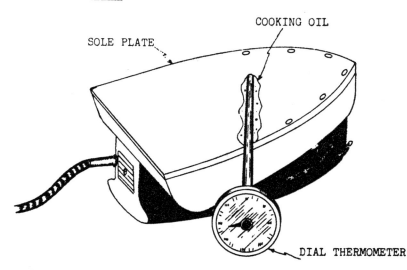

COOKING OIL

SOLE PLATE

DIAL THERMOMETER

CAUTION AND NOTE: If the thermometer pointer goes beyond the 400° F. mark when the iron is set for "synthetics," it means that the iron thermostat is jammed. Do not attempt any further checks. Disconnect the iron immediately from the wall outlet to prevent further damage to the sole plate of the iron. Jammed or otherwise defective thermostats should be replaced by qualified appliance repair technicians. If, however, the thermometer pointer indicates excessive iron temperature just above the normal range (220°-280° F.), an attempt can be made to adjust the thermostat to restore correct ironing temperatures. The procedures for adjusting the thermostat in two of the more widely used irons are given in the steps that follow.

7. Remove the iron plug from the wall outlet.

8. To reach the thermostat adjustment screw for the type of iron shown in *Figure 2*, gently pry the metal saddle plate off by grasping and lifting both sides with fingertips. A stubborn saddle plate may be removed by carefully prying one side up with the tip of a flatblade screwdriver.

   CAUTION: The saddle plate rests upon a plastic portion of the iron handle. If a screwdriver must be used, take care not to pry against the plastic handle.

9. Locate the slotted thermostat adjustment screw. (*Figure 2*) Insert the tip of a small screwdriver into the slot of the thermostat adjustment screw and give the screw a quarter turn in a clockwise direction.

10. Connect iron to wall outlet and measure the temperature of the sole plate again. Be sure to wait at least three minutes and check to see that the fabric indicator knob is on lowest "synthetics" setting. The temperature of the iron should now be lower.

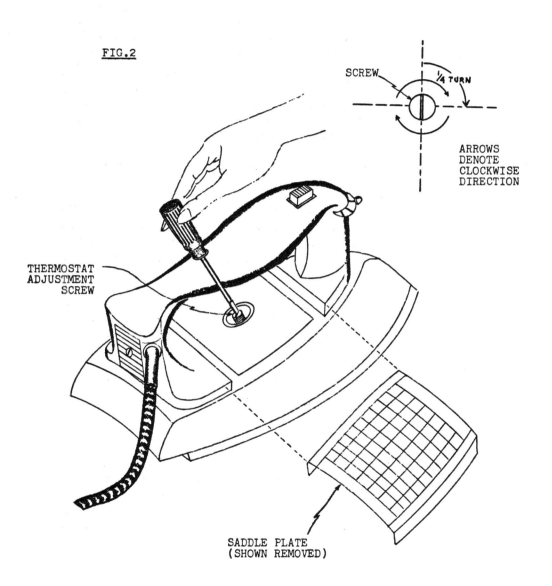

FIG.2

SCREW

¼ TURN

ARROWS
DENOTE
CLOCKWISE
DIRECTION

THERMOSTAT
ADJUSTMENT
SCREW

SADDLE PLATE
(SHOWN REMOVED)

If, however, the temperature has not been lowered enough, turn the adjustment screw again (a quarter turn at a time) until temperature falls within correct range (220°-280° F.).

11. For the final test, turn the iron off and allow it to cool to room temperature. When the iron has cooled, place the fabric indicator knob in the lowest heat position. Plug the iron into wall receptacle. If iron does not heat, it means that the thermostat did not respond to the adjustment, is defective, and must be replaced.

12. To reach the thermostat adjustment nut for the type of iron shown in *Figure 3*, bend a paper clip as shown in *Figure 3* and place the tip of the paper clip in the center of the plastic cap rivet. Press down firmly until the rivet is pushed clear through the handle.

13. Grasp the front cap of the iron handle and pull it forward. Disconnect the steam control lever from the top of the valve shaft and remove the cap. (*Figure 4*)

CAUTION: Retrieve the cap rivet, which will be found in a little well directly below its position in the handle. Set it aside carefully so that it may be reinstalled after the thermostat adjustment has been completed.

FIG.3

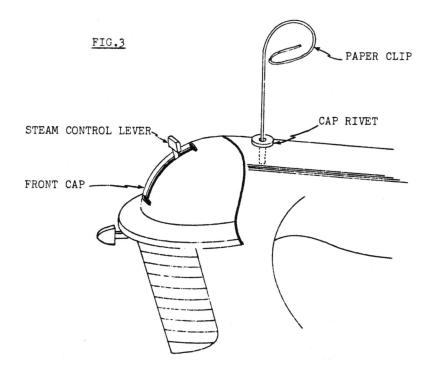

PAPER CLIP

STEAM CONTROL LEVER

CAP RIVET

FRONT CAP

FIG.4

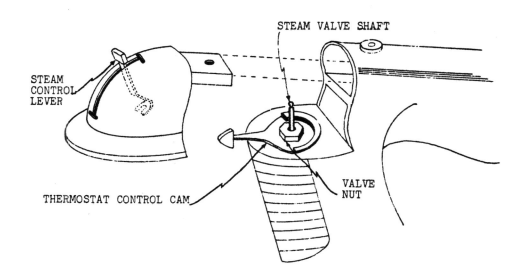

STEAM VALVE SHAFT

STEAM
CONTROL
LEVER

THERMOSTAT CONTROL CAM

VALVE
NUT

14. Unscrew the valve nut (turn counter-clockwise) with pliers and remove it. Lift off the washer and the thermostat control cam. (*Figure 5*)

15. Locate the thermostat adjustment nut. (*Figure 5*) Grasp the adjustment nut with fingers and give it a half turn in a clockwise direction. If nut is stubborn, grasp it with pliers to turn it. Use only moderate pressure.

16. After adjustment has been made, replace the thermostat control cam washer and valve nut. Tighten valve nut securely with pliers and measure temperature of iron again. Repeat the adjustment (a half turn at a time) if necessary until temperature falls within the normal range (220°-280° F.).

17. Allow the iron to cool to room temperature for the final test. Set fabric indicator knob to the lowest heat position. Plug iron into wall outlet. If iron does not heat, it means that the thermostat did not respond to the adjustment, is defective, and therefore must be replaced. If iron does heat in the lowest position, the thermostat adjustment has been successfully completed.

18. Replace the steam control lever and slide the front clip cap into place.

19. Install the cam rivet. Press rivet into place firmly with the flat side of the pliers.

FIG.5   EXPLODED VIEW

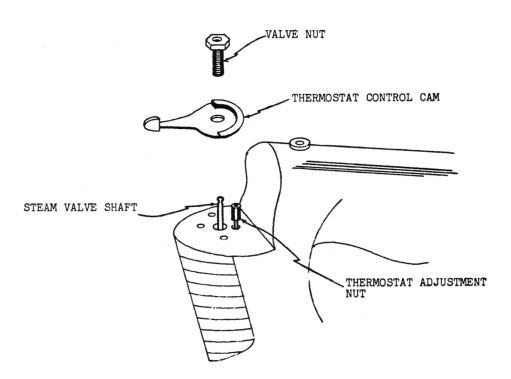

VALVE NUT

THERMOSTAT CONTROL CAM

STEAM VALVE SHAFT

THERMOSTAT ADJUSTMENT
NUT

Problem Solver #8

APPLIANCE: All Toasters

PROBLEM: **Toaster smokes.**

EXPLANATION: The annoying and often frightening occurrence of smoke arising from a toaster is in almost all cases caused by crumbs or other food (butter, margarine, sugar, etc.) coming in contact with or accumulating close to the heating element wire. The problem is generally brought about by improper use and care of a toaster.

TOOLS AND MATERIALS NEEDED:

(a) a flashlight

(b) a ½″ paintbrush

(c) clear household ammonia

SOLUTION: 1. Plug toaster into wall outlet and allow toaster to heat without bread.

NOTE: Automatic self-lowering toasters can be operated without bread by momentarily pressing down on the bread carriage with the wooden (insulated) handle of the small paintbrush. (*Figure 1*)

2. As toaster heats, peer into bread slots and locate the exact area of heating element from which the smoke originates. (*Figure 2*)

3. Remove the line cord plug from the wall outlet and allow the toaster to cool to room temperature.

4. Carefully reexamine with flashlight the area where smoke originated to locate any particles of food stuck to heating element wire.

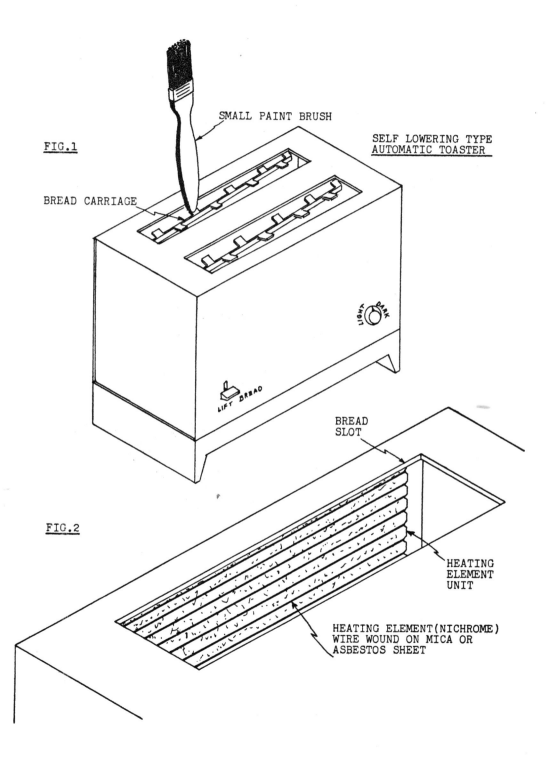

FIG.1

SMALL PAINT BRUSH

SELF LOWERING TYPE
AUTOMATIC TOASTER

BREAD CARRIAGE

LIGHT DARK

LIFT BREAD

FIG.2

BREAD
SLOT

HEATING
ELEMENT
UNIT

HEATING ELEMENT(NICHROME)
WIRE WOUND ON MICA OR
ASBESTOS SHEET

5. Insert paintbrush carefully through bread slot and gently brush the food particle off the heating element and down into the crumb tray. (*Figure 3*)

   CAUTION: Do not turn toaster upside down. Crumbs and other particles of food from the crumb tray will adhere to the heating element and cause a repetition of the smoking condition. More important, food particles coming in contact with the heating element wire produce "hot spots" (bright overheated spots on the heating element wire) that can cause the heating element to burn out.

6. Remove butter or margarine that may have gotten onto heating element or dripped into bottom of toaster by washing toaster areas with a paintbrush dipped into a solution of clear household ammonia. (*Figure 4*)

   CAUTION: Allow toaster to dry thoroughly (at least one hour) before attempting to use it.

   SPECIAL NOTE: To insure satisfactory service from your toaster:

   A. Brush the crumb tray clean regularly.

   B. Do not turn toaster upside down to remove crumbs.

   C. Avoid the practice of buttering bread *before* toasting it.

   D. Do not force oversized pieces of bread or other food items into toaster.

FIG.3

BREAD SLOTS

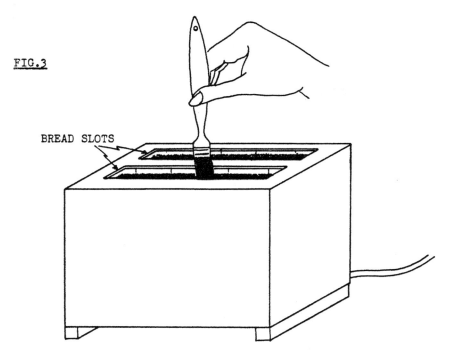

FIG.4

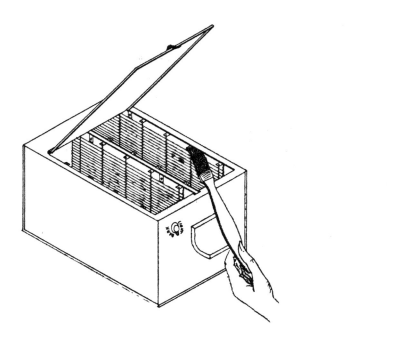

Problem Solver #9

APPLIANCE: All Toasters

PROBLEM: Toaster does not heat.

EXPLANATION: When the heating elements within a toaster do not heat, the cause can usually be traced to a blown fuse, a tripped circuit breaker, or a defective line cord.

TOOLS AND MATERIALS NEEDED:

(a) line cord (asbestos or plastic, as required by specific toaster; can be purchased completely assembled with plug and terminal connectors)

(b) a small screwdriver (sewing machine type)

(c) a pair of pliers

SOLUTION: 1. Make sure that the wall outlet has electric power. Plug a lamp or other appliance known to be in good working order into the outlet used for the toaster. If lamp or other appliance fails to operate, it can be assumed that a fuse has blown or that a circuit breaker has tripped "off," preventing electric power from reaching the wall outlet, or that the wall receptacle itself is defective. Refer to Section II, General Repair Procedures, Fuses and Circuit Breakers, for further information about this condition. However, if lamp or other appliance operates, it means that the problem is in the toaster.

2. Examine the line cord plug. Check the plug prongs for looseness. Test the condition of the line cord wires going into the plug by tugging firmly on the plug against the line cord. (*Figure 1*) If the plug prongs wiggle freely or if the plug seems to part from the line cord when pulled, the plug should be replaced. See Section II, General Repair Procedures, Plugs, for further information.

<u>FIG.1</u>

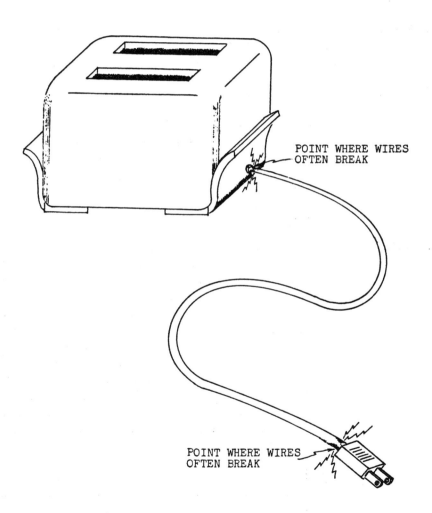

POINT WHERE WIRES
OFTEN BREAK

POINT WHERE WIRES
OFTEN BREAK

SPECIAL NOTE: While it is possible for wires to break anywhere along the length of the line cord, they are most apt to break at points where sharp bending occurs during use. These points are located where the line cord enters the plug and again where the line cord enters the toaster. When you are uncertain about breakage or whenever the line cord shows outward signs of wear, such as fraying, replace the entire line cord as outlined in the steps that follow.

CAUTION: Remove the line cord from the wall outlet before working on toaster.

3. Examine toaster shell and plastic base where line cord enters toaster. Locate and remove only those screws that fasten the section (usually part of the plastic base) through which the line cord enters the toaster. Separate this section from the toaster shell. (*Figure 2*)

4. Take careful note of the way the line cord wire ends are routed to insure correct routing of new replacement line cord wires.

5. Follow the line cord wire ends to where they end (toaster terminals) and note the kind of terminal connectors used. (*Figure 2*) If wires are attached with push-on connectors, simply grasp each connector with the fingertips and pull upward with a slight side to side motion and remove them. (*Figure 2A*)

6. If wires are attached with terminal screws, loosen the two screws with two counter-clockwise turns and remove the line cord wire ends.

NOTE AND CAUTION: If the line cord wire ends under the screws have U-shaped connectors, the wire ends will slip out from behind the terminal screws when the screws are loosened. (*Figure 2*) If the line cord wires use circular eyelets as connectors, the two terminal screws must be removed completely in order to disconnect the line cord wires.

Take care not to drop the terminal screws into the toaster if it becomes necessary to remove them. Refer to Section II, General Repair Procedures, Terminal and Wire Connectors, for further information.

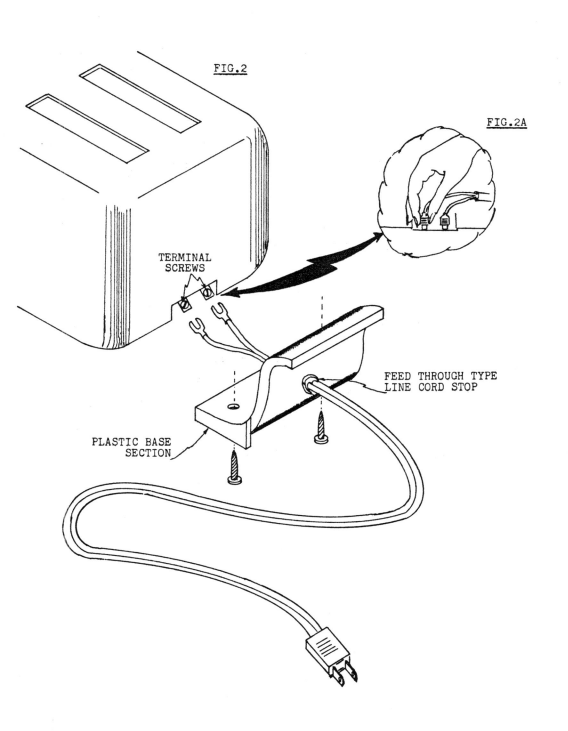

FIG.2

FIG.2A

TERMINAL
SCREWS

FEED THROUGH TYPE
LINE CORD STOP

PLASTIC BASE
SECTION

7. Free the line cord by removing the line cord stop. If line cord is held by plastic feed-through type of cord stop, grip the cord stop with the tip of a pair of pliers. (*Figure 3*) Squeeze hard on plier handles and pull cord stop and cord wire out. Set cord stop aside for reuse with new replacement line cord.

8. Feed the wire ends of the new replacement line cord through the opening in the toaster section. Place the line cord stop at a distance from the line cord wire ends equal to its original position on the old line cord.

9. Clamp cord stop down firmly on line cord with pliers and push cord stop into place.

10. Connect the line cord wire ends to the toaster terminals (screw or push-on).

11. Route the wire ends of the line cord as they were originally.

12. Reattach toaster section and secure it with screws.

CAUTION: When reassembling toaster, make certain that the line cord wires are not pinched between parts.

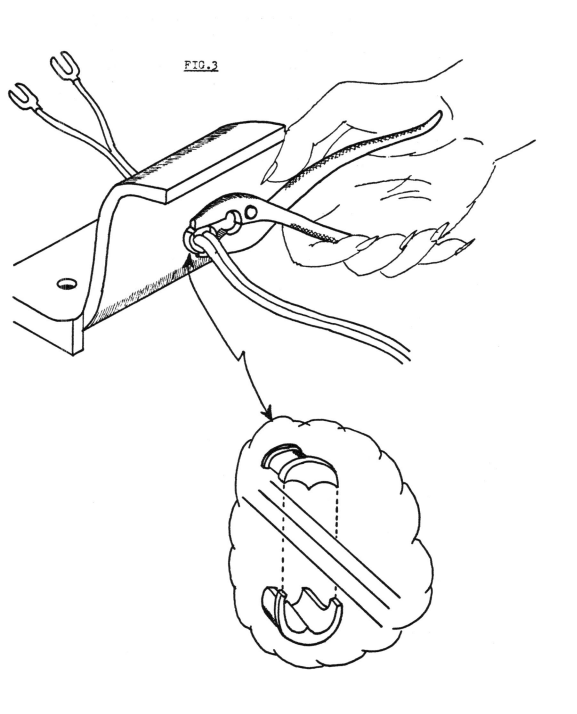

FIG.3

Problem Solver #10

APPLIANCE: All Toasters

PROBLEM: One side of bread does not toast.

EXPLANATION: A two-slice toaster may contain as many as four separate heating element units (one for each bread side). When one or more of these element units fails to heat, the side of the bread that faces the defective heating element will not be toasted. The failure of one or more heating element units to heat is usually traced to a broken or burned-out heating element (nichrome) wire.

TOOLS AND MATERIALS NEEDED:

(a) a flashlight

(b) a lead pencil (sharpened)

(c) a pair of long-nose pliers

(d) terminal connector
(solderless spade for #16 wire, available at any electrical hardware store)

SOLUTION: 1. Identify the defective heating element unit. (The heating element facing the untoasted side of the bread.)

2. Remove the line cord plug from the wall outlet and allow the toaster to cool to room temperature.

3. Use flashlight to provide light inside the toaster. Gently probe along the element wire to pinpoint the exact location of the wire break. (*Figure 1*)

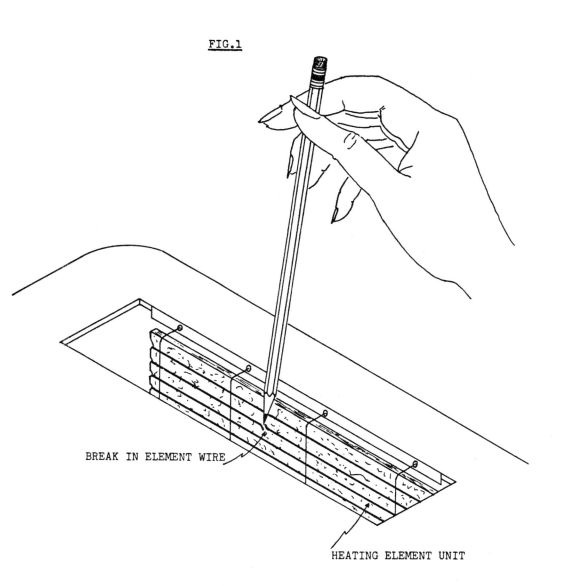

FIG.1

BREAK IN ELEMENT WIRE

HEATING ELEMENT UNIT

NOTE: Some breaks in the heating element wire are easily discovered by visual inspection, since a space may be seen between the parted wire ends. At times, however, the space between the parted element wires may be too small to be noticed and will therefore require gentle probing (with the point of a pencil) to disclose the break.

4. If a search through bread slots (at the top of toaster) fails to disclose the wire break, open or remove the bread crumb tray and continue to examine the element unit through the bottom of the toaster.

   NOTE: When a break in the heating element wire cannot be found or if, when located, the space between the two parted wire ends is more than one-half inch, the toaster should be taken to a qualified appliance service shop for further tests and repairs. If the parted wire ends are found to be close together, they may be mended as is described in the steps that follow.

5. Reach into toaster (through top bread slots or bottom with crumb tray opened) with a pair of long-nose pliers. Grasp and pull the wire ends toward each other so that they overlap or at least meet. (*Figure 2*)

   CAUTION: Use moderate force when adjusting wire ends in order to prevent further damage to them.

6. Bend a wire connector until the cylindrical sleeve breaks off from the front position of the connector. (*Figure 3*)

FIG.2

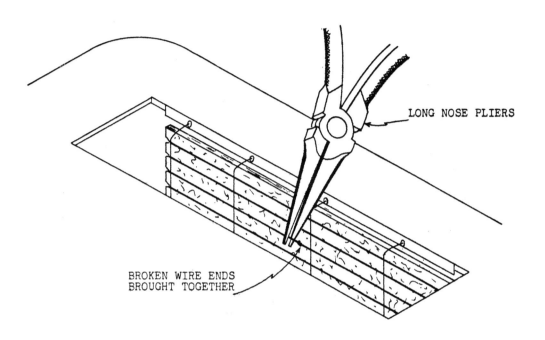

LONG NOSE PLIERS

BROKEN WIRE ENDS
BROUGHT TOGETHER

FIG.3

BREAK TERMINAL
CONNECTOR

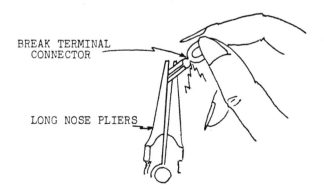

LONG NOSE PLIERS

7. Grip the connector sleeve with the tip of the long-nose pliers and slip the sleeve over both ends of the heating element wire. (*Figure 4*)

8. Carefully adjust the sleeve so that it covers both ends of the wire equally. Crush the sleeve flat between the jaws of the pliers so that both wire ends are locked together securely. (*Figure 5*)

   NOTE: To obtain greater crushing power from the long-nose pliers, grip the sleeve as far back in the plier jaws (towards the hinge) as space permits.

9. Prod the sleeve with a pencil to see that wire ends are being held firmly. Crush the sleeve again if necessary.

10. Test the toaster operation. Plug the line cord into the wall outlet, allow toaster to heat (without bread), and check the repaired element. Element should glow red.

11. Inspect the mended sleeve connection. If it glows with the same degree of redness as does the wire of the heating element, the repair has been properly completed. If, however, slight sparking is noticed at the sleeve connection or if the sleeve connection glows brighter (more white hot than red) than the rest of the element wire, it means that the sleeve connection has not been properly made (loose). The sleeve connector should therefore be removed and the connection remade with a new connector sleeve.

    SPECIAL NOTE: With normal use, the heating element units of toasters will operate for many years without failure. In most instances a defective heating element can be traced to improper use of a toaster. To avoid damaging the heating element units of your toaster, follow the suggestions listed below.

    A. Make sure that food items to be toasted do not come in contact with the heating element wires.

    B. Do not remove particles of food that have stuck to the heating element units with hard, sharp objects. Remove food particles with a brush after the toaster has cooled.

FIG.4

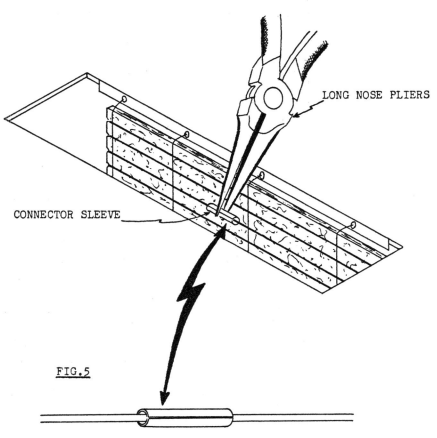

LONG NOSE PLIERS

CONNECTOR SLEEVE

FIG.5

CONNECTOR SLEEVE PLACED OVER WIRE ENDS

CONNECTOR SLEEVE CRUSHED TO SECURE WIRE ENDS

C. Do not attempt to dislodge food items that have become stuck in the bread slots with a fork; a fork may curve into and break the heating element wires.

CAUTION: Disconnect the line cord from the wall outlet before attempting to remove any food that may have become lodged in the bread slots. If food being toasted cannot be removed by lifting the bread carriage lever, carefully insert the tip of a small steak knife into the food item and pry the item straight up. Make certain that the knife blade is kept parallel with the bread slot. Never allow it to touch the heating element units.

Problem Solver #11

APPLIANCE: Automatic Pop-Up Toasters

PROBLEM: **Bread does not stay down.**

EXPLANATION: Bread is lowered and raised in a toaster by the bread carriage and rack. In its lowered position, the bread carriage engages and is locked by a latch down mechanism. Through normal use, the latching mechanism may bend out of adjustment or bind at hinged points and thus fail to lock the bread carriage in its lowered position. While many variations of latching mechanisms are used in different toaster models, most are simple in design, and their operation is easily understood.

Tools and Materials Needed:

    (a) a pair of universal pliers

    (b) a pair of long-nose pliers

    (c) a small artist's paintbrush

    (d) non-inflammable cleaning fluid
       (capable of dissolving grease)

Solution:

> NOTE: The latch down mechanism is located on the side of the toaster that contains the bread lever and toast control knobs. Access to the latch down mechanism may be achieved by disassembling the plastic base section and/or a section of the metal toaster shell. *Figures 1, 3, and 6* illustrate common varieties of construction. Other toaster models require the removal of the entire toaster shell to gain access to the latch down mechanism and should, therefore, be taken to a qualified appliance repair shop for service.

1. Identify the toaster's construction according to *Figures 1, 3, and 6.*

2. To disassemble toaster shown in *Figure 1*, remove the bread lever knob by pulling it straight out. Take care not to lose the small metal clasp that secures the knob to the lever. (*Figure 1*)

> NOTE: As an aid to removing a stubborn knob, wedge the flat tip of a screwdriver behind the knob and pry it off.

3. Remove the small toast control lever and knob set screw located on the bottom of the toaster, and pull the toast control lever and knob out. (*Figure 1*)

4. Remove the two screws that fasten the plastic base to the metal shell and remove the plastic base. (*Figure 2*)

5. Grasp the bottom edge of the front metal shell section and pull down hard until the locking tabs are freed from the locking tab slots. Lift the front metal shell section away from the toaster. (*Figure 2*)

6. Examine the operation of the latch down mechanism after the plastic base or end shell section has been removed. Operate the bread lever and note the condition that prevents the "latch" from engaging or locking onto the "latch lock." (*Figure 2A*)

7. If the latch fails to engage the latch lock (they do not make contact), examine the latch, bread lever, and bread rack for bent parts. Realign any bent part by bending it back into position with a pair of pliers.

8. If the latch engages (touches) the latch lock but does not lock, examine the electromagnetic latch release and the latch lock to see if they move freely on their pivots. (*Figure 2A*)

9. Free a stuck pivot or hinge by cleaning it thoroughly with a non-inflammable cleaning fluid applied with a small artist's brush. Work the movable latch lock and electromagnetic latch release back and forth to allow the cleaning fluid to penetrate until free movement is obtained.

   CAUTION: Do not lubricate a pivot or hinge on the latch down mechanism.

10. If the latch lock and electromagnetic latch release move freely but the latch still fails to hold, look to see that the flat, leaf-shaped spring between the solenoid coil and the electromagnetic latch release has sufficient tension to position the electromagnetic latch release to its locking position (away from the solenoid so as to engage the latch lock).

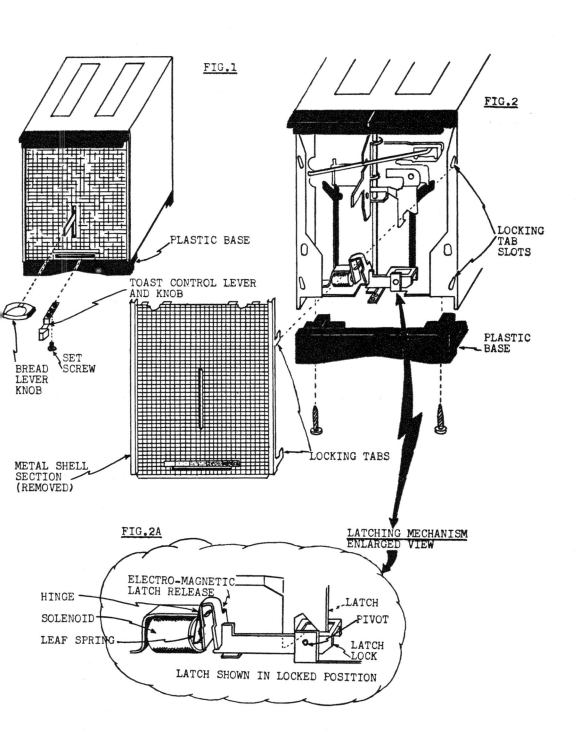

FIG.1

PLASTIC BASE

TOAST CONTROL LEVER
AND KNOB

SET
SCREW

BREAD
LEVER
KNOB

METAL SHELL
SECTION
(REMOVED)

FIG.2

LOCKING
TAB
SLOTS

PLASTIC
BASE

LOCKING TABS

FIG.2A

ELECTRO-MAGNETIC
LATCH RELEASE

HINGE

SOLENOID

LEAF SPRING

LATCH

PIVOT

LATCH
LOCK

LATCHING MECHANISM
ENLARGED VIEW

LATCH SHOWN IN LOCKED POSITION

11. If the leaf spring (*Figure 2A*) does not push the electromagnetic latch release out far enough to engage the latch lock, bend the leaf spring out slightly with long-nose pliers.

12. Reassemble toaster and test latch down action. To reassemble toaster, simply reverse the procedure outlined in steps 2, 3, 4, and 5.

    NOTE: Make certain that the locking tabs of the metal shell section are completely seated in the locking tab slots to insure satisfactory alignment of all parts.

13. To disassemble toaster shown in *Figure 3*, remove the bread lever knob and the toast control knob by pulling them straight out. (*Figure 3*)

14. Remove the plastic shell section mounting screw with a pair of pliers. (*Figure 4*)

15. Grasp the plastic shell section and pull it downward until the spring clasp that fastens it at the top to the metal shell is released to free the shell section. (*Figure 4*)

16. Examine the operation of the latch down mechanism. (*Figure 5*) Operate the bread lever and note the condition that prevents the latch from engaging or locking onto the latch lock. (*Figure 5A*)

17. If the latch does not engage (touch) the latch lock, check the position of the latch lock with respect to the latch. The latch lock should be struck by the latch when the bread carriage is lowered. Bend the latch lock toward the latch (if necessary) until correct striking action is achieved.

18. If the latch engages the latch lock but does not lock, check to see that the latch goes below the latch lock lip when the bread carriage is lowered. (*Figure 5A*) If it does not, check along the bread carriage and bread carriage guide rod for any obstruction that could prevent the bread carriage from being lowered fully.

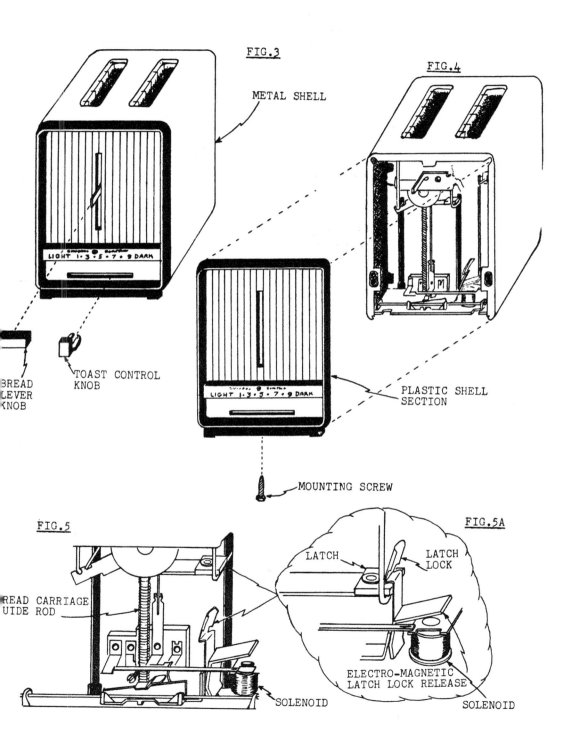

FIG.3

METAL SHELL

FIG.4

BREAD
LEVER
KNOB

TOAST CONTROL
KNOB

LIGHT 1·3·5·7·9 DARK

PLASTIC SHELL
SECTION

MOUNTING SCREW

FIG.5

FIG.5A

LATCH

LATCH
LOCK

BREAD CARRIAGE
GUIDE ROD

SOLENOID

ELECTRO-MAGNETIC
LATCH LOCK RELEASE

SOLENOID

19. Reassemble the toaster and test the latch down operation. For reassembling instructions follow steps 13, 14, and 15 in reverse order.

    NOTE: When reassembling the toaster, make sure that the metal clasp at the top of the plastic shell section engages the edge of the metal toaster shell.

20. To gain access to the latch down mechanism for the toaster illustrated in *Figure 6*, remove the toast control knob by pulling it straight out.

21. Remove the two screws that fasten the front plate. Depress the door release bar to raise the door and door handle. Lift the front plate (escutcheon) out. (*Figure 6*)

FIG.6

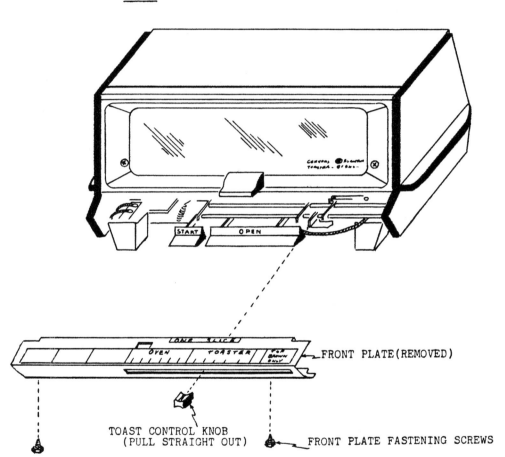

FRONT PLATE (REMOVED)

TOAST CONTROL KNOB
(PULL STRAIGHT OUT)

FRONT PLATE FASTENING SCREWS

22. Examine the operation of the latching mechanism by closing the door. (*Figures 7 and 7A*) Check to see that the door latch is aligned with the door latch pin. If necessary, bend the door latch or door latch pin with a pair of pliers until the door latch strikes the door latch pin correctly.

23. If the door latch engages the door latch pin correctly but the door does not lock, check to see that the latch spring is properly seated and that it has enough tension to operate the latch and latch lock.

24. Check for free movement of both the latch and latch lock. If either does not move freely upon its pivot, clean the pivot. (*Figure 7A*) Refer to step 9 for cleaning procedures.

25. Reassemble toaster and test the latch down operation.

FIG.7

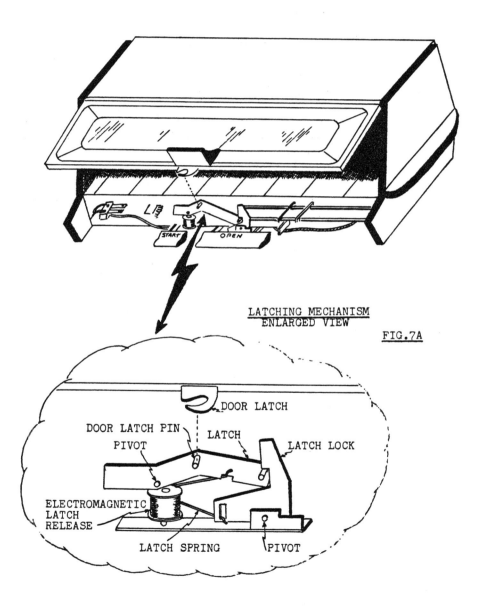

LATCHING MECHANISM
ENLARGED VIEW

FIG.7A

DOOR LATCH

DOOR LATCH PIN
PIVOT

LATCH

LATCH LOCK

ELECTROMAGNETIC
LATCH
RELEASE

LATCH SPRING

PIVOT

Problem Solver #12

APPLIANCE: Automatic Pop-Up Toasters

PROBLEM: Toaster does not pop up.

EXPLANATION: This condition occurs in automatic toasters when something goes wrong in either the latching or timer mechanisms. The latching mechanism is responsible for locking the bread carriage down during toasting, and the timer mechanism automatically limits the "down" time by tripping (unlocking) the latch to release the bread carriage after a prescribed period of toasting time has elapsed. The types of defects that can be encountered in these mechanisms are numerous. Some are serious and require the services of a qualified appliance technician. Others are relatively minor and may require only a simple adjustment or repair. The steps outlined under "solution" below cover common defects that are easily corrected.

TOOLS AND MATERIALS NEEDED:

(a)   a pair of long-nose pliers

(b)   a ¾" paintbrush

(c)   an artist's paintbrush

(d)   a #0 knitting needle

(e)   a flashlight

(f)   cleaning fluid
(non-inflammable grease solvent type)

SOLUTION: 1. Remove the line cord from the wall outlet. Depress the bread lever and latch the bread carriage down in its toasting position. Lift the bread lever (bread release knob on some toaster models) to pop up the bread carriage. If the bread carriage is difficult to raise manually, it indicates either that the carriage is jamming in the carriage support slots (*Figure 1*) or that the latching mechanism is not releasing the carriage properly. If the bread carriage can be lowered and raised manually but fails to pop up automatically, the problem is in the toaster timer.

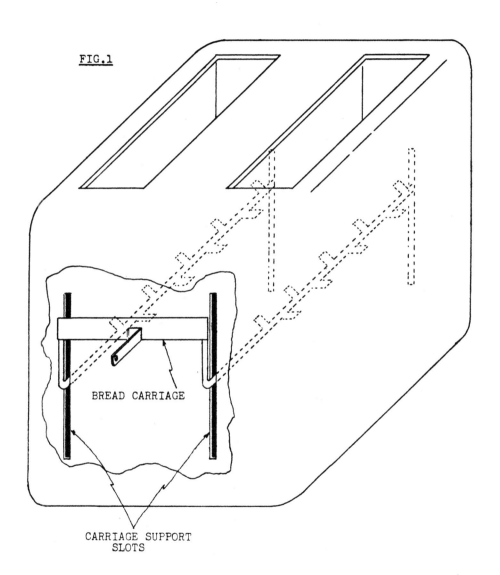

FIG.1

BREAD CARRIAGE

CARRIAGE SUPPORT
SLOTS

2. When the bread carriage fails to release properly with manual operation, check along the carriage support slots and make certain that the bread carriage is not binding. The bread carriage may bind when burned particles of food have become lodged in the carriage support slots or when the bread carriage is bent out of alignment.

NOTE: Light the inside of the toaster with a flashlight.

3. Clear burned food from carriage support slots with knitting needle and brush clean with paintbrush. (*Figure 2*)

4. Straighten bread carriage (if necessary) so that it moves up and down freely in the carriage support slots by bending slightly with the long-nose pliers. (*Figure 3*)

5. If the bread carriage moves freely when operated manually but fails to pop up automatically during use, inspect both the latching mechanism and timer.

CAUTION: Some toasters have the words "one slice" stamped on the top of the shell. When used to toast only a single slice of bread, these toasters require that the bread slice be placed in the slot indicated by arrows for correct timer operation. Failure to do so will cause bread placed in the other slot to burn long before popping up.

NOTE: Refer to Problem Solver #11 for the procedure for gaining access to and servicing the latch down mechanism of three common types of toasters.

6. After testing and servicing the latch down mechanism, retest the toaster for automatic pop-up during actual use. If bread carriage still does not pop up during use, the problem lies in the toaster timer. The toaster should then be taken to a qualified appliance service shop for further tests and repairs.

FIG.2

CARRIAGE SUPPORT SLOTS

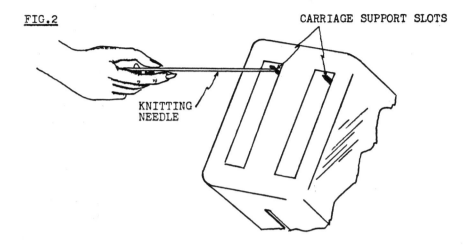

KNITTING
NEEDLE

FIG.3

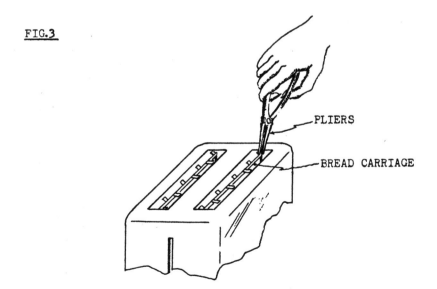

PLIERS

BREAD CARRIAGE

Problem Solver #13

APPLIANCE: Automatic Pop-Up Toasters

PROBLEM: **Bread toasts too light or too dark.**

EXPLANATION: This complaint can often be traced to the type of bread used. Since different breads may contain different quantities of moisture and ingredients such as milk, butter, sugar, and so forth, each may require a different toasting time to achieve the same degree of toast color. If, however, the resulting toast color varies on the usual control setting when the same bread is used, the toaster timer probably needs adjustment.

TOOLS AND MATERIALS NEEDED:

(a) a small screwdriver (sewing machine type)

(b) a pair of pliers

SOLUTION:

1. Check to see that the toast control knob has not been accidentally moved from the desired setting.

   SPECIAL NOTE: The toast control knob adjusts the timer mechanism to lengthen or shorten the toasting period, for darker or lighter toast. In addition to this control knob, each toaster is provided with a second timer adjustment that is used to calibrate the toast control knob so that it indicates the degree of toast color accurately. Some toaster models make this timer adjustment readily available for the user by providing a timer adjustment knob on the underside of the toaster. (*Figure 1*) Most models, however, locate a timer adjustment screw or cam inside the metal toaster shell. (*Figures 3 and 4*)

   CAUTION: Some toasters have the words "one slice" stamped on the top of the shell. When only a single slice of bread is to be toasted, these toasters require that the bread slice be placed in the slot indicated by arrows for correct timer operation. Failure to do so will cause bread placed in the other slot to toast too dark or burn long before it pops up.

2. To adjust the toaster timer (*Figure 1*), set the bread control knob to its middle position ("medium" toast). Toast two slices of bread and observe the degree of toasting.

FIG.1

UNDERSIDE VIEW

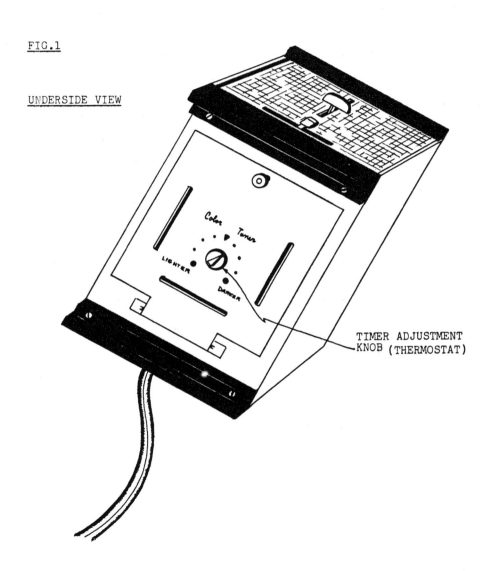

TIMER ADJUSTMENT
KNOB (THERMOSTAT)

3. If toast color is lighter than medium, remove plug from outlet, allow toaster to cool, and turn the timer adjustment knob one click toward "dark." Retest by toasting bread. Turn adjustment knob further if necessary, until desired medium toast is obtained.

4. If toast color is darker than medium, turn the timer adjustment knob one turn toward "light." Turn adjustment knob further toward "light" if necessary, until desired medium toast is obtained.

   NOTE: The toasters illustrated in *Figures 2 and 4* are examples of common types that require removal of a section of their shells in order to reach the timer adjustments.

5. Identify your toaster's construction according to *Figures 2 and 4.*

6. To gain access to the timer for the toaster shown in *Figure 2,* remove the bread lever knob and the toast control knob by pulling them straight out. (*Figure 2*)

7. Remove the plastic shell section mounting screw with a pair of pliers. (*Figure 3*)

8. Grasp the plastic shell section and pull it downward until the spring clasp that fastens it at the top to the metal shell is released to free the shell section. (*Figure 3*)

9. Locate the timer adjustment screw. (*Figure 3A*) If medium toast is too light, turn the adjustment screw (a half turn at a time) in a clockwise direction with a small screwdriver. If medium toast is too dark, turn the adjustment screw (a half turn at a time) in a counter-clockwise direction. Test toast color between each half turn of adjustment by toasting bread with the bread control set in its middle position ("medium" toast).

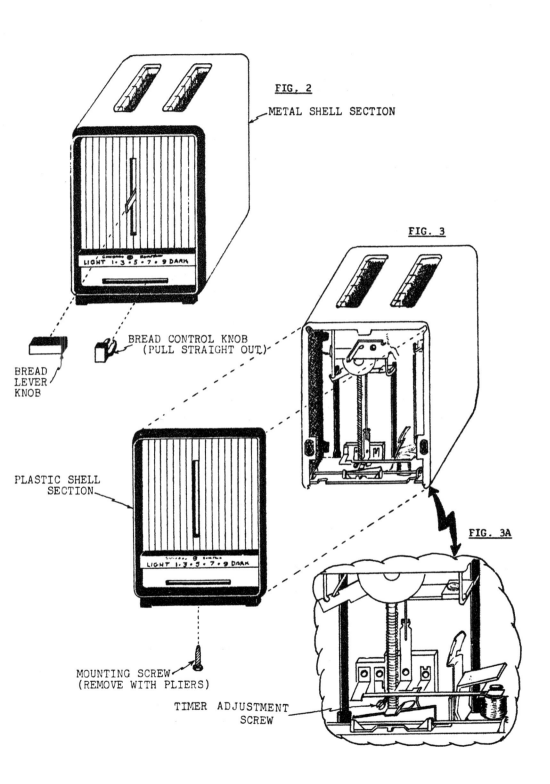

FIG. 2

METAL SHELL SECTION

FIG. 3

BREAD CONTROL KNOB
(PULL STRAIGHT OUT)

BREAD
LEVER
KNOB

LIGHT 1·3·5·7·9 DARK

PLASTIC SHELL
SECTION

LIGHT 1·3·5·7·9 DARK

FIG. 3A

MOUNTING SCREW
(REMOVE WITH PLIERS)

TIMER ADJUSTMENT
SCREW

NOTE: When reassembling the toaster, make sure that the metal clasp at the top of the plastic shell section fully engages the edge of the metal toaster shell.

10. To gain access to the timer for the toaster illustrated in *Figure 4,* remove the toast control knob by pulling it straight out.

11. Remove the two screws that fasten the front plate. Depress the door release bar to raise the door and door handle and lift the front plate (escutcheon) out. (*Figure 4*)

12. Locate the timer adjustment cam for toaster. (*Figure 4A*) If toast is too light for medium setting, insert the tip of a screwdriver into the cam slot (*Figure 4A*) and turn the cam (a quarter turn at a time) in a counter-clockwise direction. If toast is too dark for medium setting, turn adjustment cam (a quarter turn at a time) in a clockwise direction. Retest toast color after each quarter turn until desired medium toast is obtained.

CAUTION: Make certain bread slice is placed on side of toaster marked "one slice."

Problem Solver #14

APPLIANCE: All Toasters

PROBLEM: User gets an electric shock when metal shell of toaster is touched.

EXPLANATION: This condition occurs when one of the toaster components or wires that carry the electric current makes contact with any of the internal metal parts. The condition presents a serious hazard to the user of the toaster. Further use of the toaster should be discontinued until the condition has been corrected.

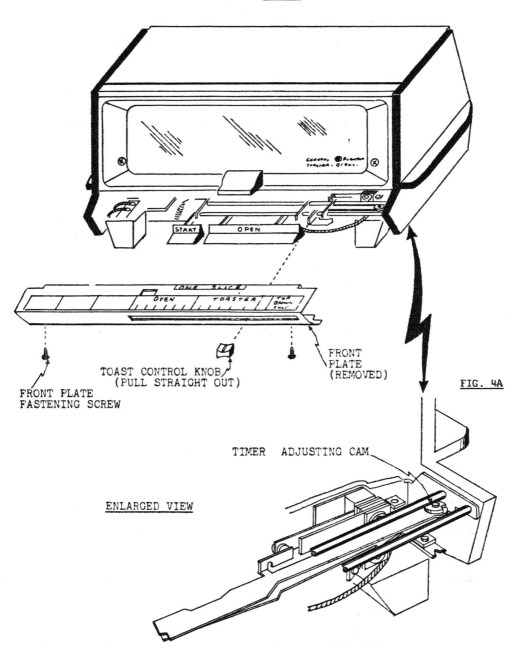

FIG. 4

START   OPEN

ONE SLICE
OVEN   TOASTER   TOP BROWN ONLY

FRONT PLATE
FASTENING SCREW

TOAST CONTROL KNOB
(PULL STRAIGHT OUT)

FRONT
PLATE
(REMOVED)

FIG. 4A

TIMER   ADJUSTING CAM

ENLARGED VIEW

Tools and Materials Needed:

    (a) a pair of long-nose pliers

    (b) a table lamp

    (c) a 6-foot extension cord

    (d) a flashlight

    (e) a #0 knitting needle

    (f) a sharp paring knife

Solution:

1. Remove the line cord from the wall outlet. If toaster is hot, allow it to cool to room temperature.

2. Latch the bread carriage down in its toasting position.

3. Light the inside of the bread slots with a flashlight and carefully examine the heating element (nichrome) wires. Check to see that the wires do not at any point contact metal parts of the toaster such as the bread carriage or the bread guard wires. (*Figure 1*) Inspection should be made through the top bread slots and bottom opening with bread crumb tray opened or removed.

   NOTE: While it is possible for unwanted contact to be made between current-carrying parts and other metal components almost anywhere within the toaster, contact occurs most often when a portion of heating element wire extends too far into the bread slot or when the bread guard wires have been bent into the heating element wire.

4. Carefully adjust heating element wires or bread guard wires with the tip of a knitting needle or a pair of long-nose pliers so that there is sufficient space between the heating element wires and other metal parts of the toaster. (*Figure 2*)

5. Test toaster to make sure that the condition has been corrected.

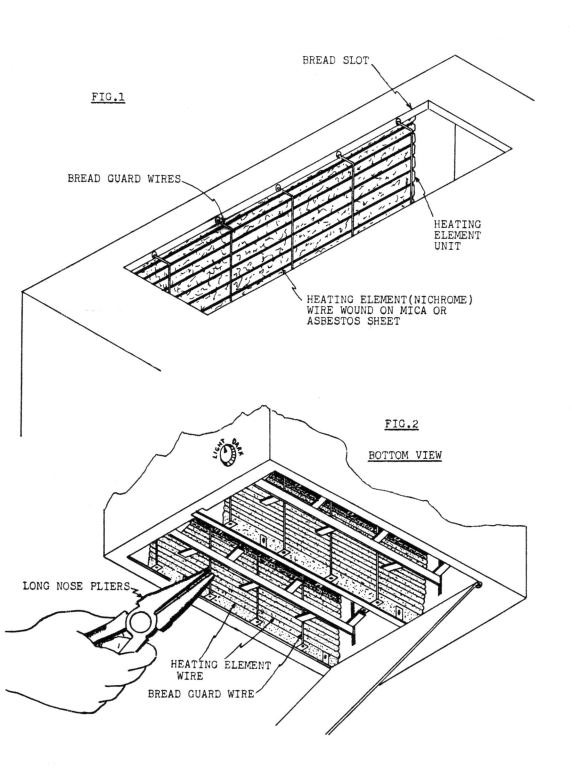

FIG.1

BREAD SLOT

BREAD GUARD WIRES

HEATING
ELEMENT
UNIT

HEATING ELEMENT(NICHROME)
WIRE WOUND ON MICA OR
ASBESTOS SHEET

FIG.2

BOTTOM VIEW

LIGHT DARK

LONG NOSE PLIERS

HEATING ELEMENT
WIRE

BREAD GUARD WIRE

SPECIAL NOTE: A simple testing circuit can be arranged with any available table lamp and a 6-foot extension cord. This testing circuit will provide an effective visual indication of whether or not the condition still exists. The procedure for arranging and using the test circuit is outlined in the steps that follow.

6. Separate the wires of the extension cord for about ten inches along the center of its length by slitting them apart with a sharp paring knife. (*Figure 3*) Guide the paring knife carefully along the center insulation of the extension cord to avoid exposing the copper wire.

7. Cut through one side of the separate extension cord wires with the paring knife. (*Figure 4*)

8. Remove about an inch of insulation from the cut wire ends. (*Figure 5*)

FIG.3

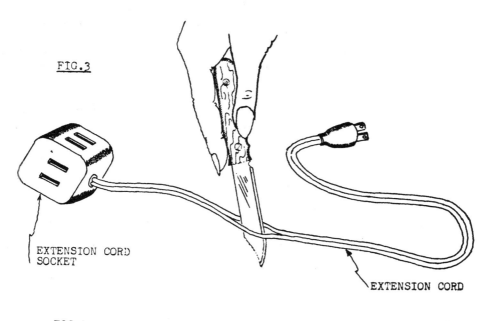

EXTENSION CORD
SOCKET

EXTENSION CORD

FIG.4

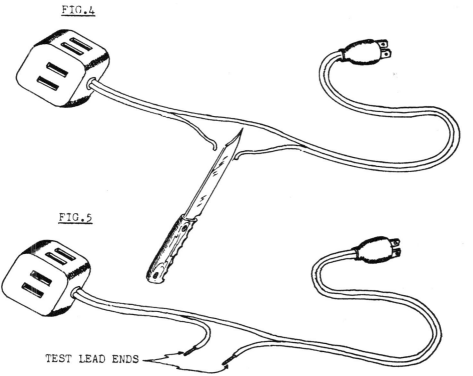

FIG.5

TEST LEAD ENDS

9. Wrap one cut wire end of the extension cord around one prong of the toaster plug. Connect the other wire end to any point on the metal shell of the toaster. Make certain wire end to toaster shell makes good contact with clean, unpainted surface. (*Figure 6*)

10. Connect lamp plug with extension cord receptacle. Connect extension cord plug with a convenient wall outlet. (*Figure 6*)

11. Turn on lamp switch. Depress bread lever down to toast position.

12. If lamp does not light, the hazardous condition has been corrected. The toaster is now safe for use.

13. If lamp lights, the condition still exists. Disconnect extension cord from wall outlet and reexamine toaster for unwanted connection between heating element wires and other metal parts. Retest toaster with test lamp circuit as before.

14. If unwanted connection cannot be located and test lamp circuit continues to indicate that the hazardous condition exists, toaster should not be used until properly repaired by a qualified appliance technician.

    SPECIAL NOTE: The extension cord that has had a wire cut for the purpose of arranging the test lamp circuit may be restored for use as an extension cord by splicing the cut wire ends together. See Section II, General Repair Procedures, How to Install Solderless Wire Connectors.

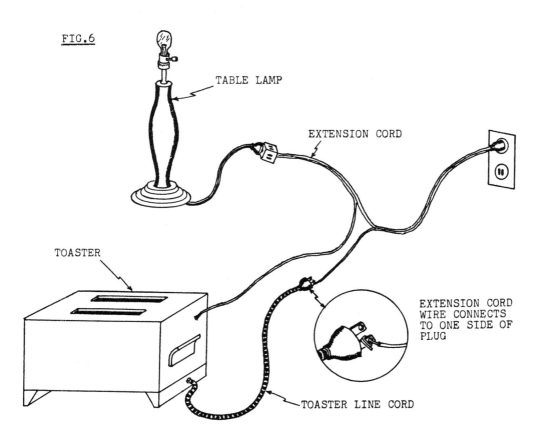

FIG.6

TABLE LAMP

EXTENSION CORD

TOASTER

EXTENSION CORD
WIRE CONNECTS
TO ONE SIDE OF
PLUG

TOASTER LINE CORD

Problem Solver #15

APPLIANCE: Non-Automatic Broilers

PROBLEM: **Heating element does not come on.**

EXPLANATION: Many simply constructed broilers have no automatic features. Most do not have an "on-off" switch, so that they heat up when the line cord is plugged into a wall outlet, and they shut off when the line cord is disconnected. When this type of broiler fails to heat up, a search will usually disclose a broken wire or wire connection.

TOOLS AND MATERIALS NEEDED:

   (a) a small screwdriver (sewing machine type)

   (b) a pair of long-nose pliers

   (c) a pair of universal pliers

   (d) one sheet of fine sandpaper (#00)

SOLUTION:

1. Make sure that the wall outlet has electric power. Plug a lamp or other appliance known to be in good working order into the outlet used for the broiler. If lamp or other appliance fails to operate, it can be assumed that a fuse has blown, a circuit breaker has tripped off, thus preventing electric power from reaching the wall outlet, or that the outlet itself is defective. Refer to Section II, General Repair Procedures, Fuses, Circuit Breakers, and Wall Outlets, for further information about this condition. If the lamp or other appliance operates, it means that the problem is in the broiler.

2. Examine the broiler line cord. (*Figure 1*) Check the female appliance plug for heat damage. If portions of the plastic body are burned away and the terminal connectors are loose and corroded, replace the female appliance plug. Refer to Section II, General Repair Procedures, Plugs, for detailed information.

FIG.1

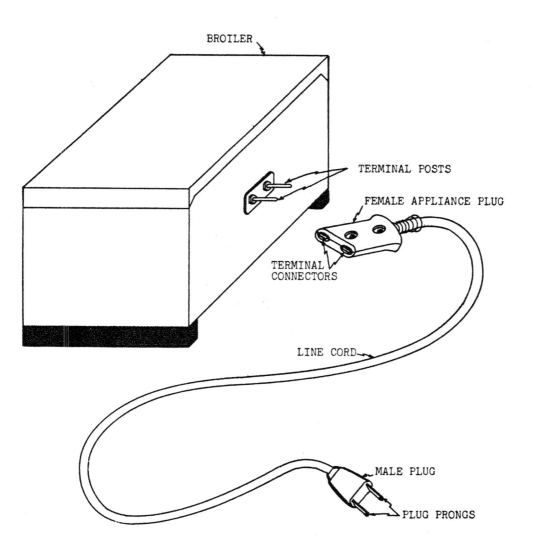

BROILER

TERMINAL POSTS

FEMALE APPLIANCE PLUG

TERMINAL
CONNECTORS

LINE CORD

MALE PLUG

PLUG PRONGS

NOTE: When in addition to a damaged female plug, examination of the line cord discloses a loose male plug and/or frayed wire covering, replace the entire line cord. The line cord may be purchased completely assembled from an appliance repair shop.

3. Inspect the terminal posts of the broiler. (*Figure 1*) If they are dark purple or black in color and are pitted (metal eaten away), clean them by rubbing with small strips of sandpaper until their surface becomes smooth and bright.

CAUTION: Do not remove too much of the surface metal with sandpaper. Reducing the thickness of the terminal posts may result in a loose fit with the female appliance plug. This will cause further deterioration of both the plug and terminal posts. Terminal posts that have worn excessively thin must be replaced by a qualified appliance technician.

4. Check terminal posts for looseness by wiggling them from side to side. Tighten loose terminal posts. Reach into broiler with pliers and turn the back nut (clockwise) until terminal post is secure. (*Figure 2*)

NOTE: The back nut may have become stuck to the thread of the terminal post. Therefore, when you turn the back nut, it may be necessary to hold the terminal post with another pair of pliers to prevent it from turning together with the back nut.

5. After the back nut has been tightened, tighten the front terminal nut to insure a good connection with the heating element wire.

6. Check the heating element wires going to the terminal posts. If wires are broken, reconnect them as outlined in Section II, General Repair Procedures, Heating Element Wire.

FIG.2

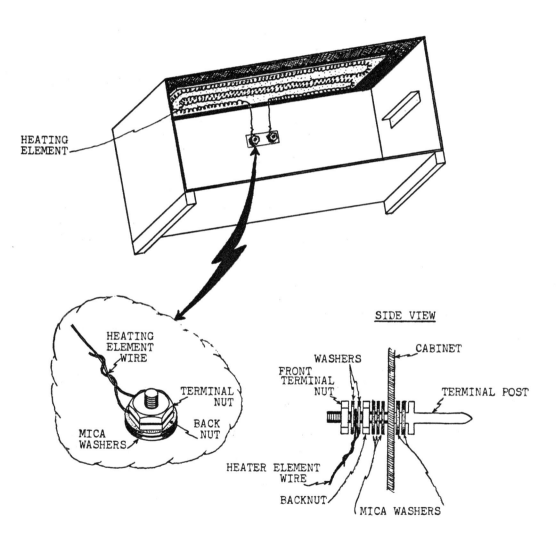

HEATING
ELEMENT

HEATING
ELEMENT
WIRE

TERMINAL
NUT

MICA
WASHERS

BACK
NUT

SIDE VIEW

WASHERS

FRONT
TERMINAL
NUT

CABINET

TERMINAL POST

HEATER ELEMENT
WIRE

BACKNUT

MICA WASHERS

Problem Solver #16

APPLIANCE: Broilers

PROBLEM: Fuse blows or circuit breaker trips when broiler is turned on.

EXPLANATION: Fuses and circuit breakers are safety devices that automatically limit the amount of electric power a line may carry. A blown fuse or tripped circuit breaker (depending on which is employed) is an indication that the demand for electric power on that particular electric line exceeded the safety limit. This can happen when too many appliances are operated on the same electric line or when an appliance (in this case a broiler) becomes defective and creates a "short circuit."

TOOLS AND MATERIALS NEEDED:

(a) a pair of long-nose pliers

(b) a screwdriver

(c) fiberglass tape (heat-proof)

SOLUTION:
1. Disconnect the broiler from the wall outlet.

2. Do not remove the blown fuse or, if circuit breaker is used, do not reset it to the "on" position.

NOTE: See Section II, General Repair Procedures, Fuses and Circuit Breakers, for further information.

3. Check to see if other appliances have gone "dead" as a result of the blown fuse. If other appliances are found not to be operating, the blown fuse or tripped circuit breaker may have resulted from the user's operating too many appliances on the same electric line.

SPECIAL NOTE: The electric power consumption of broilers (and many other heat-producing appliances) is very near the maximum safe power delivery of an electric line. Local electrical wiring regulations usually require that a separate electric line leading to a single wall outlet be provided for use by an electrical appliance. When blown fuses are experienced regularly, consult your electrician about adequate wiring.

4. If investigation of other appliances eliminates the possibility of too many appliances on one line as the cause of the blown fuse or tripped circuit breaker, it can be assumed that **a** defect in the broiler has produced a short circuit.

NOTE AND CAUTION: A short circuit is produced when an unwanted electrical connection is made within the broiler. When a short circuit is suspected, do not attempt to use the broiler until the unwanted connection is located and removed. A careful inspection of the broiler wiring will often reveal the location of the unwanted connection. This procedure is outlined in the steps that follow.

5. Remove the side shell mounting screws with a pair of pliers or a screwdriver and set them carefully aside. (*Figure 1*)

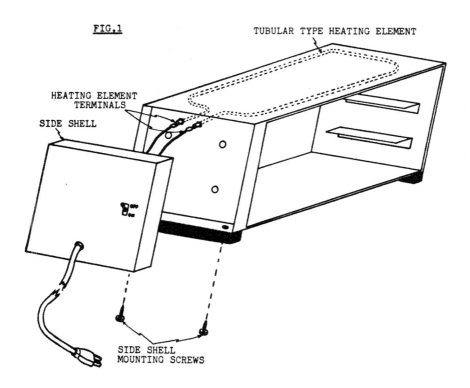

FIG.1   TUBULAR TYPE HEATING ELEMENT

HEATING ELEMENT
TERMINALS

SIDE SHELL

SIDE SHELL
MOUNTING SCREWS

6. Pry the bottom of the side shell away from the broiler with the flat blade of a screwdriver. Lift and remove the side shell.

7. Examine the heating element terminals and the wires that connect to them. (*Figures 2 and 3*) Check to see that there is no connection being made between the two terminals. Check also to see that the terminal connectors are not touching the black metal sheath of the heating element. (*Figure 3*) Adjust wires and/or terminal connectors with long-nose pliers to provide clearance when necessary.

   CAUTION: The terminal connectors of the heating element can withstand only slight bending. (*Figure 2*) If it is necessary to adjust the terminal connectors, use extreme care to avoid breakage.

8. Inspect the wires leading to the heating element terminals and the "on-off" switch for frayed insulation covering. Cover frayed sections of wires with fiberglass tape. Refer to Section II, General Repair Procedures, Terminals and Wire Connectors, for more details on how to insulate wire.

FIG.2

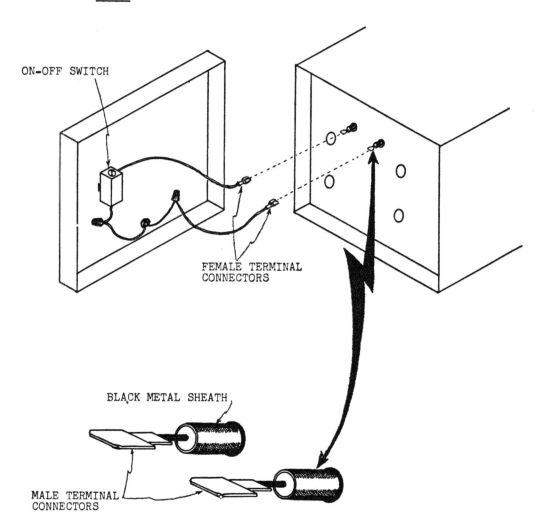

ON-OFF SWITCH

FEMALE TERMINAL
CONNECTORS

BLACK METAL SHEATH

MALE TERMINAL
CONNECTORS

9. Check to see that wires were not pinched between sharp portions of the side shell and the broiler shell. This condition is sometimes evidenced by blackened burn marks at one or more points along the wire. Cover these points with fiberglass tape.

   NOTE: If cause of short circuit cannot be established, the broiler should be taken to a qualified appliance repair shop for further tests.

10. Replace the side shell and secure it with the mounting screws. Take care not to pinch the wires between the side shell and the broiler shell. Make certain that the heating element terminals do not contact the side shell.

11. Replace the blown fuse with a new one or reset the circuit breaker to "on" and operate the broiler.

FIG.3

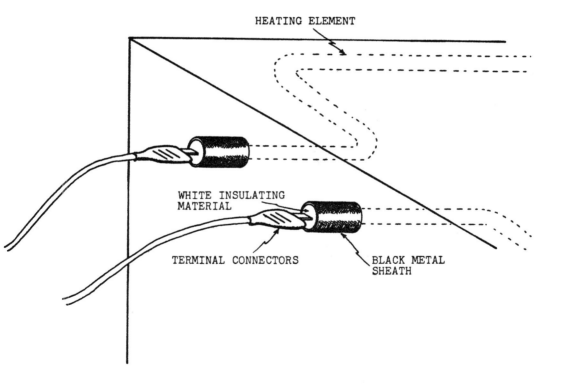

HEATING ELEMENT

WHITE INSULATING
MATERIAL

TERMINAL CONNECTORS

BLACK METAL
SHEATH

Problem Solver #17

APPLIANCE: Broilers

PROBLEM: Fuse blows or circuit breaker trips when broiler is plugged into wall outlet with switch in the "off" position.

EXPLANATION: When the fuse blows or circuit breaker trips to "off" with the broiler switch in the "off" position, it invariably points to a defective line cord. A close examination of the broiler line cord will probably disclose that the two wires that are normally insulated from each other have at some point contacted each other and caused a short circuit.

TOOLS AND MATERIALS NEEDED:

(a) a pair of pliers

(b) one heavy-duty male plug

(c) a 6-foot length of asbestos- and cloth-covered line cord wire

(d) a screwdriver

(e) fiberglass tape

SOLUTION:
1. Examine the line cord plug. If the plug shows signs of charring or if the wires going into it appear to have melted or fused together, the plug must be replaced. If no visible signs of defect are evident, pull the plug. If the plug parts from the line cord, replace the plug. See Section II, General Repair Procedures, Plugs, for information on how to replace the plug.

   NOTE: Defective wires in line cords can often be hidden beneath the outer cloth covering. Therefore, to insure the elimination of a short circuit due to the line cord, replace the entire line cord. The procedure for this is outlined in the steps that follow.

2. Remove the two screws that fasten the side shell and set them carefully aside. (*Figure 1*)

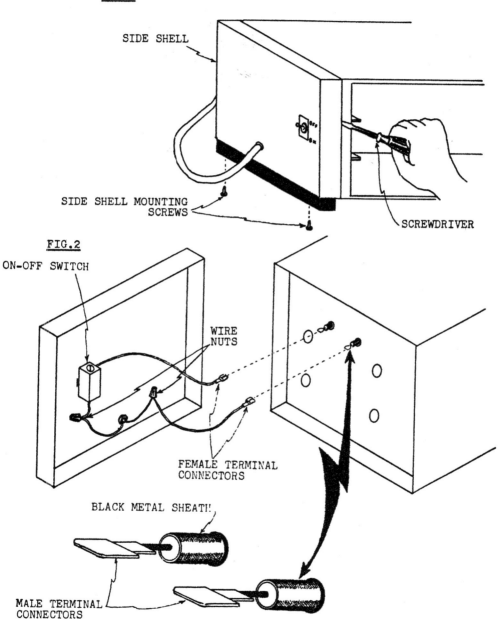

FIG.1

SIDE SHELL

OFF
ON

SIDE SHELL MOUNTING
SCREWS

SCREWDRIVER

FIG.2

ON-OFF SWITCH

WIRE
NUTS

FEMALE TERMINAL
CONNECTORS

BLACK METAL SHEATH

MALE TERMINAL
CONNECTORS

3. Pry the bottom edge of the side shell with the flat tip of a screwdriver. Lift and remove the side shell. (*Figures 1 and 2*)

4. Remove the wire nuts by unscrewing them in a counter-clockwise direction. (*Figure 3*)

5. Twist apart the line cord wire ends from the wires to which they are connected. (*Figure 3*)

6. Free the line cord from the side shell by removing the line cord stop. The feed-through type cord stop is removed by gripping it with the tip of a pair of pliers. (*Figure 4*) Squeeze hard on the handles of the pliers, and pull the cord stop and line cord wire out. Set the cord stop carefully aside for reuse with new replacement line cord.

7. Feed the wire ends of the new replacement line cord through the opening in the side shell. Place the line cord stop at a distance from the line cord wire ends equal to its original position on the old line cord.

8. Clamp the cord stop firmly on the line cord with pliers and push the cord stop into place in the side shell.

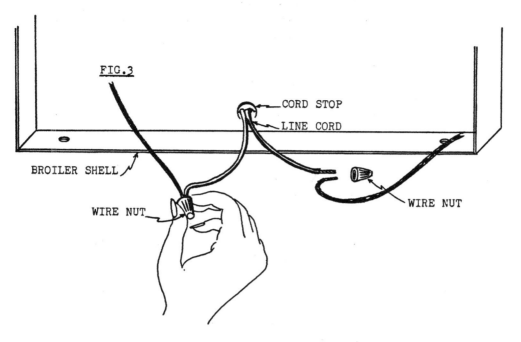

FIG.3

CORD STOP

LINE CORD

BROILER SHELL

WIRE NUT

WIRE NUT

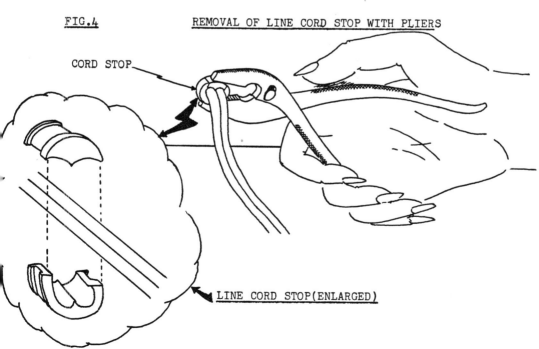

FIG.4   REMOVAL OF LINE CORD STOP WITH PLIERS

CORD STOP

LINE CORD STOP(ENLARGED)

9. Remove about an inch of insulation from each line cord wire end.

    CAUTION: Do not remove any more of the asbestos (white fluffy material) from the wire ends than is necessary.

10. Wrap the individual line cord wires with fiberglass tape. (*Figure 5*)

11. Reconnect the line cord wire ends to other wire ends as they were in the original line cord and replace the wire nuts. Refer to Section II, General Repair Procedures, Terminals and Wire Connectors, for more detailed information.

12. Reattach the side shell and secure it with screws.

    CAUTION: When reassembling, make sure wires are not pinched between sharp edges of side shell and broiler shell.

FIG.5

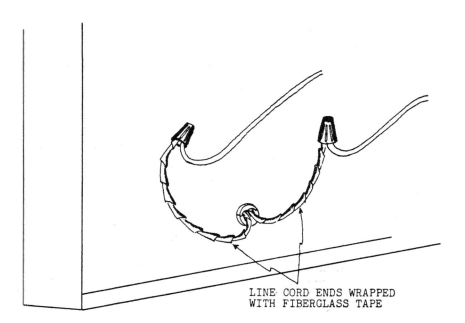

LINE CORD ENDS WRAPPED
WITH FIBERGLASS TAPE

Problem Solver #18

APPLIANCE: Coffee Makers (Electric)

PROBLEM: **Coffee has poor flavor.**

EXPLANATION: Coffee flavor may vary with different brands, and some are preferred because of their distinctive flavor. Some coffee, however, tastes bitter because the coffee maker has not been properly maintained. Good coffee maker maintenance should include cleaning that removes coffee residue and mineral deposits contained in hard water. These contaminants often accumulate in inaccessible areas within the coffee maker and are not readily removed by normal cleaning methods.

TOOLS AND MATERIALS NEEDED:

(a) one cup of white vinegar

(b) baking soda

(c) dishwashing detergent

(d) ordinary cooking pot

SOLUTION: 1. See *Figure 1* for illustration showing typical coffee maker and its component parts.

2. Rinse coffee maker, coffee basket, and pump tube thoroughly with clear water in order to remove coffee grounds.

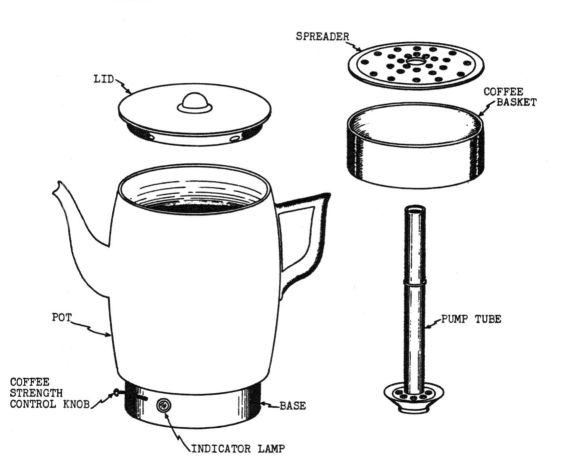

FIG.1

SPREADER

COFFEE
BASKET

LID

POT

PUMP TUBE

COFFEE
STRENGTH
CONTROL KNOB

BASE

INDICATOR LAMP

3. Place coffee basket and pump tube in cooking pot. Add dishwashing detergent and fill pot to brim with hot water. Allow to soak for at least 15 minutes. (*Figure 2*)

   NOTE: Some coffee makers are designed with sealed bases and are featured as "completely immersible" models. Water is prevented from entering the working parts of these units for as long as the seals remain intact. Since the possibility of water leaking into the sealed base is ever present and since there is no greater cleaning advantage gained by immersing the entire coffee maker, it is advisable to follow the soaking method described as additional insurance to prolong satisfactory service.

4. Using dishwasher detergent and water, scrub coffee maker, coffee basket, and pump tube thoroughly with dishcloth. (*Figure 3*)

   CAUTION: Avoid use of abrasive cleaners and pads, which produce minute scratches in metal surfaces.

5. Rinse all parts well with warm water. Allow to dry completely before storing.

   SPECIAL NOTE: The foregoing cleaning and care procedures have been suggested for "after each use" care. The cleaning procedures to be described in the steps that follow are suggested as periodic treatments to remove any accumulation of deposits.

6. To remove mineral deposits, fill coffee maker with a solution of equal parts of white vinegar and water. Place coffee basket and pump tube in coffee maker and allow vinegar solution to boil through as when making coffee.

7. To remove coffee residue, dissolve approximately two teaspoons of baking soda (for 8-cup coffee makers) in water. Allow solution to boil through as when making coffee.

FIG.2

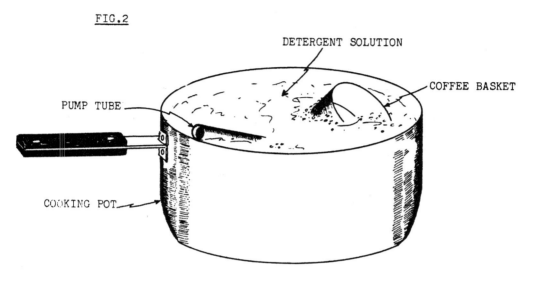

DETERGENT SOLUTION

COFFEE BASKET

PUMP TUBE

COOKING POT

FIG.3

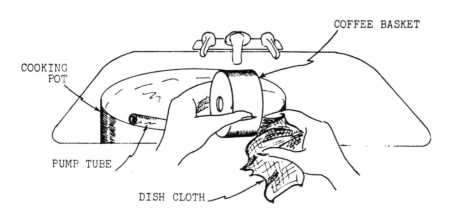

COFFEE BASKET

COOKING
POT

PUMP TUBE

DISH CLOTH

Problem Solver #19

APPLIANCE: Coffee Makers (Electric)

PROBLEM: Water boils but does not enter coffee basket in percolator-type coffee maker.

EXPLANATION: The perking action in an electric coffee maker is controlled by a floating disc-shaped valve located at the base of the pump tube. If the valve disc fails to close, as might happen when a particle of coffee or coffee residue causes it to jam in its open position, there will be no perking action.

TOOLS AND MATERIALS NEEDED:

(a) a toothpick

(b) baking soda

SOLUTION:

NOTE: Make certain that the pump tube is fully seated in the heater well before each use. (*Figure 1*)

1. Inspect the heater well to see that it is free of anything that might prevent the pump tube from seating fully. (*Figure 2*)

FIG.1

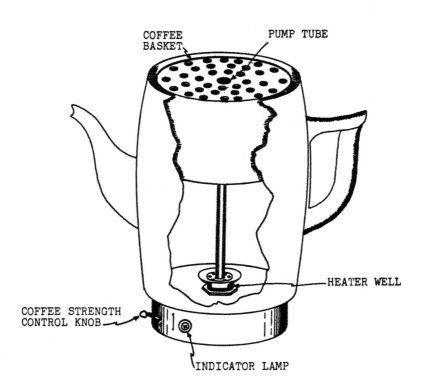

COFFEE BASKET

PUMP TUBE

HEATER WELL

COFFEE STRENGTH CONTROL KNOB

INDICATOR LAMP

2. Inspect the base of the pump tube. If it is distorted or dented, replace the pump tube. This part can be purchased from any appliance service shop. Make certain an exact replacement is used.

3. If the base of the pump tube is not distorted or dented, proceed to check the pump valve.

4. Hold the pump tube in a vertical position and shake it up and down. If free, the valve disc can be heard to clatter.

5. If the valve disc does not clatter, poke it up and down with the tip of a toothpick. If the valve disc does not move freely, examine the pump tube base carefully for coffee residue or a particle of ground coffee that may be jamming the valve disc. Pick clean with the tip of a toothpick the area round the valve disc until the valve moves freely. (*Figure 3*)

SPECIAL NOTE: An accumulation of coffee residue can be removed and prevented by soaking the appliance in dishwashing detergent regularly and boiling with baking soda solution periodically.

FIG.2

HEATER WELL

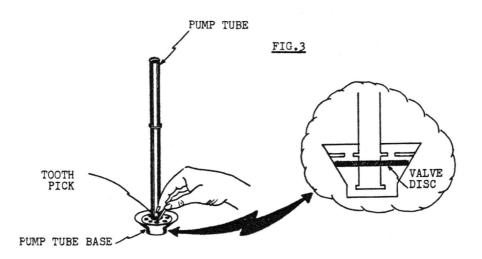

PUMP TUBE

FIG.3

TOOTH PICK

PUMP TUBE BASE

VALVE DISC

Problem Solver #20

APPLIANCE: Coffee Makers (Electric)

PROBLEM: **Coffee is too weak or too strong for desired setting.**

EXPLANATION: Many factors are involved in controlling the strength of percolated coffee. The most important points to consider are proportion of coffee and water used, temperature of the water, and the length of perking time.

TOOLS AND MATERIALS NEEDED:

(a) a screwdriver

(b) a toothpick

SOLUTION:
1. Check the directions on the can of your brand of coffee for the correct coffee measurement. Use an accurate measuring utensil.

2. Fill the coffee maker with water to the proper cup level for quantity of coffee used.

   NOTE: Always use water at tap temperature (50°-70° F.). Never use hot water to start the coffee. Pre-heated water will cause the perking action to stop too soon, thus producing weak coffee.

3. If all of the above precautions have been taken and the coffee is still too weak, check the valve disc located in the base of the pump tube. When the valve disc fails to close completely, insufficient perking action results. Clean the areas directly above and below the valve disc of any coffee residue that could prevent the valve disc from moving freely. (*Figure 1*)

4. Check the pump tube base to see that it seats fully into the heater well. If the base of the pump tube is dented or distorted, replace the pump tube. This part may be purchased from appliance parts and service shops.

FIG.1

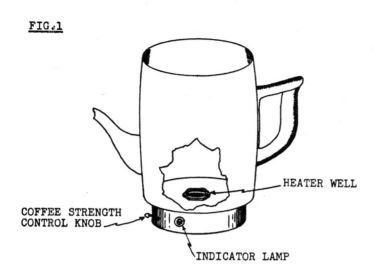

HEATER WELL

COFFEE STRENGTH
CONTROL KNOB

INDICATOR LAMP

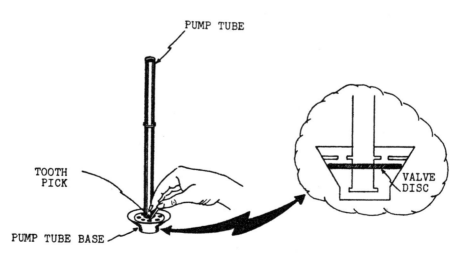

PUMP TUBE

TOOTH
PICK

PUMP TUBE BASE

VALVE
DISC

(PS#20)

SPECIAL NOTE: The length of perking time is automatically controlled by a thermostat. Different coffee blends packaged under different brand labels may require slightly different settings of the coffee strength control knob to suit individual tastes. If, however, the coffee produced is excessively weak (no flavor or color) or excessively strong (bitter), it would indicate that the thermostat is not functioning correctly. The steps that follow list the procedures for uncovering the thermostat and the visual clues that help in evaluating the working condition of the thermostat.

CAUTION: Remove appliance plug from maker before proceeding.

5. Remove the coffee strength control knob by pulling it off, and remove the screw (or screws) that fastens the base section to the pot. Carefully take off the base. (*Figure 2*)

CAUTION: The base section of completely immersible coffee makers should be disassembled by a qualified appliance technician in order to guarantee waterproof assembly.

6. Inspect the wires that are routed to and around the movable thermostat blade. (*Figure 3*) Wires that lie against the blade could prevent its free movement during operation. Move the wires aside.

7. Inspect the thermostat blade and its electrical contact points for corrosion and/or stuck condition. Reassemble coffee maker and test.

NOTE: Water seepage into the base section of the pot (due to leaks or improper cleaning techniques) will cause the thermostat and other working parts to corrode and malfunction. If this condition exists, the coffee maker should be taken to an authorized appliance service shop for repair.

SPECIAL NOTE: To insure satisfactory service from your coffee maker:

A. Carefully follow the manufacturer's instructions on use and care.

B. Do not allow water or coffee spills to run into the base section of the pot.

C. Have qualified service technicians investigate the slightest evidence of coffee leakage into base section as quickly as possible to avoid further damage.

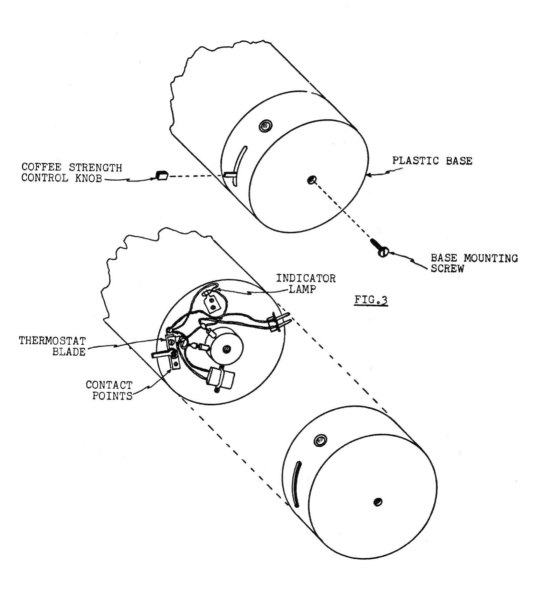

FIG.2

COFFEE STRENGTH
CONTROL KNOB

PLASTIC BASE

BASE MOUNTING
SCREW

INDICATOR
LAMP

FIG.3

THERMOSTAT
BLADE

CONTACT
POINTS

Problem Solver #21

APPLIANCE: Coffee Makers (Electric)

PROBLEM: Lid falls off when user pours coffee.

EXPLANATION: The lid of most coffee makers is held firmly on top of the pot by a number of small bumps which protrude around the edge of the lid. Through normal use these bumps can become worn or flattened so that they no longer exert the correct pressure against the pot to hold the lid firmly in place.

TOOLS AND MATERIALS NEEDED:

    (a) a hammer

    (b) a block of wood

    (c) a sardine can opener (key)

SOLUTION: 1. Remove the lid from the coffee maker. (*Figure 1*)

    2. Take off the glass lid knob to avoid damaging it. Glass lid knobs are removed by twisting them counter-clockwise and lifting them out.

    NOTE: If the knob is stuck or otherwise difficult to remove, allow knob to remain but be careful not to break it.

    3. Place lid on wood block with lid bump contacting wood. (*Figure 2*)

FIG.1

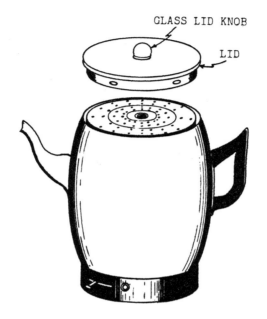

GLASS LID KNOB

LID

FIG.2

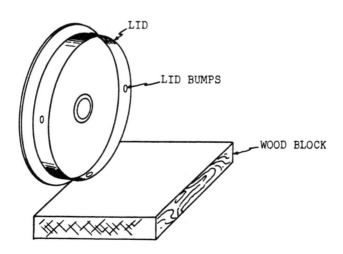

LID

LID BUMPS

WOOD BLOCK

4. Place tip of sardine can opener into lid bump cavity and tap the top of can opener with hammer (*Figure 3*)

   NOTE: Examine the lid bump after tapping to determine how far bump has been extended. In most cases, the lid bumps need be extended only slightly to restore correct lid fit.

5. Rotate lid and tap out remaining lid bumps. Test fit of lid after tapping each lid bump so as to prevent making the lid fit too tightly.

6. If lid is too tight, flatten bumps *slightly* by tapping them with wood block. (*Figure 4*)

Problem Solver #22

APPLIANCE: Coffee Makers (Electric)

PROBLEM: Indicator lamp does not operate.

EXPLANATION: In some coffee percolators, a small red lens lights up to indicate that percolation has stopped and the coffee is ready. The lens light is provided by a small lamp located directly behind the lens. If the percolator works satisfactorily but the lamp fails to indicate, the fault can be corrected by simply replacing the lamp. This is an inexpensive repair and can usually be completed at an appliance repair shop while you wait. However, the procedure for replacing the indicator lamp is described below for those who decide to do it themselves.

FIG.3

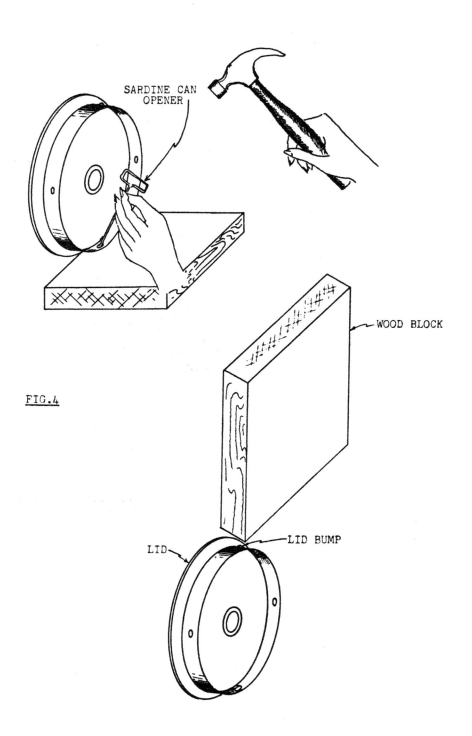

SARDINE CAN OPENER

WOOD BLOCK

FIG.4

LID

LID BUMP

Tools and Materials Needed:

   (a) a screwdriver

   (b) a pair of pliers

   caution: Disconnect appliance plug from coffee maker.

Solution:

1. Remove the coffee strength selector knob by pulling it straight off.

2. Remove the screw (or screws) used to fasten the plastic base of the percolator to the pot and carefully take off the base. (*Figure 1*)

3. Locate and identify the indicator lamp.

   note: Two basic types of lamps are presently in use: incandescent lamps and neon lamps. The incandescent lamps resemble the kind of lamp used in flashlights and are usually found in older percolator models. This type is secured in the lamp socket in one of two ways. One is screwed into the socket and is referred to as a screw-base lamp. The other is pushed into the socket and twisted. Two little pins on its base secure this second lamp in the socket. This is known as a bayonet lamp. The neon lamp is more often found in newer model percolators. This lamp does not require a lamp socket. It is connected to the electric wiring of the percolator by two thin wire leads.

4. If a screw-base incandescent lamp is used, remove it from its socket by turning it counter-clockwise. Take the burned out lamp to the nearest appliance repair shop and ask for a replacement.

   note: A qualified appliance technician can usually identify the lamp to be replaced by numbers printed on its base and other code marks. It is a good idea to take along also the manufacturer's name and the model number of the percolator to insure purchase of the correct replacement lamp. (*Figure 1*)

   caution: Before replacing plastic base, make certain that the lamp is correctly aligned behind red lens. The lamp socket bracket may be bent slightly if necessary.

5. To remove bayonet lamp, hold the lamp socket with one hand to prevent it from being forced out of position. Grasp the lamp with the other hand, push into the socket, and twist it counter-clockwise. The lamp can then be pulled straight out of the socket. (*Figure 2*)

FIG.1

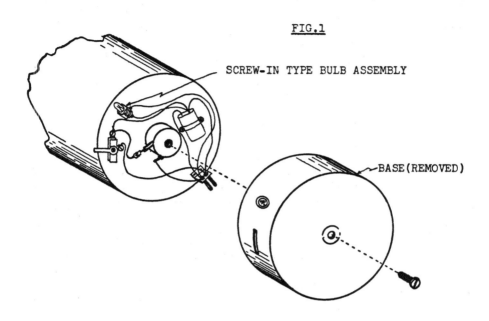

SCREW-IN TYPE BULB ASSEMBLY

BASE(REMOVED)

FIG.2

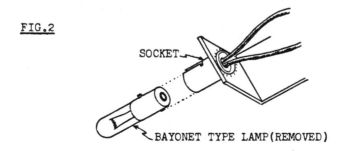

SOCKET

BAYONET TYPE LAMP(REMOVED)

6. To install a replacement bayonet lamp, align the two pins on the base of the lamp with the two channels on the lamp socket. Press the lamp into the base as far as it will go, twist the lamp clockwise, and release it.

7. Align the lamp socket so that the lamp will be positioned directly behind the red lens. Replace the plastic base and secure it to the pot with screw (or screws).

8. If neon lamp is used, check first to see that the lead wires of the lamp are securely connected to their terminals. (*Figure 3*)

   NOTE: Neon lamps do not as a rule burn out. Unless the glass bulb actually breaks, failure of these lamps to operate can usually be traced to broken or loose wire leads. These lamps are purchased and replaced as an entire assembly that can include lamp, insulating sleeves, terminals, and in some models an additional part called a resistor. (*Figure 3A*)

FIG.3

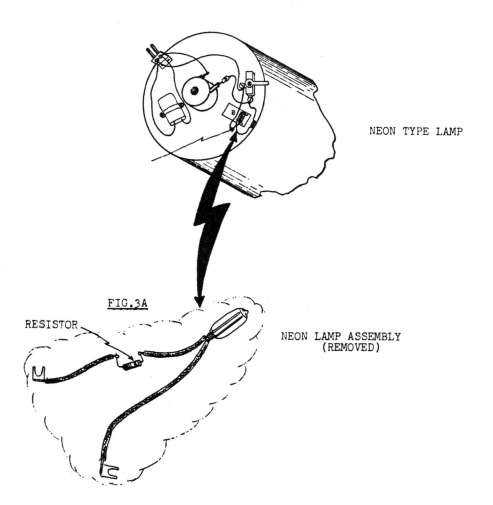

NEON TYPE LAMP

FIG.3A

RESISTOR

NEON LAMP ASSEMBLY
(REMOVED)

9. To replace neon lamp assembly, loosen terminal screws or nuts by turning counter-clockwise about two full turns and remove the lamp lead terminals. This will release the lamp assembly. (*Figure 4*)

   NOTE: In some models the lamp is held in position behind the lens by a small clamp. If so, slip the lamp out of the clamp to release it.

10. To install new lamp assembly, place lead wire terminal under terminal screws (or nuts) and tighten securely. Place lamp under clamp. (*Figure 5*)

   CAUTION: Make certain that wire leads of clamp are positioned away from other parts. Handle lamp wires carefully to prevent them from breaking. Do not bend them sharply or tug them too hard.

11. Secure plastic base to pot with screw (screws) and replace coffee strength control knob.

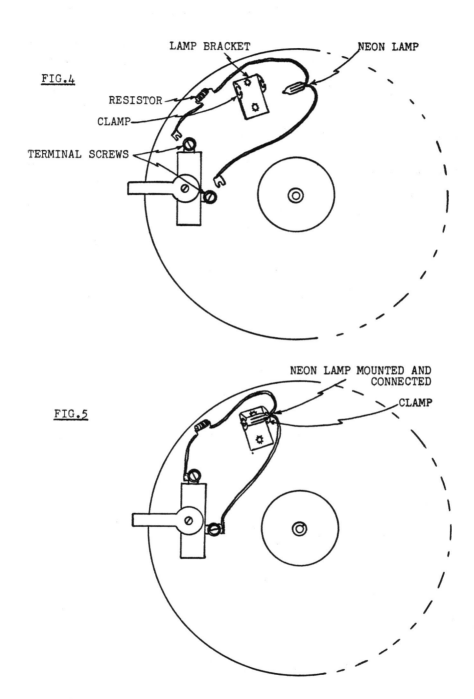

FIG.4

LAMP BRACKET

NEON LAMP

RESISTOR

CLAMP

TERMINAL SCREWS

FIG.5

NEON LAMP MOUNTED AND
CONNECTED

CLAMP

Problem Solver #23

APPLIANCE: Vaporizers

PROBLEM: House lights dim or fuse blows when vaporizer is plugged into wall outlet.

EXPLANATION: When any appliance causes house lights to dim, it should serve as a warning that more electric power is being demanded than can be supplied by the electric line. This can happen when too many appliances are connected to the same electric line or when the appliance itself is not working properly. A blown fuse or tripped circuit breaker (when used) serves as fairly reliable evidence that the power demand has exceeded the safety limit.

TOOLS AND MATERIALS NEEDED:

(a) instructional literature (supplied by manufacturer)

(b) a long-handled spoon

SOLUTION:
1. Check for and disconnect other heavy wattage appliances operating in the same room or on the same electric line. If lights still dim or fuse blows again, follow procedure outlined below.

2. Read and carefully follow manufacturer's instructions on use of vaporizer.

   NOTE: Modern vaporizers depend upon a saline (salt and water) solution for operation. When the proportion of salt added is too great, a vaporizer will draw an excessive amount of electricity. This can cause lights to dim and/or a fuse to blow.

3. Spill out contents of vaporizer and refill with fresh clear water.

4. Add *correct* amount of salt to water and stir with spoon to dissolve all salt. (*Figure 1*)

5. Plug unit into wall outlet and allow at least two minutes for steam vapor to appear.

   CAUTION: Do not add more salt to hasten or increase steam vapor. Also do not add medication to the water. Most vaporizers contain a special well near the steam spout for any medication. (*Figure 1*)

FIG.1

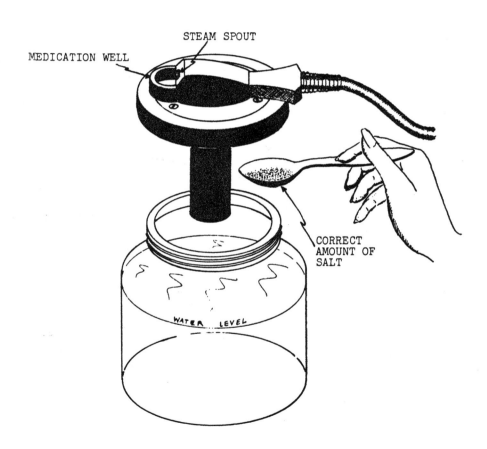

STEAM SPOUT

MEDICATION WELL

CORRECT
AMOUNT OF
SALT

WATER LEVEL

Problem Solver #24

APPLIANCE: Vaporizers

PROBLEM: **Vaporizer produces little or no steam.**

EXPLANATION: The simpler of two causes of this problem is improper filling and preparation of the vaporizer. The second and more serious cause develops over a period of time through normal use and requires the cleaning or replacement of two electrodes that produce the steam.

TOOLS AND MATERIALS NEEDED:

(a) instructional literature (supplied by manufacturer)

(b) a small phillips screwdriver

(c) a medium size screwdriver (flatblade)

(d) two emery boards (used for fingernails)

(e) a long-handled spoon

(f) a pair of pliers

SOLUTION: 1. Read and carefully follow manufacturer's instructions on use of vaporizer.

NOTE: For satisfactory operation, vaporizers depend upon a correct proportion of salt and water. When not enough salt is used, vaporizers will not produce a sufficient quantity of steam. It is wise, therefore, to make sure that the manufacturer's recommended quantity of salt is carefully measured.

2. Spill out contents of vaporizer and refill with fresh clear water.

3. Add *correct* amount of salt to water and stir with spoon to make certain all salt is dissolved.

4. Plug unit into wall outlet and allow at least two minutes for steam vapor to appear.

CAUTION: Do not add more salt to hasten or increase steam vapor. If vaporizer still does not produce enough steam, proceed to solution steps below.

FIG.1

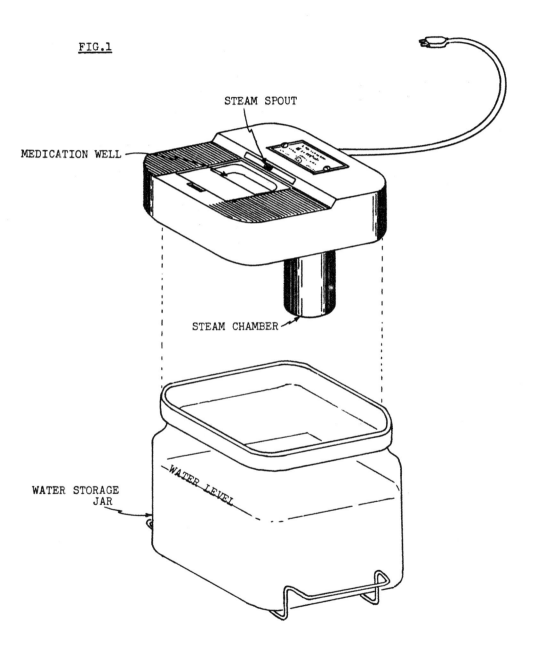

STEAM SPOUT

MEDICATION WELL

STEAM CHAMBER

WATER STORAGE
JAR

WATER LEVEL

5. Disconnect vaporizer from wall outlet.

6. Remove vaporizer steam chamber from the water jar. (*Figure 1*) Allow water to drain from steam chamber into water jar.

7. Remove the screws that fasten the steam chamber cover. (*Figure 2*)

8. Examine the electrodes. They will probably be encrusted with heavy deposits of minerals and salt. (*Figure 3*)

9. Carefully scrape off mineral deposits with an emery board until metal electrodes are thoroughly clean. (*Figure 4*)

CAUTION AND NOTE: Take care when cleaning electrodes not to disturb or break the ceramic insulator that separates the two electrodes. The metal electrodes must never touch each other. Cleaning of electrodes is usually all that is required to restore proper steam supply. However, if examination of electrodes shows that large portions of the electrodes have been eaten away by corrosion, the electrodes must then be replaced.

SPECIAL NOTE: In most vaporizers, the electrodes are the only "working" parts. Replacing the electrodes with new ones can restore the operation of a vaporizer to "like new" condition. The procedure for replacing the electrodes is outlined in the steps that follow.

FIG.2

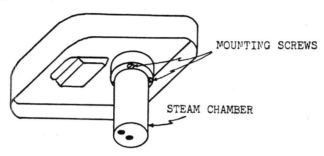

MOUNTING SCREWS

STEAM CHAMBER

FIG.3

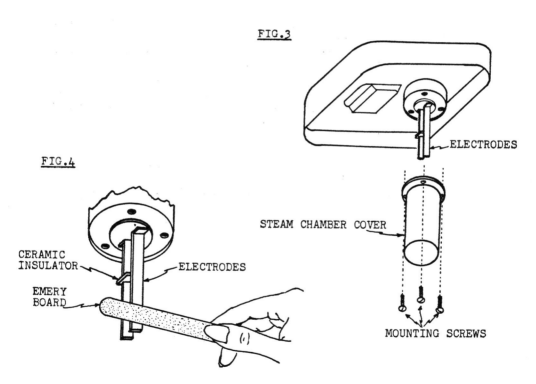

ELECTRODES

FIG.4

STEAM CHAMBER COVER

CERAMIC
INSULATOR

ELECTRODES

EMERY
BOARD

MOUNTING SCREWS

10. Remove the screws that fasten the terminal cover plate and lift off the cover plate. (*Figure 5*)

11. Remove the terminal nuts (turn counter-clockwise) with a pair of pliers. (*Figure 6*)

12. Lift the line cord terminal connectors off the threaded terminal screws. Remove the two washers and set them carefully aside for reuse with new electrodes. (*Figure 6*)

13. Grasp electrodes and remove them by pulling them straight out.

14. Insert new replacement electrodes in the same position as original ones. Make certain the two neoprene seals (*Figure 6*) are in place and are seated correctly to prevent water and steam from entering the electrical terminal compartment. Broken or worn seals should be replaced. These may be purchased at an authorized service center.

15. Hold electrodes in position and replace washers. Replace line cord terminal connectors. Thread terminal nuts down and tighten them with pliers. Make sure that terminal connectors do not touch each other.

16. Replace terminal cover plate and steam chamber cover to complete the repair.

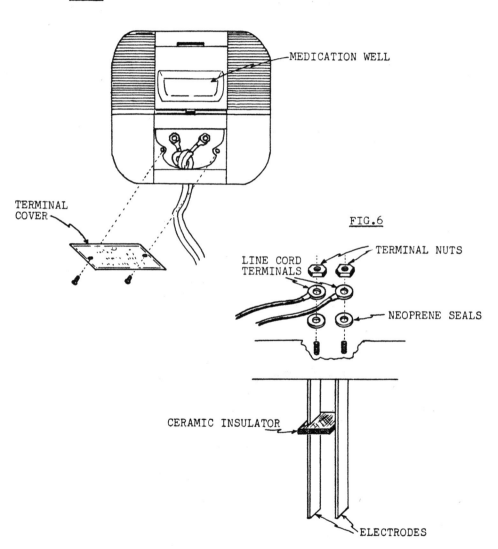

FIG.5

MEDICATION WELL

TERMINAL
COVER

FIG.6

LINE CORD
TERMINALS

TERMINAL NUTS

NEOPRENE SEALS

CERAMIC INSULATOR

ELECTRODES

Problem Solver #25

APPLIANCE: Electric Fry Pans and Cookers

PROBLEM: **Appliance does not heat.**

EXPLANATION: Modern fry pans and cookers are constructed so that they have two major working sections. These are: (1) the pan (or pot), which contains the heating element; and (2) the control unit, which contains the thermostat and, on some models, an indicator lamp. When this type of appliance does not heat, the cause must be traced to one of the two sections. Once the malfunctioning section has been identified, the repair is best completed by replacing the entire section.

TOOLS AND MATERIALS NEEDED:

(a) a table lamp (with 40 watt bulb or less)

(b) 6-foot extension cord

(c) a handful of fine steel wool (or abrasive cleaning pad)

(d) a paring knife

SOLUTION: 1. Disconnect control unit from the pan (or pot) and examine the terminal pins for signs of discoloration or corrosion. (*Figure 1*)

2. If terminal pins are found to be discolored or corroded, clean them with steel wool. Retest pan to see if it heats. If appliance still fails to heat, proceed to the test outlined on the following pages.

FIG.1

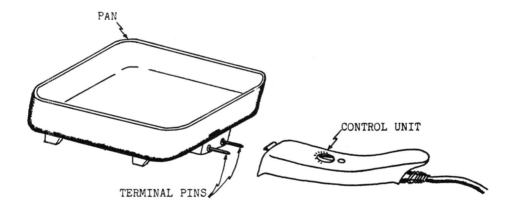

PAN

CONTROL UNIT

TERMINAL PINS

SPECIAL NOTE: A simple testing circuit can be arranged with any available table lamp and a 6-foot extension cord. This testing circuit will provide an effective visual indication that can be used to determine which of the two sections (pan or control unit) is defective. The procedure for arranging and using the test circuit is outlined in the following steps.

3. Separate the wires of the extension cord for about ten inches along the center of its length by slitting them with a sharp paring knife. (*Figure 2*) Guide the paring knife carefully along the insulated center of the extension cord in order to avoid exposing the copper wire.

4. Cut through one side of the separate extension cord wires with the paring knife. (*Figure 3*)

5. Remove about an inch of insulation from the cut wire ends. (*Figure 4*)

FIG.2

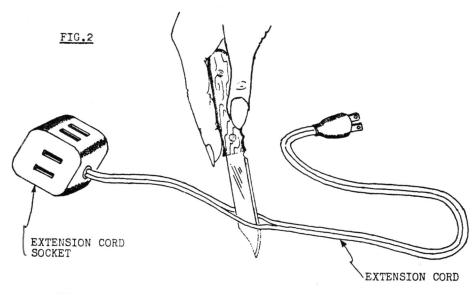

EXTENSION CORD
SOCKET

EXTENSION CORD

FIG.3

FIG.4

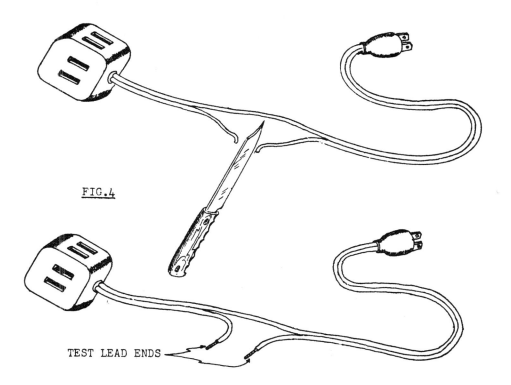

TEST LEAD ENDS

6. Wrap the cut wire ends of the extension cord around each terminal pin on the pan. (*Figure 5*)

7. Screw a small wattage bulb (40 watts or less) into the lamp. Connect the lamp plug into the extension cord receptacle. Connect the extension cord plug into a convenient wall outlet. (*Figure 5*)

8. Turn the lamp switch on. If lamp does not light, it means that the heating element in the pan is not working.

   NOTE: The heating element is usually embedded in the casting of the pan or pot and cannot be removed. Replacement, therefore, will require the purchase of a new pan or pot. This section can be purchased at any appliance repair shop.

9. If the lamp lights, it means that the heating element is working and that the malfunction is in the control unit.

   NOTE: Because of the exacting tolerances within which the control unit must operate, service and repairs to this unit should be performed only by a qualified appliance technician.

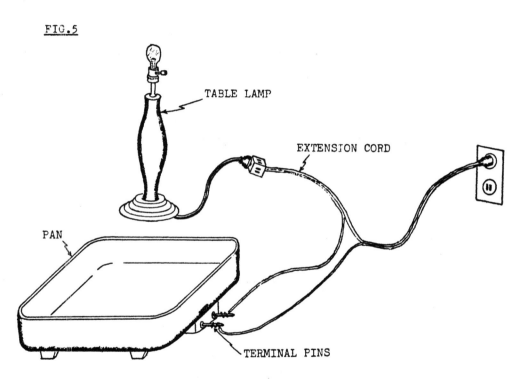

FIG.5

TABLE LAMP

EXTENSION CORD

PAN

TERMINAL PINS

Problem Solver #26

APPLIANCE: Electric Deep Fryers; Fry Pans (Not Teflon Coated)

PROBLEM: **Pan-fried food sticks and/or burns at prescribed settings.**

EXPLANATION: This complaint usually indicates that the surface temperature of the pan is too high. This can occur when the thermostat located in the control unit of the appliance becomes defective. However, since other factors may also contribute to the burning of food, the operation of the thermostat should be tested before it is unnecessarily condemned and replaced.

TOOLS AND MATERIALS NEEDED:

(a) a dial thermometer
(used for candymaking and deep frying)

SOLUTION:

NOTE: Two methods of testing the operation of the thermostat will be described in the steps that follow. The first method can be used on deep fryers that have an indicating lamp. The second method can be employed with those that do not have an indicating lamp.

1. Pour about two inches of water into the pot.

2. Turn the temperature control knob to its highest setting (400° F.) and allow the water to come to a rolling boil. (*Figure 1*)

3. Allow water to continue to boil for about three minutes. Then turn control knob slowly back toward the lower temperature settings until indicator light goes out.

4. Stop turning the knob when the indicator lamp goes out and read the temperature that the knob points to on the dial.

FIG.1

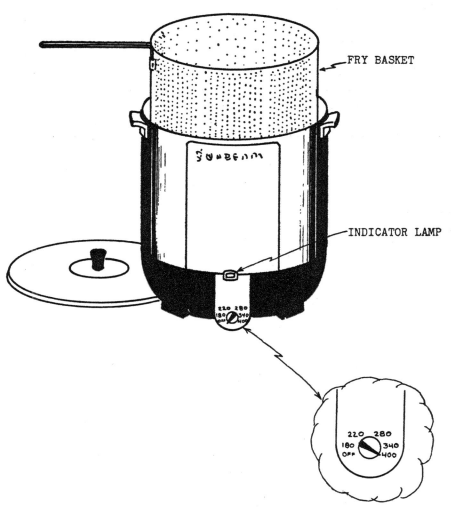

TEMPERATURE CONTROL KNOB SET TO 400°

5. If the knob points to a temperature between 190° and 230° F., you can assume that the thermostat is functioning correctly. If the light does not go out or if the knob points to a temperature that is not between the range given above, it means that the thermostat control unit is defective and must be repaired or replaced. The appliance should be taken to an appliance repair shop for further testing and service.

6. To test the thermostat control unit for fry pans and/or cookers that do not have an indicator lamp, pour at least two inches of clear cooking oil into pan or pot and set the temperature control knob to 300° F. (*Figure 2*)

7. Connect line cord plug into wall outlet and allow oil to heat for at least six minutes.

8. Place a dial thermometer (used for candymaking or deep frying) into the oil and measure the temperature. (*Figure 3*)

   CAUTION: Make sure sensitive stem portion of thermometer is immersed at least two inches into the heated oil.

9. If the thermometer reading is between 270° and 330° F., it means that the thermostat control unit is functioning properly.

10. If the thermometer reading is less than 270° F. or more than 330° F., it means that the thermostat control unit is defective and should be taken to an appliance repair shop for service.

    SPECIAL NOTE: Cooking oil, shortening, and butter behave differently when used for frying. Some of these products contain a large quantity of food solids that produce smoke at high frying temperatures. This condition is often mistakenly thought to be caused by defective operation of the pan or cooker. Selection of oil or shortening that has been refined for frying can eliminate unnecessary smoke.

FIG.2

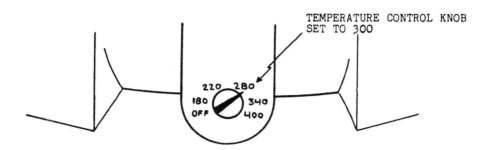

TEMPERATURE CONTROL KNOB
SET TO 300

FIG.3

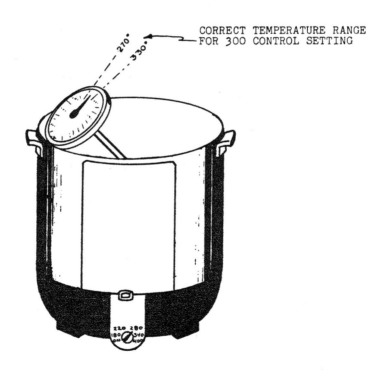

CORRECT TEMPERATURE RANGE
FOR 300 CONTROL SETTING

Problem Solver #27

APPLIANCE: Teflon Coated Electric Fry Pans and Cookers

PROBLEM: **Teflon coating is deteriorating.**

EXPLANATION: Teflon is the modern plastic material used to coat the inside surface of pots and pans for a no-stick surface. When properly cared for, the Teflon coating can last the life of the pan or cooker. If abused, the coating can be ruined.

TOOLS AND MATERIALS NEEDED:

(a) manufacturer's use and care literature

SOLUTION: Read and carefully follow manufacturer's instructions on the use and care of Teflon coated pans and cookers.

SPECIAL NOTE: Preventive care is the only solution for preventing damage or further deterioration of the Teflon coating. The first products employing Teflon were often coated too thinly to withstand even normal use. Special plastic utensils had to be used to protect the Teflon coating from damage. Owners of these products were cautioned by the manufacturer to avoid using metal utensils to stir cooking ingredients. Many people continued to use metal utensils. This practice invariably resulted in portions of the Teflon coating being scratched or chipped away. However, recent improvements and moderate care should insure the effectiveness of the Teflon coating for the life of the product. Moreover, some manufacturers now claim that ordinary metal utensils may be used with the Teflon coating without fear of damage.

The following precautions are offered for prolonging the effectiveness of Teflon coatings used in electric cookers.

1. Avoid the use of sharp metal utensils for stirring or scraping.

2. Avoid the use of abrasive cleaning pads.

3. Never allow an empty pan or pot to heat to high temperatures. This can scorch the Teflon coating and cause it to discolor and deteriorate.

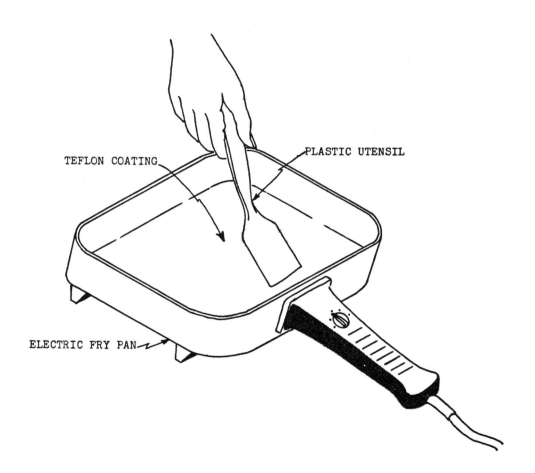

FIG.1

TEFLON COATING

PLASTIC UTENSIL

ELECTRIC FRY PAN

Problem Solver #28

APPLIANCE: Electric Sandwich Grill and Waffle Baker
(Not Teflon Coated)

PROBLEM: **Waffles stick to grill.**

EXPLANATION: Removing a waffle that has stuck to the hot grills of a waffle baker can be a nuisance and a hazard. The secret of how to prevent this from happening lies in the preparation and cleaning care of the surfaces of the grills.

TOOLS AND MATERIALS NEEDED:

(a) scouring pad

(b) clear, light cooking oil (nonsmoking type)

(c) basting brush

(d) paper towels

SOLUTION: 1. Allow waffle baker to cool to room temperature before attempting to handle grill sections.

2. Clean grill surfaces carefully with scouring pad. Make certain all burned-on waffle residue is removed. (*Figure 1*)

3. Rinse grills thoroughly with warm water. Make sure all traces of cleaning agent (soap or detergent) are removed. (*Figure 2*)

FIG.1

WAFFLE BAKER
GRILL

SCOURING PAD

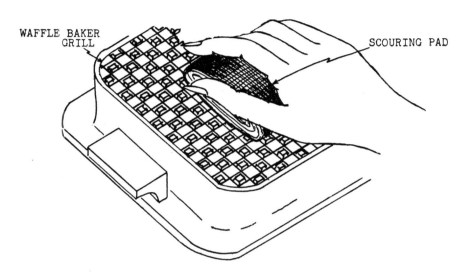

FIG.2

WET RAG (RINSE)

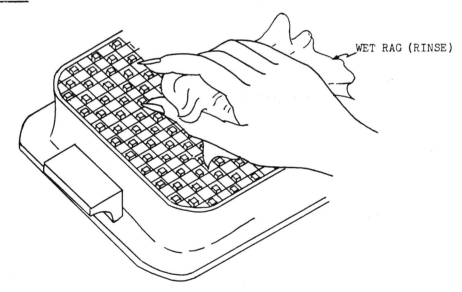

CAUTION: Do not hold grill under running water since there is danger that some water may get into the area below the base and come into contact with electrical connections. Use a wet cloth or rag to rinse.

4. Dry the grills thoroughly with a clean cloth or towel.

5. Apply a nonsmoking cooking oil to the baking surfaces of the grills with a basting brush. Make certain that the surfaces are completely coated. (*Figure 3*)

6. Wipe the surfaces of the grills with paper towels until all excess oil has been absorbed. (*Figure 4*)

7. Waffle baker is now ready for use.

SPECIAL NOTE: Waffle grills are especially designed with finely pitted surfaces. The pitting acts much like very small wells that can store small quantities of cooking oil evenly over the entire surfaces of the grills.

Once the surfaces of the grills have been treated as described above, the waffle baker can be used continuously without further need for oiling the surfaces. In between use, the surfaces need only to be wiped clean with dry towels and should not be cleaned with detergents or scouring pads.

If, however, an occasional cleaning becomes necessary, as would be the case after a long period of storage, the cleaning and treatment as described in the solution steps 1 through 7 should be followed.

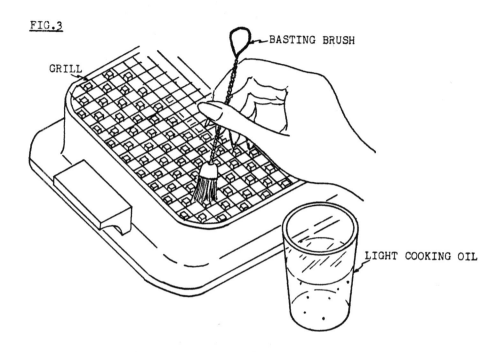

FIG.3

BASTING BRUSH

GRILL

LIGHT COOKING OIL

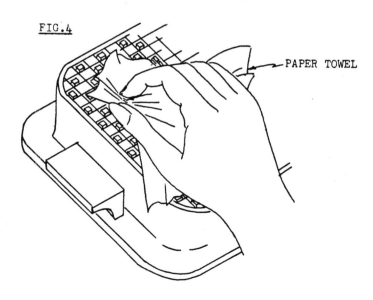

FIG.4

PAPER TOWEL

Problem Solver #29

APPLIANCE: Electric Sandwich Grill and Waffle Baker

PROBLEM: **No heat on one or both waffle grills.**

EXPLANATION: Heating element wires are located behind both the top and bottom grills of waffle bakers. In some waffle baker models, the heating element wires of each grill operate independently; therefore, a broken or burned-out element wire in one grill would not prevent the other grill from heating. In other waffle baker models, the heating element wires operate together. In this kind of waffle baker, a break or burn-out in either heating element wire would prevent both grills from heating. However, the solution to the heating problems that may be encountered in either type is the same. The exact point at which the wires have broken or burned apart must be located and repaired.

TOOLS AND MATERIALS NEEDED:

(a) a medium size screwdriver (flatblade)

(b) a pair of long-nose pliers

(c) one 6-32 ¼″ long roundhead brass screw

(d) one 6-32 brass nut

SOLUTION: 1. Remove the line cord plug from the wall outlet.

2. Remove both grills. (*Figures 1 and 2*)

   NOTE: Waffle grills are secured to the baker with either screws or clips. (*Figures 1 and 2*)

FIG.1

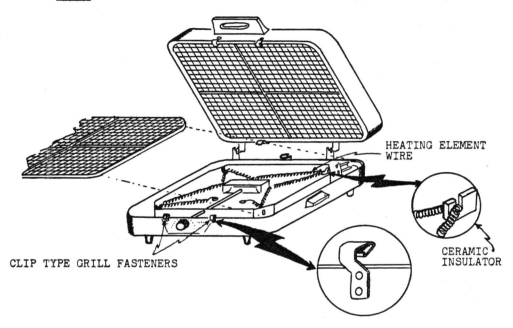

HEATING ELEMENT
WIRE

CERAMIC
INSULATOR

CLIP TYPE GRILL FASTENERS

FIG.2

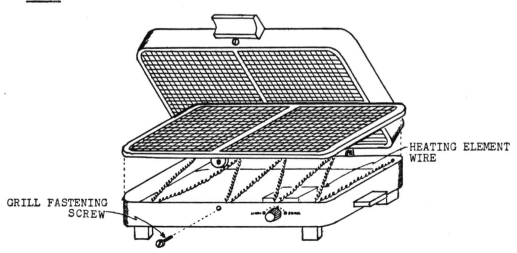

HEATING ELEMENT
WIRE

GRILL FASTENING
SCREW

3. Examine the heating element wires carefully until the break (point at which wire has parted) is located. (*Figure 3*)

4. Form each wire end into a loop, or eyelet, with long-nose pliers. (*Figure 4*) Each eyelet opening should only be large enough to allow a size 6-32 screw to pass through it freely. Do not form too large an eyelet.

5. Insert the brass screw through both eyelets and secure them by threading the brass nut onto the screw.

6. Hold the nut with the long-nose pliers and tighten the screw securely with a screwdriver. (*Figure 5*)

7. Inspect the heating element wire to make certain that it is supported securely by the ceramic insulators. Also, make certain that the element wire does *not* contact the metal housing of the baker anywhere along its route. Carefully bend the wire away from the metal housing whenever necessary.

8. Replace the grills to complete the repair.

NOTE: Other solutions for the repair and replacement of heating element wire are given in Section II, General Repair Procedures, Heating Element Wire.

FIG.3

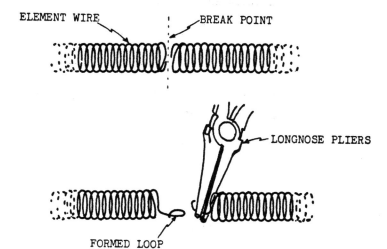

ELEMENT WIRE   BREAK POINT

FIG.4

LONGNOSE PLIERS

FORMED LOOP

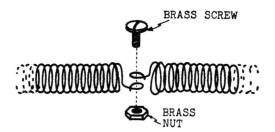

BRASS SCREW

BRASS NUT

FIG.5

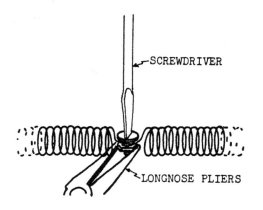

SCREWDRIVER

LONGNOSE PLIERS

Problem Solver #30

APPLIANCE: Space Heaters (All Types)

PROBLEM: Plug becomes excessively hot.

EXPLANATION: Space heaters require large quantities of electric power over long operating periods. It is not uncommon to operate this appliance continuously throughout a night or day. Extra care, therefore, must be taken to insure perfect electrical contact between the appliance and its source of power. An overheated plug is an indication that a poor connection exists at the wall outlet. Moreover, it represents a potential fire hazard and should be eliminated as quickly as possible.

TOOLS AND MATERIALS NEEDED:

(a) a medium size screwdriver (flatblade)

(b) a sharp paring or pocket knife

(c) one two-prong male plug
(heavy-duty, rubber appliance type)

SOLUTION: 1. Remove the line cord plug from the wall outlet.

2. Examine the plug. Check to see that the prongs are firmly attached to the plug body. (*Figure 1*) If the plug prongs wiggle freely or if the plug body shows signs of charring (deterioration due to heat), the plug should be replaced. Refer to Section II, General Repair Procedures, Plugs, for complete replacement procedure.

TWO DIFFERENT MODELS OF SPACE HEATERS

NOTE: ALTHOUGH DESIGN OF HEATER
      MAY CHANGE,OPERATING
      PRINCIPLES REMAIN THE SAME.

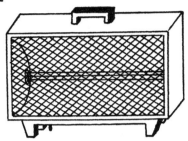

FIG.1

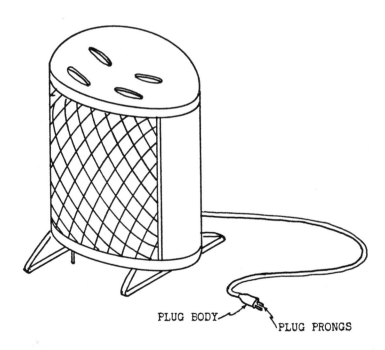

PLUG BODY   PLUG PRONGS

3. If the plug prongs are firmly attached and the plug body does not show signs of heat damage, check the fit of the plug in the wall outlet for looseness.

NOTE: Firm pressure should be required to insert and remove the plug from the wall outlet.

4. If the plug shows evidence of looseness, spread both prongs of the plug slightly by inserting the flat blade of a screwdriver between the folded layers of each prong. (*Figure 2*)

SPECIAL NOTE: A loose fit can be caused by either the plug or a worn-out wall outlet receptacle. Some appliances have been originally equipped with plugs having prongs fashioned from folded strips of metal. When new, the folded type prongs have the necessary thickness to insure good contact with the wall outlet receptacle. With use, however, the folded metal prongs become flattened, and looseness results. If the plug still fits loosely after the prongs have been spread, it can be assumed that the wall outlet receptacle is worn and should be replaced.

NOTE: Most local electrical codes state that house wiring, wall outlets, and electrical fixtures must be installed and repaired by licensed electricians.

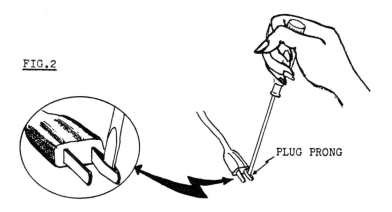

FIG.2

PLUG PRONG

Problem Solver #31

APPLIANCE: Space Heaters (Reflector Type)

PROBLEM: **Heating element glows red, but not enough heat can be felt.**

EXPLANATION: Space heaters are used normally to supplement the existing heating system. Their effectiveness depends upon their ability to throw heat into a small space or section of a larger area that requires additional heat. The reflector space heater moves heat into a space by reflecting the heat produced by the heating element. This heater cannot operate efficiently if the chromed surface of its reflector has become clouded with dust or dirt.

TOOLS AND MATERIALS NEEDED:

(a) two soft rags

(b) commercial metal polish

(c) a flatblade screwdriver (medium size)

SOLUTION: 1. Remove the plug from the wall outlet.

NOTE: *Figures 1 and 3* illustrate two typical reflector space heaters.

2. Remove the front guard. (*Figures 2 and 4*)

3. To remove the front guard of the space heater (*Figure 1*), grasp the front guard close to where the guardrail ends are inserted into holes in the edge of the bowl reflector. Bend the guard until the rail ends are removed from the holes. (*Figure 2*)

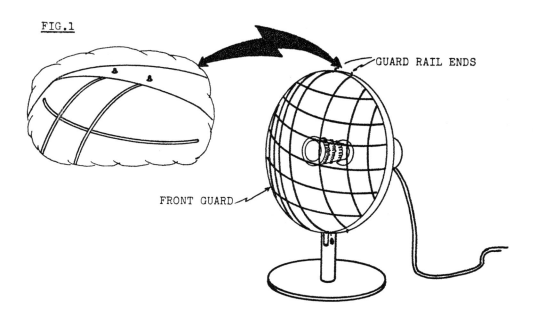

FIG.1

GUARD RAIL ENDS

FRONT GUARD

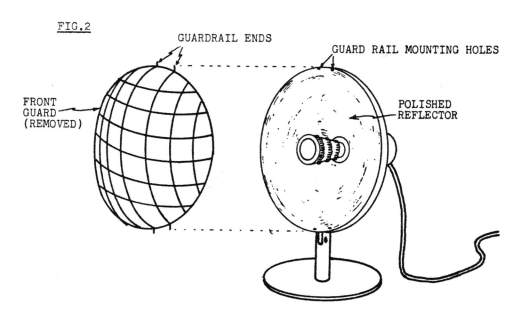

FIG.2

GUARDRAIL ENDS

GUARD RAIL MOUNTING HOLES

FRONT GUARD (REMOVED)

POLISHED REFLECTOR

4. To remove the front guard of the space heater (*Figure 3*), remove two screws located in the lower corners of the guard. (*Figure 4*) Tilt the top cover back slightly and lift out the guard.

5. Clean and polish the reflector with metal polish applied to a soft rag. Use a dry soft rag to remove all traces of the metal polish.

   CAUTION: When cleaning the reflector of the kind of space heater shown in *Figure 3*, take care not to press against the heating element wires.

Problem Solver #32

APPLIANCE: Space Heaters

PROBLEM: The heater does not heat.

EXPLANATION: In space heaters, as in other heat-producing appliances, heat is produced by the effect of an electric current passing through the heating element wire. When the electric current is prevented either from reaching the heating element wire or from passing completely through it, the space heater will fail to operate. The flow of electricity is stopped when a house fuse is blown or when a component of the space heater becomes defective.

TOOLS AND MATERIALS NEEDED:

(a) a flatblade screwdriver (medium size)

(b) a pair of long-nose pliers

(c) a tube of graphite lubricant

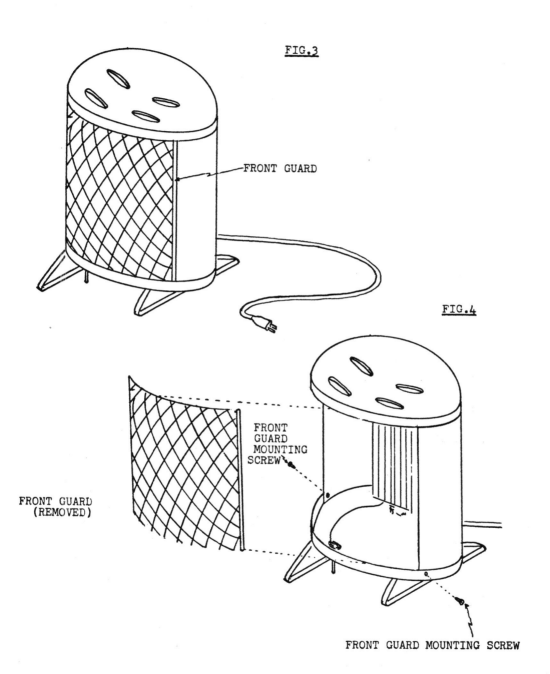

FIG.3

FRONT GUARD

FIG.4

FRONT
GUARD
MOUNTING
SCREW

FRONT GUARD
(REMOVED)

FRONT GUARD MOUNTING SCREW

SOLUTION: 1. Make certain that the wall outlet has electric power. Plug a lamp or other appliance known to be in good working order into the outlet used for the space heater. If the lamp or other appliance fails to operate, it can be assumed that a fuse has blown or that a circuit breaker has tripped off, thus preventing electric power from reaching the wall outlet, or that the wall outlet itself is defective. Refer to Section II, General Repair Procedures, Fuses and Circuit Breakers, for further instructions about this condition. If, however, the lamp or other appliance used for testing the wall outlet operates, it means that the problem is in the space heater.

2. Examine the line cord plug. Check the plug prongs for looseness. Test the condition of the line cord wires going into the plug by tugging firmly on the plug against the line cord. (*Figure 1*) If the plug prongs wiggle freely or if the plug parts from this line cord when pulled upon, the plug should be replaced. See Section II, General Repair Procedures, Plugs, for further information.

SPECIAL NOTE: Many space heater models employ a safety switch that shuts the space heater off automatically if it is tipped over. (*Figure 2* illustrates such a safety switch.) Whenever the space heater is used, the safety switch should be checked to see that it is functioning properly.

3. Examine the operation of the safety switch. Place the heater on a table so that the switch is at eye level. Check to see that the contact points come together (close) when the heater rests on the table and that they part (open) when the heater is lifted off the table.

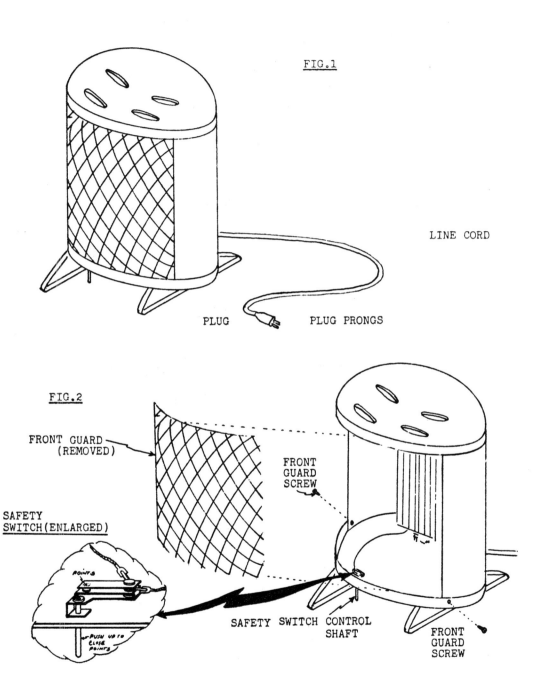

FIG.1

LINE CORD

PLUG   PLUG PRONGS

FIG.2

FRONT GUARD
(REMOVED)

FRONT
GUARD
SCREW

SAFETY
SWITCH(ENLARGED)

POINTS

PUSH UP TO
CLOSE POINTS

SAFETY SWITCH CONTROL
SHAFT

FRONT
GUARD
SCREW

4. If the contact points of the switch do not close when the heater rests on its stand, check the switch control shaft to see that it moves up and down freely.

5. Operate the switch control shaft by pushing it up manually. The control shaft should move up freely and then return to its lower position automatically.

6. If the switch control shaft does not move freely, coat the shaft with graphite lubricant sprayed from a plastic dispenser. (*Figure 3*)

7. If the switch control shaft moves up and down freely, but the contacts do not come together when the heater is rested on its stand, it means that the switch control shaft is not extending up far enough to move the contact points together.

8. Check to see that the switch control shaft extends down to the table surface far enough to be lifted when the heater is resting on its stand. If the shaft is not lifted sufficiently, bend the heater stand slightly by pressing down on both ends. (*Figure 4*) This should allow the shaft to protrude further past the heater stand for proper operation.

FIG.3

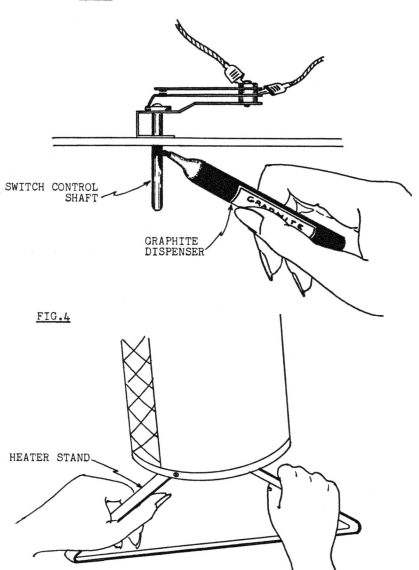

SWITCH CONTROL
SHAFT

GRAPHITE
DISPENSER

FIG.4

HEATER STAND

9. If examination of the safety switch proves that it is functioning properly but the heater still does not operate, check the terminal connectors of the heater element wire and the element wire itself to see that there are no loose connections or broken wires. (*Figure 5*)

10. Remove the front guard by removing the two screws located at both lower corners of the heater. (*Figure 2*) Lift up the top of the heater and lift out the front guard.

11. Grasp each connector and wiggle it to check for looseness. Replace any connector that feels loose. Refer to Section II, General Repair Procedures, Terminal and Wire Connectors, for complete instructions.

NOTE: The type of heating element wire used in the space heater shown in *Figure 5* is assembled in the factory as a complete unit. This type of heater element cannot be repaired practically. When broken (burned out), this heater element must be purchased and replaced as an entire unit. The procedure for replacing the heating element is given in the steps that follow.

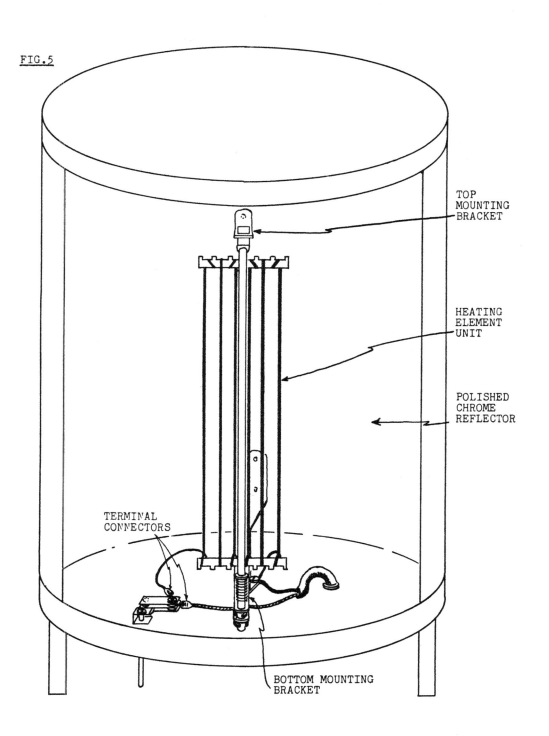

FIG.5

TOP
MOUNTING
BRACKET

HEATING
ELEMENT
UNIT

POLISHED
CHROME
REFLECTOR

TERMINAL
CONNECTORS

BOTTOM MOUNTING
BRACKET

12. Grasp the lower retaining (horseshoe-shaped) clip with a pair of long-nose pliers and pull it off the heater element mounting shaft. (*Figure 6*)

13. Disconnect the heater element by grasping the terminal connectors manually and pulling them off the terminals. (*Figure 6*)

14. Grasp the heating element unit by the mounting rod and lift the entire heater unit up and out of the bottom mounting bracket. Slide the heating unit out of the top mounting bracket to free it completely. (*Figure 7*)

    NOTE: An exact replacement heating element unit may be purchased from an authorized appliance service shop.

15. Install the new replacement heater element unit by *reversing* the procedures in steps 12 through 14 above.

FIG.6

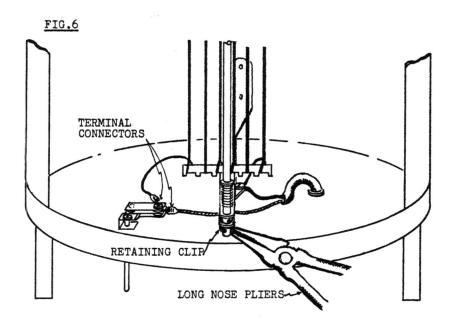

TERMINAL
CONNECTORS

RETAINING CLIP

LONG NOSE PLIERS

FIG.7

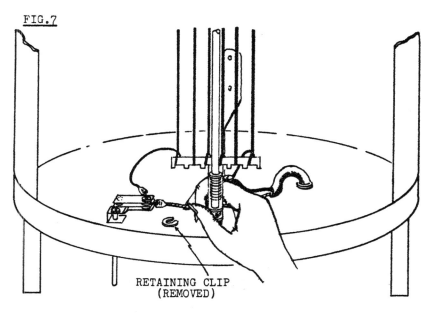

RETAINING CLIP
(REMOVED)

NOTE: The space heater illustrated in *Figure 8* does not employ a safety switch. When this type of space heater fails to operate, the heating element unit should be checked. The steps that follow describe the procedure for checking, repairing, and/or replacing the heater element.

16. Disconnect the line cord plug from the wall outlet.

17. Grasp the heating element and unscrew it (by turning it counter-clockwise) from its socket. Inspect the heating element closely at the terminal screws. (*Figure 9*) Check to see that the terminal screws are tight. Turn them in a clockwise direction with a screwdriver.

18. If terminal screw connections appear to be good, carefully inspect the element wire along its entire length on the cone-shaped ceramic form.

19. If heating element wire is found to be parted (burned-out or broken), replace the entire heating element.

    NOTE: This type of heating element is usually readily available from any appliance repair shop.

FIG.8

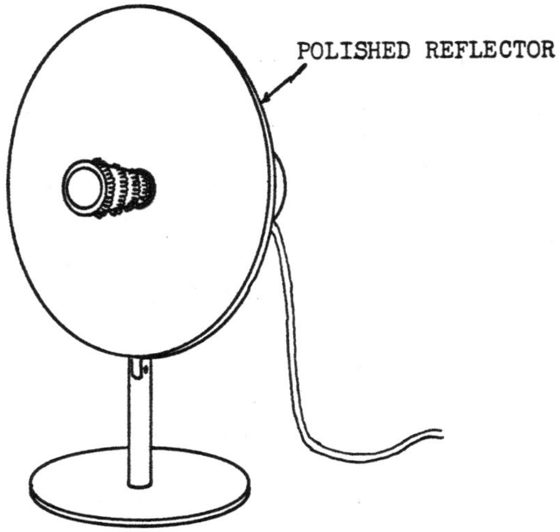

POLISHED REFLECTOR

FIG.9

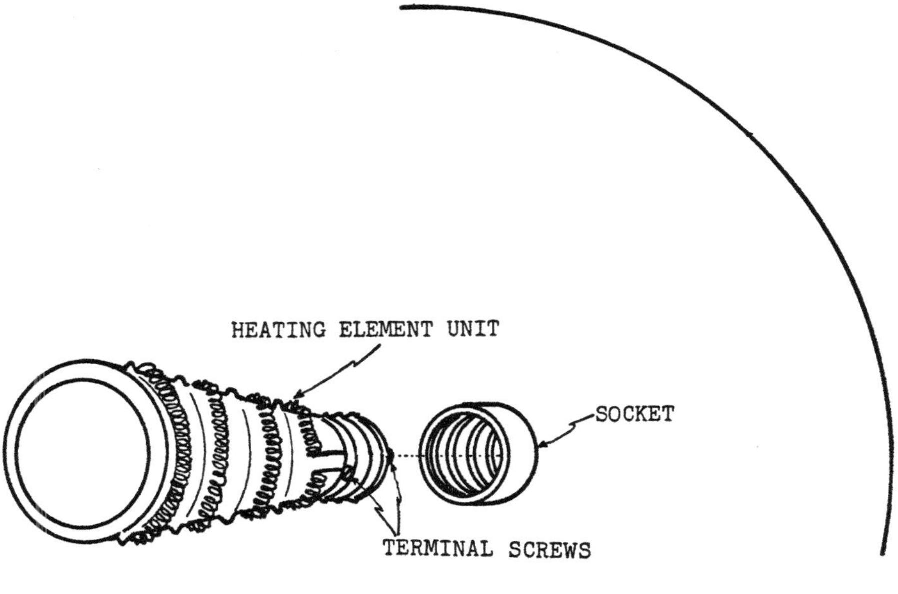

HEATING ELEMENT UNIT

SOCKET

TERMINAL SCREWS

Problem Solver #33

APPLIANCE: Vacuum Cleaner (Canister or Tank Type)

PROBLEM: **Does not pick up.**

EXPLANATION: Weak suction is invariably the cause when a canister or tank type vacuum cleaner does not pick up. Weak suction most often results when the suction air flow becomes restricted or completely clogged by excessive dirt in the dust bag or when an accumulation of hair, lint, solid objects, etc., obstructs the hose.

TOOLS AND MATERIALS NEEDED:

    (a) a broom

    (b) a clean dust bag (if needed)

    (c) a paper bag

SOLUTION:

1. Check the dust bag. Replace it if filled. Re-test pick-up action of cleaner. If suction is still weak, check hose for obstruction. (*Figure 1*)

2. Push broom handle through hose to clear obstruction. (*Figure 2*)

3. Attach hose to vacuum cleaner air outlet fitting and "blow" out debris not cleared by broom handle. (*Figure 3*)

    CAUTION: Place free end of hose in a paper bag for step 3 to prevent dust from blowing out into room.

4. Re-check suction with hose attached to cleaner. Suction strength at hose end should be equal to suction strength felt at vacuum cleaner suction fitting. Suction strength may be tested by placing palm of hand over suction openings. Good suction strength will draw hand with considerable force.

    SPECIAL NOTE: If the hose again becomes clogged with lint soon after it was properly cleared, either a portion of the inner hose liner has torn loose or the spring wire that forms the hose has broken and is jutting into the hose air passage, collecting lint. A hose so damaged should be replaced. (See Problem Solver #34 for detailed instructions for hose replacement.)

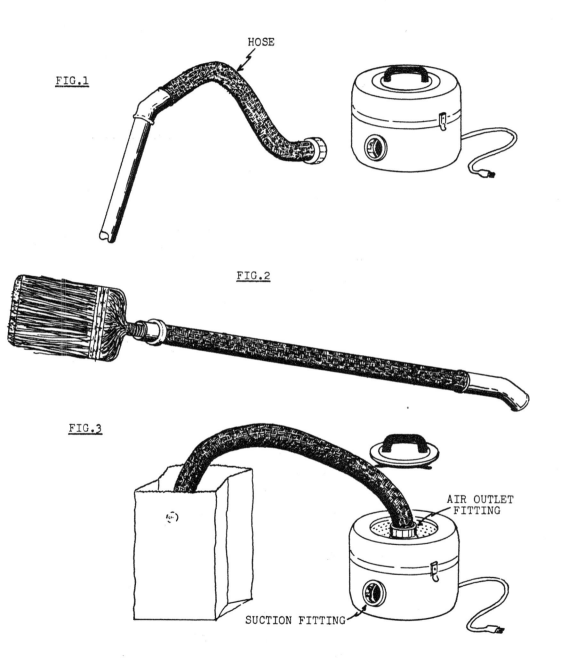

FIG.1 HOSE

FIG.2

FIG.3 AIR OUTLET FITTING

SUCTION FITTING

Problem Solver #34

APPLIANCE: Vacuum Cleaner (Canister or Tank Type)

PROBLEM: **Broken hose.**

EXPLANATION: A vacuum cleaner hose can break in a number of ways. Two visible types of breaks become obvious when either the outer fabric (cloth or plastic) covering tears or the spring wire collapses at some point along the length of the hose, sharply reducing the hose diameter at that point. Not all hose breaks are obvious, however. A portion of the inner fabric liner can often tear, or the spring wire break, without collapse of the hose. Both of these conditions would not be easily noticed. All breaks in the hose, however, would greatly reduce the suction strength of the vacuum cleaner and therefore require that the hose be replaced.

TOOLS AND MATERIALS NEEDED:

    (a) a flatblade screwdriver (medium size)

    (b) a pair of diagonal wire cutting pliers (or poultry shears)

    (c) a pair of pliers

    (d) a small bottle of white (resin type) glue

    (e) a replacement vacuum cleaner hose (purchased from vacuum cleaner service shop or general appliance repair shop)

SOLUTION: 1. Examine both ends of broken hose to determine type of hose end construction.

NOTE: The metal pieces (fittings) at both ends of the hose are not to be considered part of the hose. Replacement hoses are made available without these fittings. Fittings must therefore be removed and reinstalled on the replacement hose. They are attached to the hose ends in either of two ways. The construction of the hose ends gives the clue as to the method used. In one, hose ends are finished with heavy molded rubber covers. (*Figure 1*) In the other type of construction, the hose ends insert directly into the fittings. No rubber molding can be seen. (*Figure 4*)

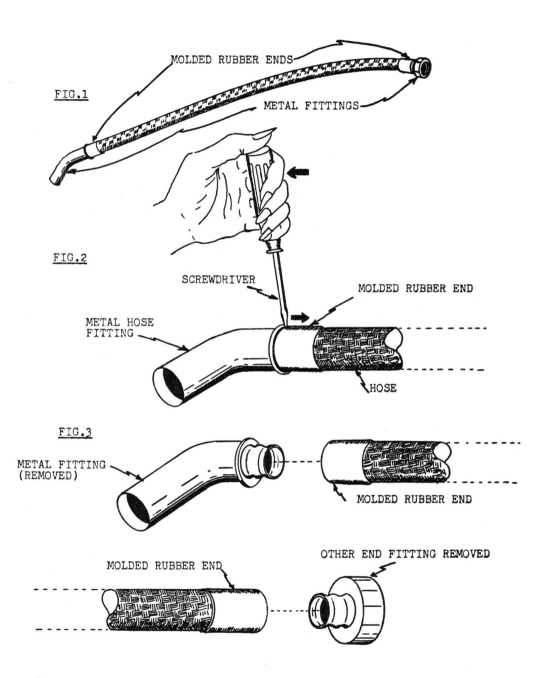

FIG.1

MOLDED RUBBER ENDS

METAL FITTINGS

FIG.2

SCREWDRIVER

METAL HOSE FITTING

MOLDED RUBBER END

HOSE

FIG.3

METAL FITTING (REMOVED)

MOLDED RUBBER END

MOLDED RUBBER END

OTHER END FITTING REMOVED

2. If hose is constructed with molded rubber ends, remove metal fittings by prying molded end of hose loose with a medium size screwdriver. (*Figure 2*) Then grasp the metal fitting with one hand and the hose end with the other and remove the fitting using a twisting, pulling motion.

   NOTE: Take old hose to appliance shop when purchasing new hose, to match replacement hose.

3. Attach fittings from defective hose onto new replacement hose. Use twisting, pushing motions to insert metal fittings into hose. (*Figure 3*) This will complete the replacement of this type of hose.

4. If hose to be replaced does not have molded rubber ends (as shown in *Figure 4*), proceed as in the steps that follow.

5. Cut through the hose (fabric and spring wire) at a point approximately two inches from each metal fitting. Use a pair of diagonal wire cutting pliers or a pair of heavy poultry shears. (*Figure 5*)

6. Grasp cut end of spring wire with a pair of pliers and pull wire straight away from metal fitting. Continue to pull until spring wire is completely removed from metal fitting. (*Figure 6*)

   NOTE: Considerable force may be necessary to tear spring wire free. If necessary, have an assistant hold metal fitting while spring wire is being pulled.

7. Pull out as much of the remaining fabric as possible.

8. Push metal collar of fitting forward (away from hose end) as far as it will go to expose the metal fitting end. (*Figure 7*)

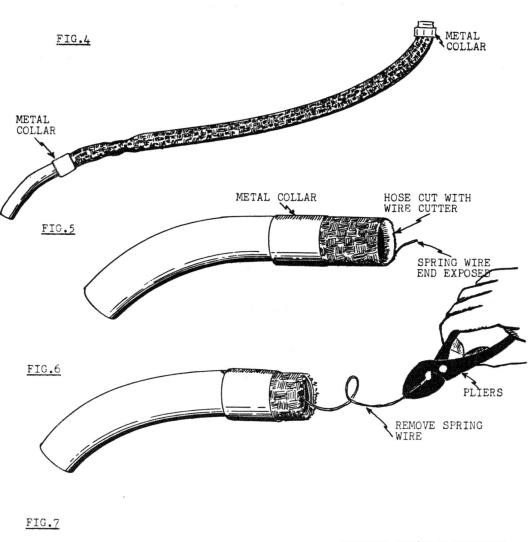

FIG.4

METAL
COLLAR

METAL
COLLAR

METAL COLLAR

HOSE CUT WITH
WIRE CUTTER

FIG.5

SPRING WIRE
END EXPOSED

FIG.6

PLIERS

REMOVE SPRING
WIRE

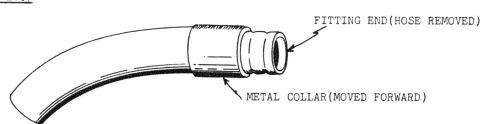

FIG.7

FITTING END(HOSE REMOVED)

METAL COLLAR(MOVED FORWARD)

9. Scrape off any residue which may have stuck onto fitting end from old hose with the flatblade screwdriver.

10. Lightly coat the fabric ends (about one inch) of the new replacement hose with white glue and allow to dry for about ten minutes. (*Figure 8*)

    NOTE: The fabric ends of this type of replacement hose can easily become frayed during normal handling. The thin coating of glue will prevent fraying and help facilitate its installation.

11. Coat the fitting end liberally with white glue, and push the hose end over it as far as it can go. (*Figure 9*)

12. Coat the hose end liberally with white glue and pull the fitting collar over the hose end to complete the repair. (*Figure 10*)

13. Repeat the procedure to install the cleaner attachment fitting to opposite hose end.

    CAUTION: Allow at least two hours for glue to dry before using the cleaner.

    SPECIAL NOTE: To help prolong the life of a vacuum cleaner hose, never store hose tightly coiled or twisted.

FIG.8

COAT WITH GLUE

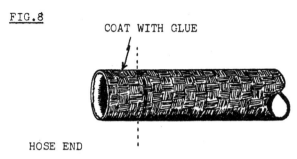

HOSE END

FIG.9

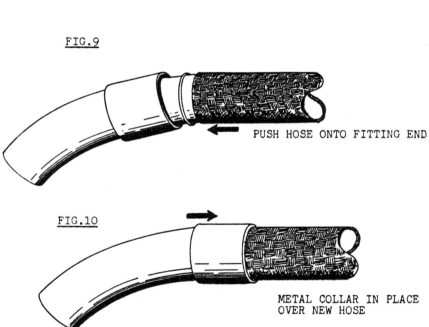

PUSH HOSE ONTO FITTING END

FIG.10

METAL COLLAR IN PLACE
OVER NEW HOSE

Problem Solver #35

APPLIANCE: Vacuum Cleaner (Canister or Tank Type)

PROBLEM: **Weak suction.**

EXPLANATION: During normal use, dust, lint, etc., is drawn into the vacuum cleaner and collected in the dust bag. Some of the finer particles of dust, however, do manage to get through the dust bag. Once past the dust bag, they would be drawn into the vacuum cleaner motor to clog it and eventually cause its failure. Motor filters are the cloth or fibrous screens located between the dust bag and the vacuum cleaner motor to protect the motor. Over a period of time, these filters can accumulate enough dust to restrict the passage of vacuum air through the cleaner and cause weak suction. They must, therefore, be periodically cleaned or replaced depending upon their condition.

TOOLS AND MATERIALS NEEDED:

    (a) a pair of pliers

    (b) a pair of scissors

    (c) a flatblade screwdriver (medium size)

    (d) a phillips screwdriver (medium size)

    (e) a replacement filter (purchased from vacuum cleaner or general appliance repair shop)

SOLUTION: 1. *Figures 1, 4, and 9* illustrate three of the more common types of tank and canister vacuum cleaners in use. Identify your vacuum cleaner with one of those shown.

      NOTE: Before proceeding to check the filter, make certain that the "weak suction" is not due to an over-filled dust bag or defective hose as described in Problem Solvers #33 and #34.

    2. To locate filter for vacuum cleaner illustrated in *Figure 1*, disconnect the cleaner from electric outlet. Open front suction lid and remove dust bag. (*Figure 2*)

TANK TYPE VACUUM CLEANER

FIG.1

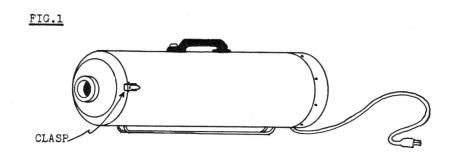

CLASP

FIG.2

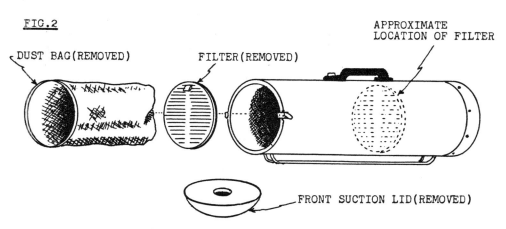

APPROXIMATE
LOCATION OF FILTER

DUST BAG(REMOVED)   FILTER(REMOVED)

FRONT SUCTION LID(REMOVED)

FIG.3   FILTER DISASSEMBLED

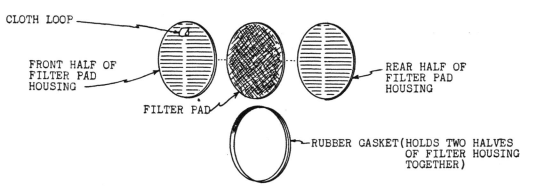

CLOTH LOOP

FRONT HALF OF
FILTER PAD
HOUSING

REAR HALF OF
FILTER PAD
HOUSING

FILTER PAD

RUBBER GASKET(HOLDS TWO HALVES
OF FILTER HOUSING
TOGETHER)

NOTE: Older model tank type cleaners are equipped with cloth type permanent dust bags. The cloth fibers of this kind of bag eventually become impregnated with dust so that a normal flow of air through it is excessively impeded. The bags should, therefore, be periodically washed with soap (detergent) and water, then rinsed and allowed to dry before using.

3. Locate disc-shaped filter directly behind the dust bag.

4. Reach into tank and grasp filter (or cloth loop if provided) and pull it out. (*Figure 2*)

NOTE: The filter pad may be found housed in a metal frame for support. If so, remove the filter from its frame and set frame aside to be used with new filter. (*Figure 3*)

5. Install new replacement filter.

NOTE: The filter material most often used in older tank type cleaners is felt. Do not attempt to clean this kind of filter, since embedded dust is difficult to remove. If original felt type material (or size) cannot be purchased, cut a circular piece of filtering material out of any fibrous room air conditioner filter, which can be purchased at most appliance service shops. Use the original filter as a template to cut new filter to exact size for vacuum cleaner.

6. Install clean dust bag and replace front suction lid to complete work on this type of cleaner.

7. To locate filter for vacuum cleaner illustrated in *Figure 4*, remove the top section of cleaner by releasing the two clasps.

8. Disconnect vacuum cleaner from electric outlet.

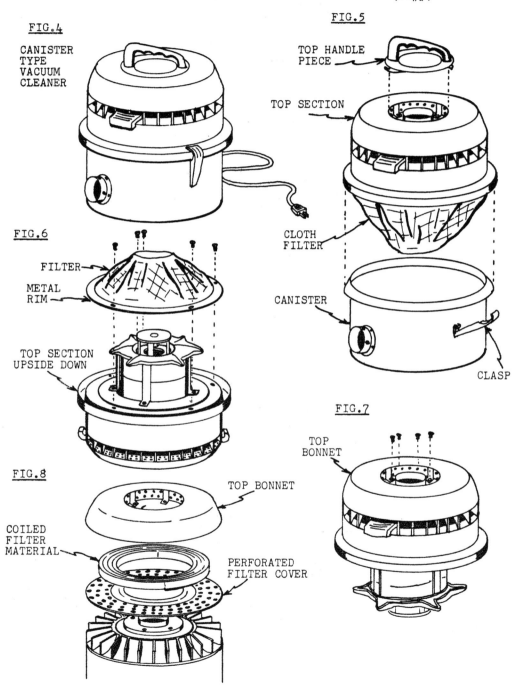

(PS#3)

FIG.4

CANISTER
TYPE
VACUUM
CLEANER

FIG.5

TOP HANDLE
PIECE

TOP SECTION

CLOTH
FILTER

CANISTER

CLASP

FIG.6

FILTER

METAL
RIM

TOP SECTION
UPSIDE DOWN

FIG.7

TOP
BONNET

FIG.8

TOP BONNET

COILED
FILTER
MATERIAL

PERFORATED
FILTER COVER

9. Remove top handle piece (twist counter-clockwise) and place the top section of cleaner upside down on table. (*Figures 5 and 6*)

NOTE: The motor filter for this particular cleaner is the cloth fabric which completely covers the motor. An additional filter enclosed in the upper portion of this section of the cleaner is used to prevent any dust which may have gone through both the dust bag and motor filter from getting out into the room. The additional air filter will be discussed later in this Problem Solver.

10. Remove five screws around rim of filter with a flatblade screwdriver. Grasp filter and lift it off. (*Figure 6*) Set screws carefully aside to avoid losing them.

11. Wash the filter with soap (detergent) and warm (not hot) water by hand (as you would any heavily soiled cloth). Allow to dry before replacing it.

12. While filter is drying, inspect the additional air filter located in the bonnet of the top section.

13. To gain access to the additional air filter, turn top section right-side up.

14. Locate and remove four screws around the top air outlet fitting. (*Figure 7*)

15. Lift off the bonnet from the top section. (*Figure 8*)

16. Pull out the perforated filter cover and pull out the filter material which is coiled around inside the bonnet. (*Figure 8*)

NOTE: This material (fiber batting) cannot be cleaned successfully and, therefore, should be replaced. If original filter material cannot be purchased, use strips cut from a fiberglass-type room air conditioner filter. Room air conditioner filters can be purchased from any major appliance service shop.

<u>FIG.9</u>

VARIATION OF CANISTER TYPE VACUUM CLEANER

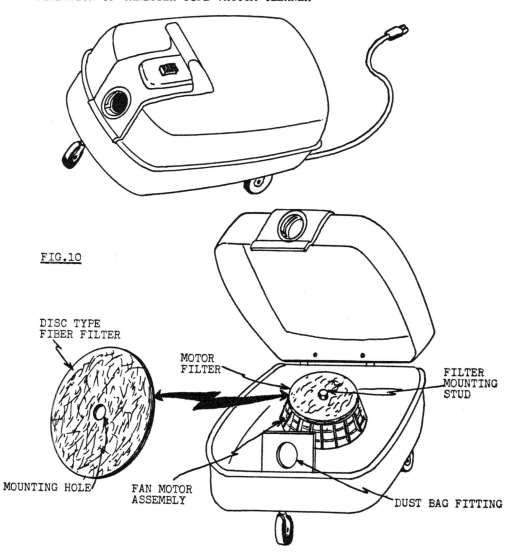

<u>FIG.10</u>

DISC TYPE
FIBER FILTER

MOTOR
FILTER

FILTER
MOUNTING
STUD

MOUNTING HOLE

FAN MOTOR
ASSEMBLY

DUST BAG FITTING

17. Replace new air filter material in the bonnet. Place the perforated filter cover over the filter material and fasten the bonnet to the top section of the cleaner with the four screws.

18. Turn top section upside down again and replace the motor filter cloth (when dry), to complete the work on this type of vacuum cleaner.

19. To locate the motor filter for the vacuum cleaner illustrated in *Figure 9*, lift top section of cleaner to expose dust bag and motor-fan assembly. (*Figure 10*)

20. Locate disc-shaped motor filter on top of the motor-fan assembly. (*Figure 10*)

    NOTE: The material used for this type of filter is usually fiberglass.

21. Remove the filter by forcing it over and off the center mounting stud.

22. Replace the filter with one of similar material, thickness, and diameter.

    SPECIAL NOTE: To maintain vacuum cleaner efficiency, empty the dust bag frequently. Never operate cleaner without dust bag.

Problem Solver #36

APPLIANCE: Vacuum Cleaner (Upright Type)

PROBLEM: Does not pick up lint from rug.

EXPLANATION: The rug cleaning ability of an upright vacuum cleaner depends a great deal upon the spinning action of the beater-brush assembly and the rubber belt which drives it. When this type of cleaner fails to remove lint, thread, etc., from rugs, the problem can usually be traced to one or both of these components.

TOOLS AND MATERIALS NEEDED:

        (a)   a flatblade screwdriver (medium size)

        (b)   a hammer

        (c)   a paring knife

SOLUTION:

1. Test the operation of the beater-brush assembly and its rubber drive belt. Lay the cleaner down on the floor horizontally. (*Figure 1*) Connect the cleaner to electric outlet and operate it. Observe the beater brush. It should rotate rapidly. If it rotates satisfactorily, the rubber drive belt is intact and a closer inspection of the beater brush itself must be made. If the beater brush does not rotate, or rotates slowly or intermittently, the rubber drive belt should be inspected.

   CAUTION: Disconnect cleaner from electric power for the next checks.

2. To inspect the beater-brush assembly for worn brushes, scan the bottom opening of the vacuum cleaner. (*Figure 2*) Rotate the beater brush slowly by hand so that each row of brush bristles moves past the opening. If the brush bristles cannot be seen above the bottom opening (about 1/16-inch), they are worn and must be replaced.

   NOTE: The procedure for replacing brush segments or the entire beater brush is described in steps 7 to 20 that follow.

FIG.1

BEATER-BRUSH

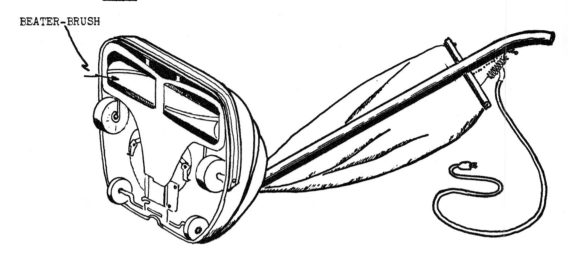

FIG.2

BRUSH BRISTLES

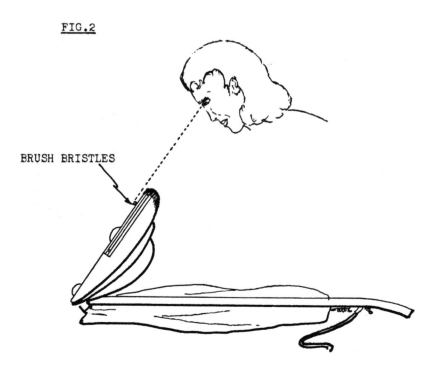

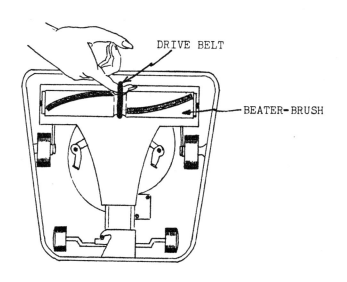

DRIVE BELT

BEATER-BRUSH

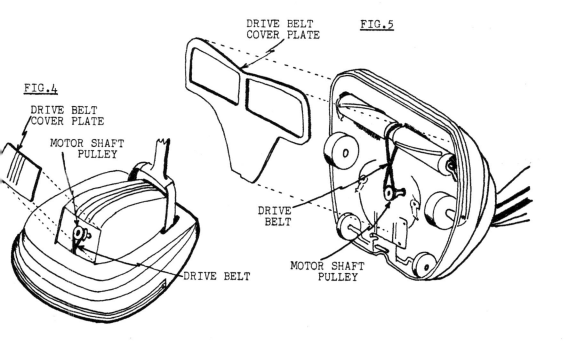

DRIVE BELT
COVER PLATE

FIG.5

FIG.4

DRIVE BELT
COVER PLATE

MOTOR SHAFT
PULLEY

DRIVE BELT

DRIVE
BELT

MOTOR SHAFT
PULLEY

3. Check the rubber drive belt for elasticity. Grasp the belt and tug on it. (*Figure 3*) If belt is not resilient, the rubber has probably dried out and become brittle thus losing its gripping ability.

4. Inspect the drive belt for worn spots by feeling along the entire length of the belt for depressions.

5. If rubber drive belt has become brittle or is found to be worn, it will not rotate the beater-brush assembly properly and should, therefore, be replaced.

6. To replace the drive belt, remove the belt cover plate. (See *Figures 4 and 5* for location of different type cover plates.) Slip the belt off the motor shaft pulley. (*Figures 4 and 5*)

   NOTE: To complete the removal of the drive belt, the beater brush assembly must be removed from the cleaner.

7. To remove the beater brush, lift up the rug guard (if used) located across the bottom opening. (*Figure 6*)

8. Examine the ends of the beater brush assembly for latching levers.

   NOTE: The methods used to secure the beater brush in its holder vary with the different manufacturers. In some model vacuum cleaners, the ends of the beater brush are simply held in a tight fitting rubber cavity. In other models, a metal lever clasps each end of the beater brush to latch it.

9. If beater-brush assembly employs latching levers, pry the levers open with the flatblade of a screwdriver. (*Figure 7*) Grasp the beater brush and pull it out. (*Figure 8*) .

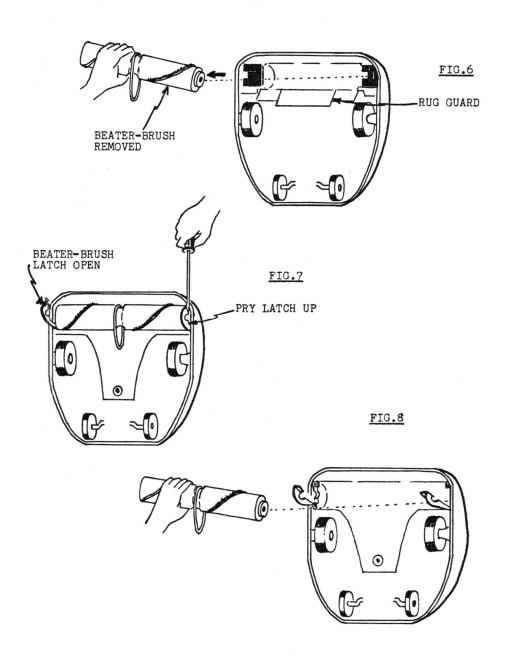

FIG.6

BEATER-BRUSH
REMOVED

RUG GUARD

BEATER-BRUSH
LATCH OPEN

FIG.7

PRY LATCH UP

FIG.8

10. If no latching levers are used, the beater brush is removed by pulling it sharply out.

11. Slip the drive belt off the beater brush to complete the belt removal.

    NOTE: At this point the belt and/or beater-brush assembly have been removed and can now be replaced. When purchasing a new drive belt, it would be wise to have with you the make and model of the vacuum cleaner written on a slip of paper and, if at all possible, the old defective drive belt. The beater brush (now removed from the cleaner) can be brought as a complete unit to an authorized appliance service shop to be either rebuilt or replaced with a new unit. It would, however, be more economical to service the beater-brush assembly yourself, at home. The steps that follow below outline the procedure to be used for restoring the beater-brush assembly.

12. Remove hair, thread, lint, etc., which usually accumulate at the ends of the beater brush and prevent it from spinning freely. Use the point of a paring knife to loosen and cut hair and thread wound around beater-brush ends. (*Figure 9*)

13. If brushes are worn (determined by test in step 3), replace the individual brush segments.

    NOTE: Two methods are commonly used to attach the brush segments to the beater-brush assembly. In one, each brush segment is held by two screws, one at each end of the brush segment. In the other, the brush segments are fitted into grooved channels in the beater-brush assembly. Procedures for removing both types are given below.

FIG.9

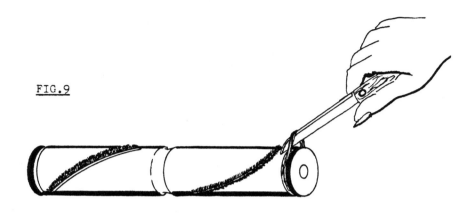

FIG.10

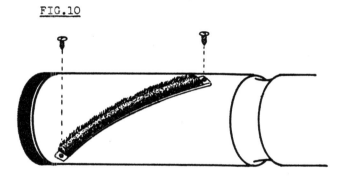

FIG.11

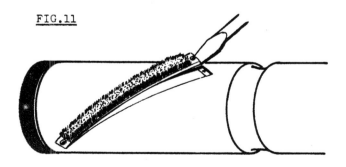

14. To remove brush segments that are attached with screws, remove both screws at each end of the brush segment. (*Figure 10*) Pry brush segment out with the tip of a flatblade screwdriver. (*Figure 11*)

15. To remove the channel held type brush segments, first remove one of the end plates. This is done by grasping both end plates and twisting them in opposite directions until one plate comes off. (*Figure 12*)

16. Pry out the remaining end section with the tip of a flatblade screwdriver. (*Figure 13*)

17. Tap the end of the center shaft with the back of a hammer handle. (*Figure 14*)

    CAUTION: To avoid damage, do not strike shaft end with hammer head or other metal objects.

18. Pull the center shaft out of the beater-brush assembly. (*Figure 15*)

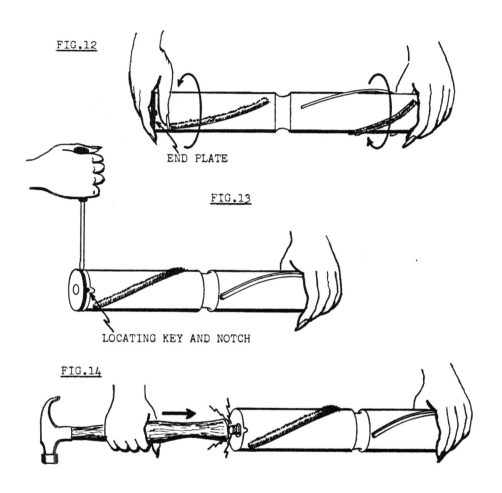

FIG.12

END PLATE

FIG.13

LOCATING KEY AND NOTCH

FIG.14

FIG.15

19. Push the brush segments out of their channels with the tip of a screwdriver. (*Figures 16 and 17*)

20. Replace new brush segments by reversing the above procedure. Take special note and care when replacing the center shaft to make sure that the locating key on the center shaft lines up with the notch on the beater-brush drum. (*Figure 13*)

    NOTE: Brush segments have their identifying part numbers stamped either on their sides or tops. When purchasing new brush segments, make sure they are exact replacements.

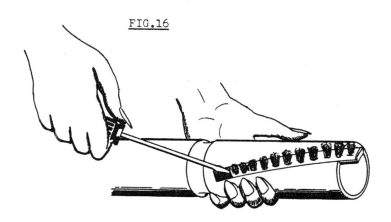

FIG.16

FIG.17

BRUSH SEGMENT CHANNEL

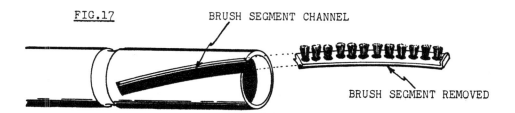

BRUSH SEGMENT REMOVED

Problem Solver #37

APPLIANCE: Electric Broom

PROBLEM: **Broom has weak suction and burning odor.**

EXPLANATION: When this type of appliance gives off a burning odor, it almost always means that a problem exists with the electric motor. The nature of the motor problem can be serious or minor. One of the most common and minor causes of motor problems (and resulting burning odor) can be traced to worn or otherwise defective motor brushes. They should, therefore, be carefully inspected and serviced before other motor components are considered.

TOOLS AND MATERIALS NEEDED:

    (a)   a flatblade screwdriver

    (b)   two pipe cleaners

    (c)   a paper towel

SOLUTION: 1. Disconnect the cleaner from electric outlet.

    2. Locate the two motor brush caps, one on each side of the motor housing. (*Figure 1*)

    SPECIAL NOTE: Motor brushes are composed of a carbon (graphite) material. They are usually bar-shaped in appearance and are used to provide electrical contact between the stationary and rotating parts of a motor. They are recessed in the motor housing and are retained with plastic insulated screw caps.

    3. Place a screwdriver into the slot in the motor brush cap and turn the cap counter-clockwise until it is removed. (*Figure 2*)

    CAUTION: Remove the motor brush cap slowly to avoid the danger of the brush springs popping out and becoming lost.

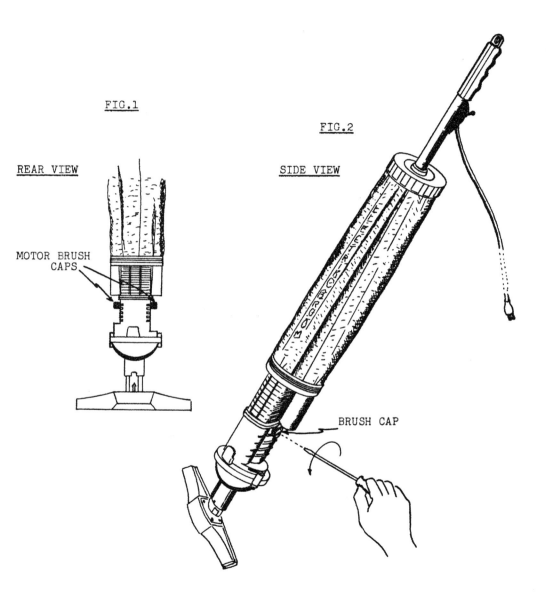

FIG.1

REAR VIEW

MOTOR BRUSH
CAPS

FIG.2

SIDE VIEW

BRUSH CAP

4. Grasp the motor brush spring, which is attached to the brush, and lift out both spring and brush. (*Figure 3*)

.5. Remove other motor brush by repeating steps 3 and 4 above.

6. Examine both motor brushes for wear. A good brush will appear as shown in *Figure 4*. A worn brush will appear as shown in *Figure 5*.

7. Examine brush springs. Compress each spring. It must have sufficient tension to return to its original length when released.

NOTE: In some model cleaners, the motor brush and brush spring are a complete unit and are purchased as such. In other model cleaners, the motor brushes may be purchased separately from the brush spring. However, it is advisable that the brushes and brush springs be replaced whenever either or both are found to be defective. Motor brushes and springs may be purchased from any qualified appliance repair or parts supply store. Be sure to take along the old motor brush and spring to insure purchase of an exact matching set.

8. If inspection of motor brushes and springs proves that they are in good order, they may be reinstalled in the motor, but only after proper cleaning and preparation. The procedure for cleaning and preparing the motor brushes is the same as the procedure required to install new replacement motor brushes and is given in steps 9 through 12.

FIG.3

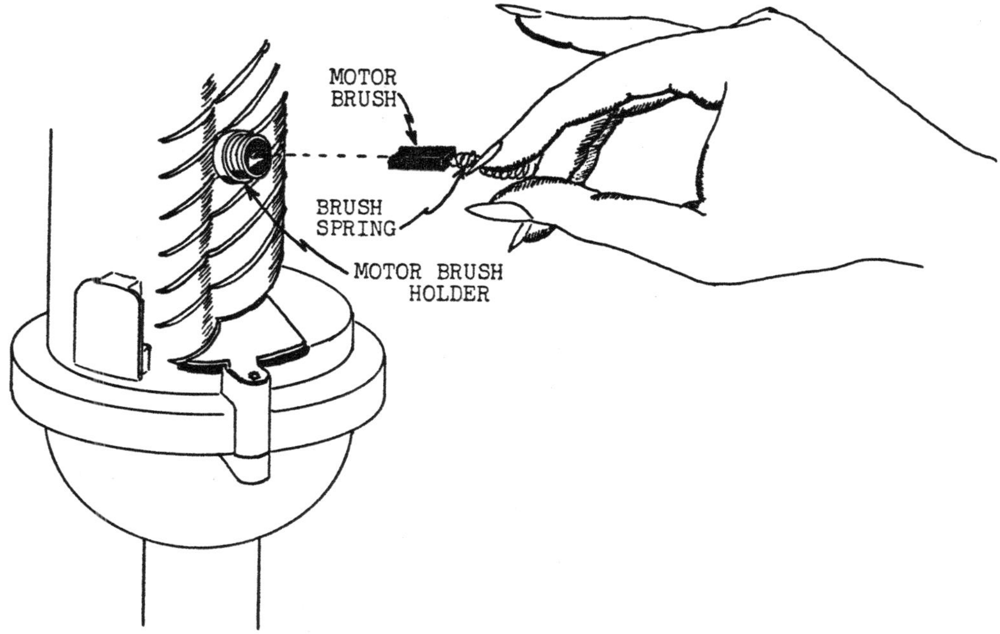

MOTOR
BRUSH

BRUSH
SPRING

MOTOR BRUSH
HOLDER

FIG.4

GOOD BRUSH

FIG.5

WORN BRUSH

9. Fold a pipe cleaner in half and with a back-and-forth motion, wipe the inside of the recessed brush holder. (*Figure 6*) Do the same to the other brush holder using a fresh pipe cleaner.

10. Clean all four sides of each brush. Place a paper towel on a flat surface (kitchen table). Lay the motor brush on one of its sides atop the paper towel. Hold the brush firmly and rub it along the surface of the towel. Repeat strokes until all dust, oil, or grease film is removed. Clean the remaining three sides in the same manner. (*Figure 7*)

CAUTION: Make certain that motor brush is held firmly against flat towel surface to maintain square corners on brush. Do not allow brush corner to become rounded. Do not remove brush material by "over-cleaning" as this will reduce the size of the brush and cause it to fit too loosely in the recessed holder.

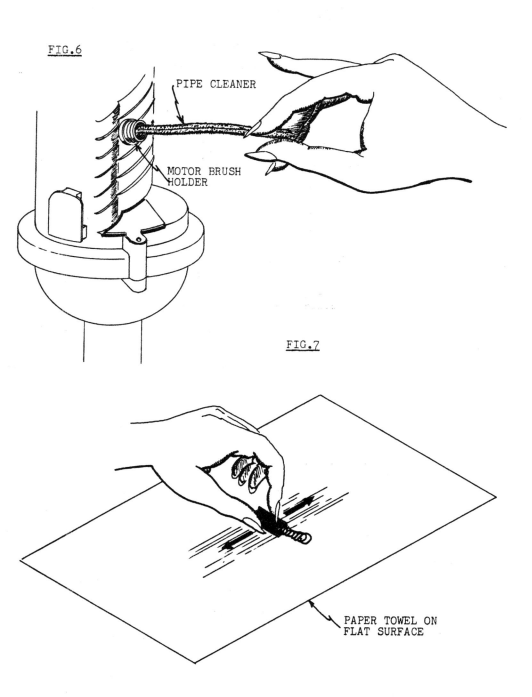

FIG.6

PIPE CLEANER

MOTOR BRUSH HOLDER

FIG.7

PAPER TOWEL ON FLAT SURFACE

11. Test to see that each motor brush has free movement in its recessed holder. Hold the motor brush so that its concave end is in correct relationship to the motor. (*Figure 8*) Insert the brush into its holder. Grasp the brush spring and move the brush in and out of the holder. Brushes should move freely without binding. If either or both brushes do not move freely repeat cleaning of recessed brush holder and brushes as in steps 9 and 10.

12. Complete the replacement of brushes by placing brush caps over brush springs and screw caps (clockwise) on securely. (*Figure 9*)

13. Test the operation of the electric broom.

    NOTE: If electric broom continues to have weak suction and burning odor after motor brushes have been serviced or replaced, a more serious motor problem is indicated. Discontinue use of the cleaner immediately and take it to a qualified appliance repair shop for further testing.

FIG.8

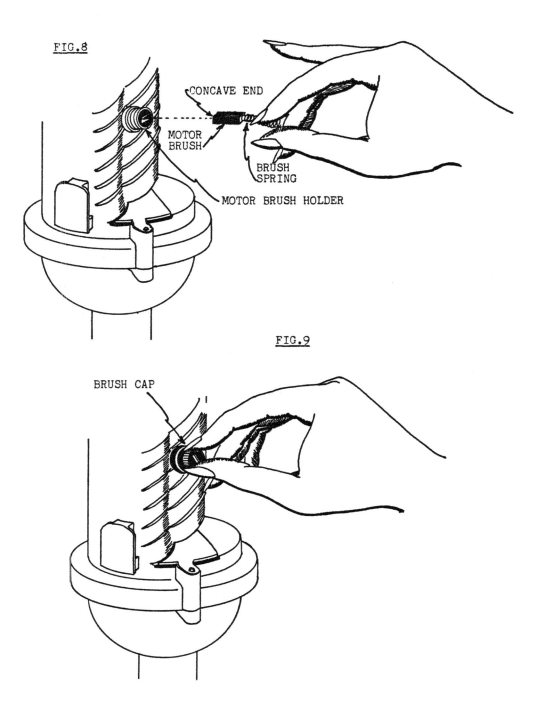

CONCAVE END

MOTOR
BRUSH

BRUSH
SPRING

MOTOR BRUSH HOLDER

FIG.9

BRUSH CAP

Problem Solver #38

APPLIANCE: Food Mixer (Portable Type)

PROBLEM: Motor runs but one or both beaters do not turn.

EXPLANATION: Gears are used in food mixers to transfer the turning
                  motion of the electric motor to the beaters. There-
                  fore, if the motor runs without turning the beaters, the
                  cause can usually be traced to worn or broken gears.

TOOLS AND MATERIALS NEEDED:

(a) a flatblade screwdriver

(b) a phillips screwdriver

(c) a tube of lubri-plate (white grease)

SOLUTION: 1. Examine mixer for screws that are used to hold the
                     top and bottom halves of the case together. These
                     are usually located on the bottom half of the mixer
                     case. (*Figure 1*)

                  CAUTION: Disconnect the mixer from electric outlet.

FIG.1

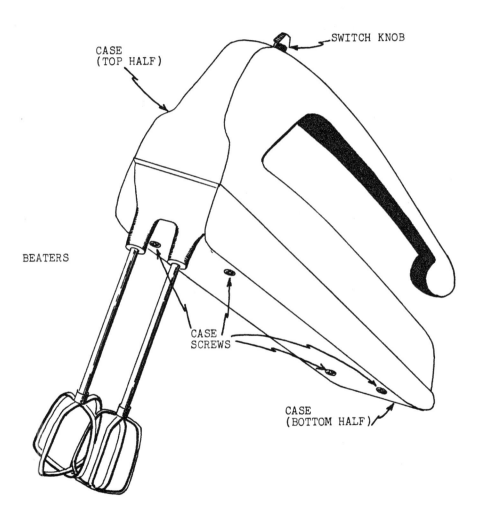

SWITCH KNOB

CASE
(TOP HALF)

BEATERS

CASE
SCREWS

CASE
(BOTTOM HALF)

2. Remove (eject) the beaters.

3. Remove the case screws with an appropriate screw-driver (flatblade or phillips type screwdriver depending upon the type of screw head used). (*Figure 2*)

4. Remove switch knob (if switch knob prevents removal of top case section) by pulling it straight off. (*Figure 3*)

FIG.2

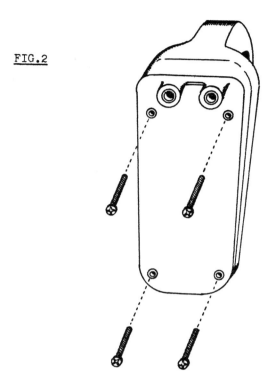

FIG.3

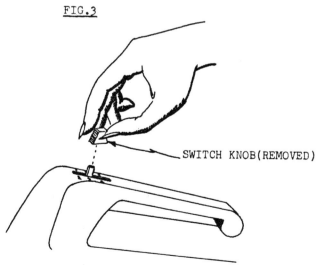

SWITCH KNOB(REMOVED)

5. Lift the top half of the mixer case off and examine the plastic or fiber worm gears for broken or worn teeth. (*Figure 4*) An example of a worm gear that has broken teeth is shown in *Figure 5*. *Figure 6* illustrates an example of a worm gear with worn teeth.

NOTE: In some model food mixers the gears are contained in an additional enclosure called the gear case. For these models, the gear case cover must be removed to gain access to them. (*Figure 7*)

FIG.4

WORM SHAFT

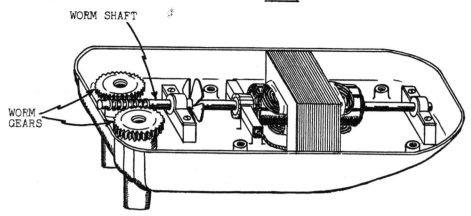

WORM
GEARS

FIG.5

DEFECTIVE WORM GEAR

FIG.6

DEFECTIVE WORM GEAR

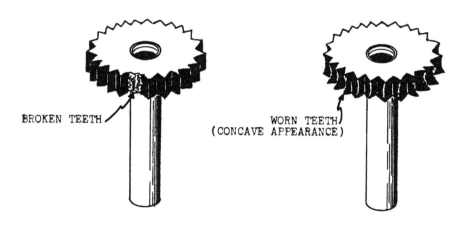

BROKEN TEETH

WORN TEETH
(CONCAVE APPEARANCE)

6. To remove defective worm gear(s), lift the gear straight up and out of the lower case section. (*Figure 8*)

   NOTE: It is advisable to replace both worm gears as a set (left worm gear and right worm gear) even though only one appears to be defective. These gears can usually be purchased from your local appliance service shop. If not available locally, they may be ordered directly from the manufacturer's parts supply division. Be sure to specify complete model or catalog number together with the names of the parts: "left worm gear" and "right worm gear."

7. Before installing new replacement worm gears, apply a light coat of grease to the gear spindles with fingertip. (*Figure 9*)

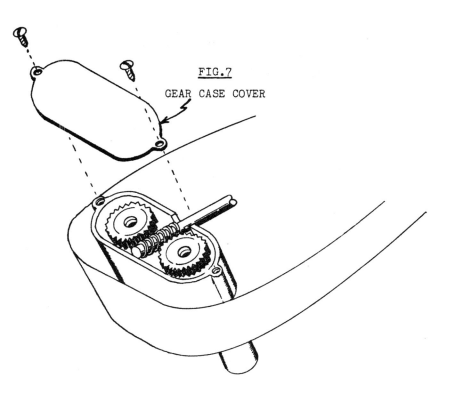

FIG.7

GEAR CASE COVER

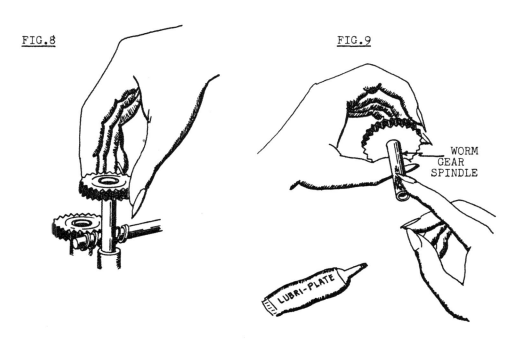

FIG.8

FIG.9

WORM
GEAR
SPINDLE

LUBRI-PLATE

8. Insert the worm gear spindles part way into the spindle shafts. Turn the worm gears until the alignment indicating marks (if provided) face each other; then, press them into place on the worm shaft. (*Figure 10*)

   NOTE: Worm gears are usually marked with an arrow, dot, etc. The mark on the left worm gear must be aligned with the mark on the right worm gear to prevent the beaters from clashing. When the new replacement gears are not marked, their correct relationship must be found through trial and error.

9. To install unmarked worm gears, insert the gears fully into the spindle shafts, then attach the beaters. If beaters touch each other, re-position one of the worm gears (turn it clockwise or counter-clockwise) until the beaters mesh without clashing. (*Figure 11*)

10. After worm gears have been installed, apply a small amount of white grease to the worm shaft with fingertip.

11. If mixer construction includes a gear case, redistribute some of the original grease contained in the gear case over the worm shaft.

FIG.10

ALIGNMENT MARKS

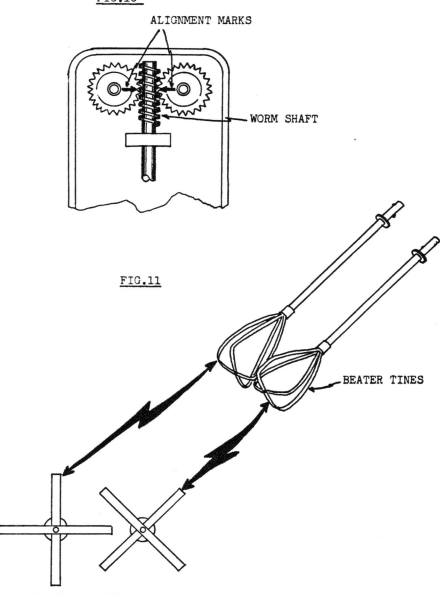

WORM SHAFT

FIG.11

BEATER TINES

CORRECT POSITION OF BEATER TINES

Problem Solver #39

APPLIANCE: Food Mixer (Portable Type)

PROBLEM: Mixer runs hot.

EXPLANATION: It is normal for food mixers as well as for other motor-driven appliances to undergo a temperature rise during operation. The electric motor normally generates a certain quantity of heat. Abnormal conditions, however, which prevent removal of motor heat or which cause the motor to generate an excessive amount of heat, can cause severe damage.

TOOLS AND MATERIALS NEEDED:

    (a) a pipe cleaner

SOLUTION:
1. Examine the air vent slots located in the mixer case to see that they have not become clogged with food (flour, egg, etc.) which may have splattered during beating. (*Figures 1 and 2*)

   NOTE: While the appearance of the air vent slots for different makes and models varies, their function remains the same. A small fan driven by the mixer motor draws air into the vent slots at one end of the mixer and discharges it through the vent slots at the other; thereby cooling the motor. If the vent slots are clogged, air circulation is restricted and overheating can result.

2. Clean vent slots with pipe cleaner. Fold a pipe cleaner in half and insert folded end into vent slots to remove food residue. (*Figure 3*)

3. Re-examine air flow through mixer after cleaning. Place hand over vent slots (front and rear) while operating the mixer. Air must be felt leaving the vent slots at one end (front or rear) of the mixer.

   SPECIAL NOTE: Occasionally, a mixer may overheat even though air circulation through it is good. This could be caused when the mixer is subjected to abnormally heavy work loads (thick batter, etc.) at low speed for long periods during operation. Other, more serious conditions which can cause overheating involve the electric motor itself. If overheating persists after proper cleaning, mixer should be brought to a qualified appliance repair shop.

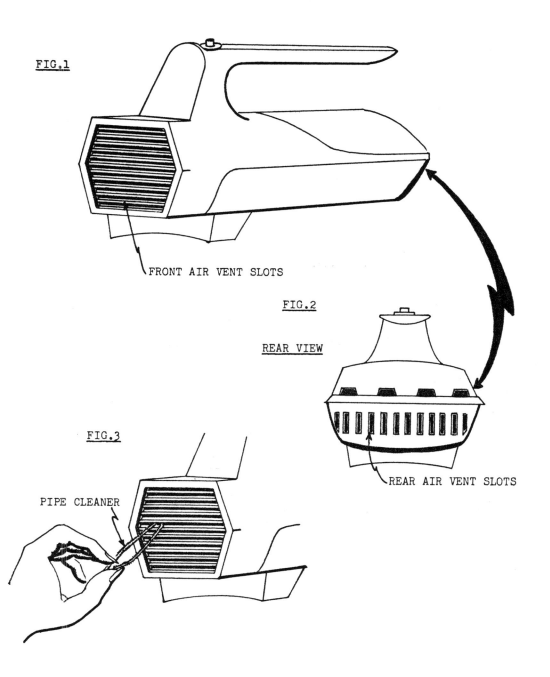

FIG.1

FRONT AIR VENT SLOTS

FIG.2

REAR VIEW

REAR AIR VENT SLOTS

FIG.3

PIPE CLEANER

Problem Solver #40

APPLIANCE: Food Mixer (Portable Type)

PROBLEM: Excessive noise during operation.

EXPLANATION: Noise is defined as any clicking, banging, or rubbing sound that is not part of the normal sound made by a food mixer when it operates. All abnormal noise should be quickly investigated, as it usually means that some part has become loose or worn, and that one part is striking against another.

TOOLS AND MATERIALS NEEDED:

    (a) a pair of pliers

    (b) a phillips screwdriver

    (c) a flatblade screwdriver (small size, sewing machine type)

SOLUTION:
1. Operate mixer with beaters installed and notice if noise occurs.

2. Operate mixer with beaters removed and listen for noise.

   NOTE: If noise occurs only when beaters are used, it means that the beaters are clashing. This can happen when the beater tines are loose or bent.

3. Check the beaters for bent tines. (*Figure 1*) If the beater tines are only slightly bent, they may be re-aligned by bending them back into their original shape with a pair of pliers. (*Figure 2*) Make slight adjustment bends and re-test mixer between each adjustment until noise disappears.

FIG.1

FIG.2

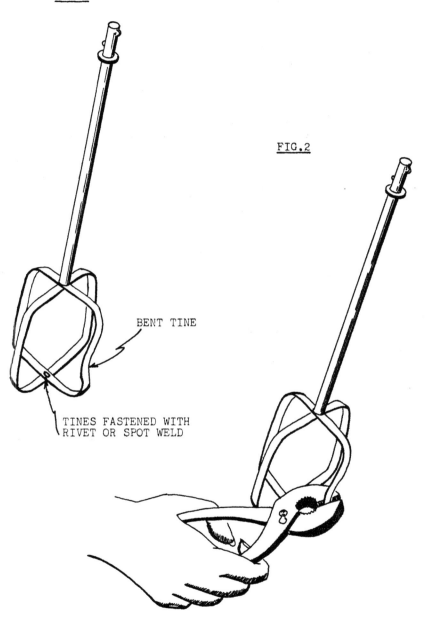

BENT TINE

TINES FASTENED WITH
RIVET OR SPOT WELD

NOTE: If beater tines are found to be badly distorted, as might happen when the mixer is accidentally dropped, or if the beater is found to be loose because of a broken spot weld or rivet (*Figure 1*), the beater should be replaced with a new one. Replacement beaters are available for purchase from most local appliance repair shops. If not available locally, they may be ordered directly from manufacturer's parts supply division.

4. Excessive noise that can be heard even with the beaters removed is caused by something within the mixer. It will be necessary to disassemble the mixer case to gain access into the mixer to determine the origin of the noise.

   NOTE: Disconnect the mixer from electric outlet before proceeding.

5. Remove the top half of the mixer case by removing the case screws with a phillips screwdriver. (*Figure 3*)

6. If speed control knob prevents removal of top half of mixer case, remove the knob by pulling it straight up. (*Figure 4*)

FIG.3

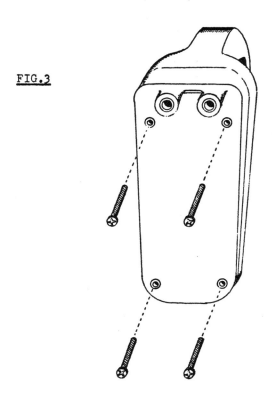

FIG.4

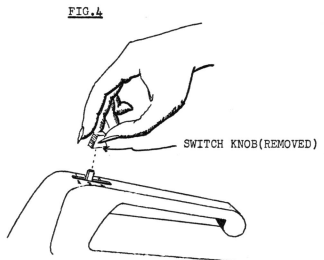

SWITCH KNOB(REMOVED)

7. Check for proper clearance between motor fan and other stationary mixer parts by rotating the fan slowly by hand for at least one complete revolution. (*Figure 5*) Fan blades must not come in contact with any other part, such as wires, case, etc.

8. If fan is striking a wire, bend wire away from fan. Make certain wire will not spring back to contact fan blades again. A small piece of plastic electrical tape can be used to secure a loose wire in place. (*Figure 6*) Carefully reassemble the case to complete the repair.

<u>FIG.5</u>

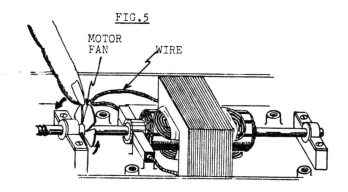

MOTOR
FAN   WIRE

<u>FIG.6</u>

WIRE HELD WITH PLASTIC ELECTRICAL TAPE

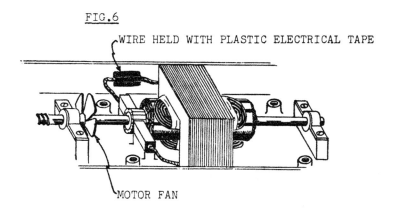

MOTOR FAN

9. If fan blade(s) is striking a portion of the case (or another stationary part), check the fan for bent (mis-aligned) blades. (*Figure 7*) Re-align bent blade(s) by bending it back into alignment with the other blades. (*Figure 8*) Carefully reassemble the case to complete the repair.

NOTE: If inspection of fan blades discloses that they were not bent or otherwise distorted, a check must be made of the amount of free movement the fan blade and the motor shaft on which it is mounted has from end to end (called end play). If the end play of the motor shaft is too much, the fan during operation can strike a stationary portion of the mixer. Some mixer models are provided with a screw that can be adjusted to eliminate excessive end play, should it exist.

FIG.7

BENT FAN BLADE

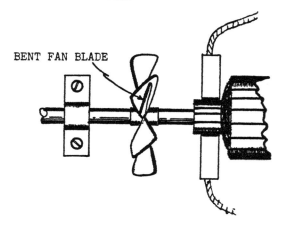

FIG.8

CORRECTLY ALIGNED FAN BLADES

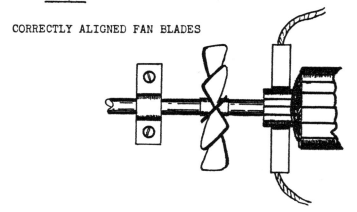

10. To test for excessive end play, grasp the fan and push it alternately toward the front end and the rear end of the mixer. (*Figure 9*) If movement of motor shaft in either direction is sufficient to cause the fan to come into contact (no matter how slight) with other parts, the amount of end play is excessive and should be adjusted.

NOTE: Correct motor shaft end play should allow the motor shaft to move only about .024 inches (or the approximate thickness of a match book cover).

11. To adjust the motor shaft end play, loosen the adjustment screw lock nut by turning one full turn counter-clockwise. (*Figure 10*)

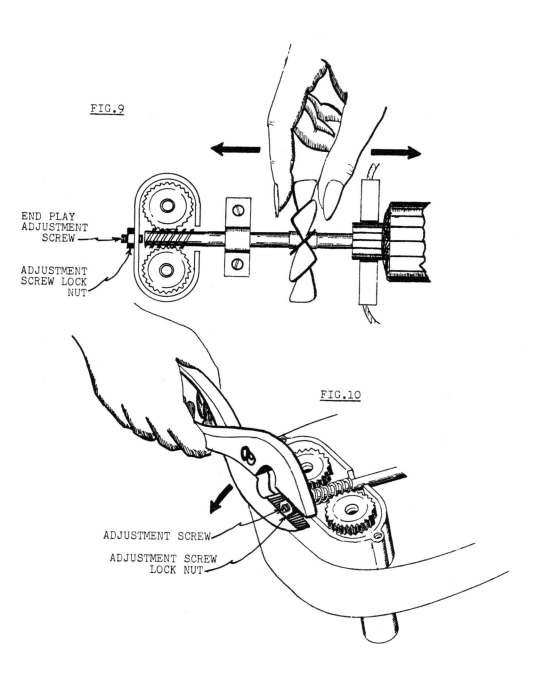

FIG.9

END PLAY
ADJUSTMENT
SCREW

ADJUSTMENT
SCREW LOCK
NUT

FIG.10

ADJUSTMENT SCREW

ADJUSTMENT SCREW
LOCK NUT

12. Insert small flatblade screwdriver into slot of adjustment screw and turn it ¼ turn (clockwise). (*Figure 11*) Re-check amount of end play. Make additional ¼ turn adjustments (if needed) and re-check end play after each adjustment until correct adjustment is obtained.

13. When correct adjustment is obtained, hold adjustment screw in final position with small screwdriver and tighten adjustment lock nut (clockwise) to lock the adjustment screw in place. (*Figure 12*)

    CAUTION: Make certain correct amount of end play remains after adjustment lock nut is tightened. Not enough end play will cause motor shaft to bind and could result in damage to the mixer motor.

14. Reassemble the mixer case to complete the repair.

FIG.11

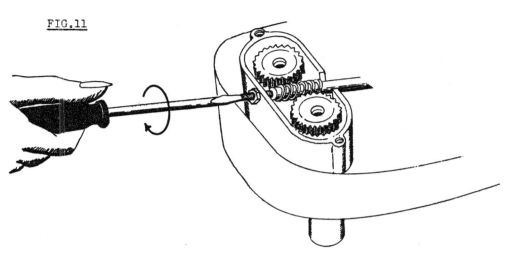

FIG.12

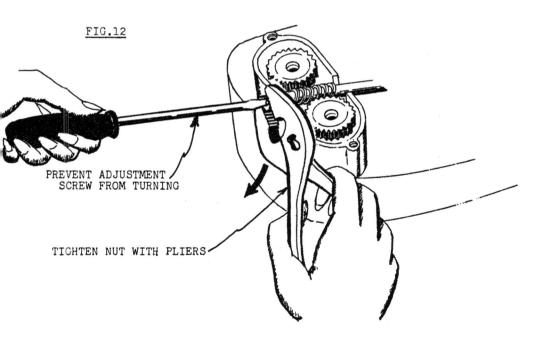

PREVENT ADJUSTMENT
SCREW FROM TURNING

TIGHTEN NUT WITH PLIERS

Problem Solver #41

APPLIANCE: Food Mixer (Portable and Stand Type)

PROBLEM: **Motor stops and starts during operation.**

EXPLANATION: Intermittent operation is invariably caused by a loose or broken wire connection. Since the line cord is subjected to constant bending and tugging stress during normal use, a broken wire is more likely to occur there than anywhere else in the food mixer.

TOOLS AND MATERIALS NEEDED:

    (a)   a flatblade screwdriver (small size)

    (b)   a pair of universal pliers

    (c)   a paring knife

    (d)   a pair of cutting pliers or kitchen poultry shears

    (e)   2 insulating wire nuts (#2)

SOLUTION:

1. Plug the mixer into an electric outlet and turn it on.

2. Shake the line cord vigorously while the mixer is running. If the mixer motor stops and starts as the line cord is being wiggled, the line cord must be carefully inspected for broken wires or loose connections.

   SPECIAL NOTE: Two basic types of line cords are being used for food mixers. The first is an older system which permanently wires the line cord into the mixer. (*Figure 1*) The newer type line cord is detachable and connects to the mixer by means of a female plug. (*Figure 2*)

3. Check to see that the two-prong male plug (used on both types of line cords) fits securely in the wall outlet. (*Figure 3*) If male plug is loose in wall outlet, spread each plug prong with a screwdriver to provide better contact. (*Figure 4*)

FIG.1

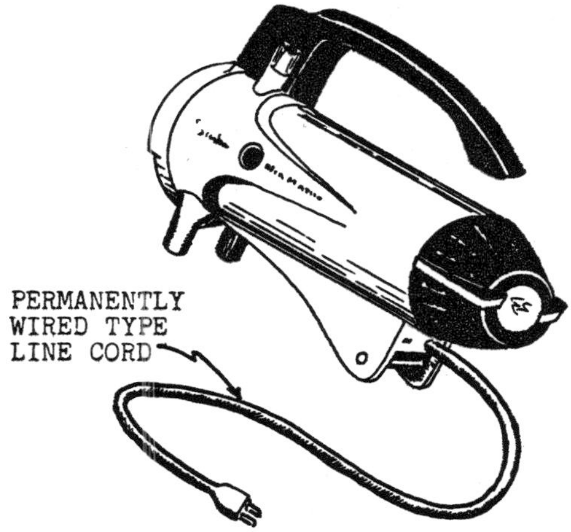

PERMANENTLY
WIRED TYPE
LINE CORD

FIG.2

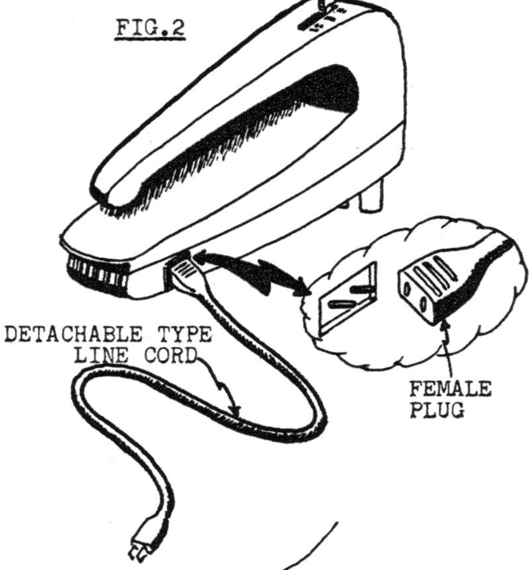

DETACHABLE TYPE
LINE CORD

FEMALE
PLUG

FIG.4

FIG.3

TEST MALE PLUG FOR LOOSE
FIT IN WALL OUTLET

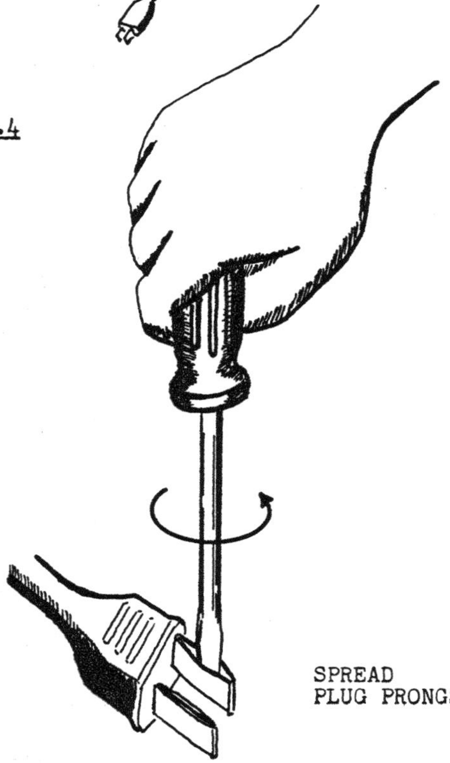

SPREAD
PLUG PRONGS

4. Re-test operation of food mixer after adjusting the male plug prongs.

    NOTE: If line cord being tested is the detachable type, the female plug should also be adjusted to insure good electrical contact with the appliance.

5. To adjust the female plug of the line cord, place half the plug between the jaws of a pair of universal pliers and squeeze the pliers firmly to tighten the plug contact. (*Figure 5*) Repeat this for the other contact.

    NOTE: If mixer continues to operate intermittently after male and female plug prongs have been adjusted, the entire line cord should be replaced with a new one. No special procedure is required to replace detachable type line cords since these simply plug into the mixer. Detachable type line cords may be purchased from most local appliance repair shops. If not available locally, they may be ordered by mail from the manufacturer's parts supply division. Be sure to specify model number and color of food mixer. Replacement of permanently wired type line cords can be accomplished by following the procedure outlined in the steps below.

    CAUTION: Remove the line cord from the wall outlet.

6. Remove the food mixer from its stand and lay it down on its side with bottom facing you.

7. Locate and remove the terminal cover plate screw (turn counter-clockwise) with a flatblade screwdriver. (*Figure 6*)

FIG.5

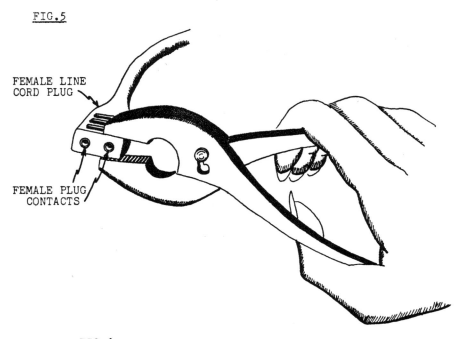

FEMALE LINE
CORD PLUG

FEMALE PLUG
CONTACTS

FIG.6

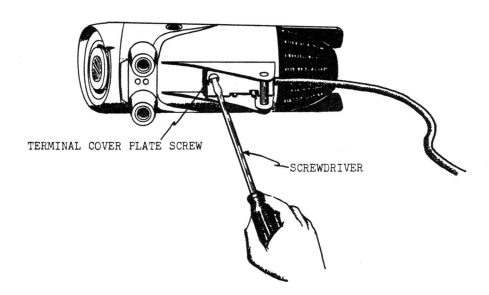

TERMINAL COVER PLATE SCREW

SCREWDRIVER

8. Remove the terminal cover plate by lifting it out. (*Figure 7*)

9. Cut both line cord wire ends just below the plastic-covered connections with wire cutting pliers or kitchen poultry shears. (*Figure 8*) Pull old line cord out through hole to remove it.

FIG.7

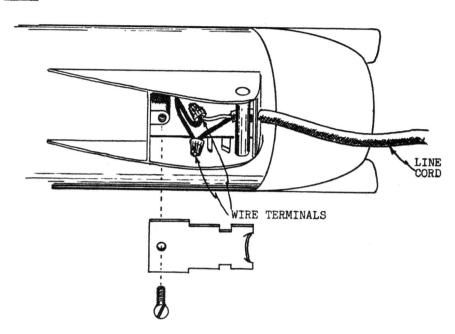

LINE CORD

WIRE TERMINALS

FIG.8

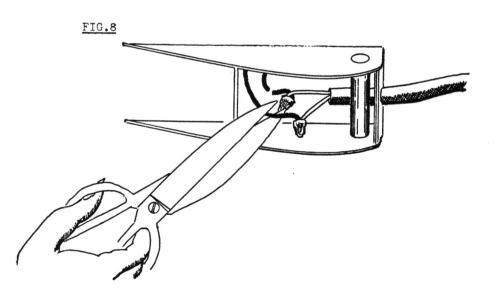

10. Carefully remove about ¾ of an inch of the insulation from the mixer's terminal wire ends with a paring knife. (*Figure 9*)

   CAUTION: Take care not to cut or otherwise remove any of the copper wire strands when removing the insulating covering.

11. Twist the loose wire strands together as shown in *Figure 10*.

FIG.9

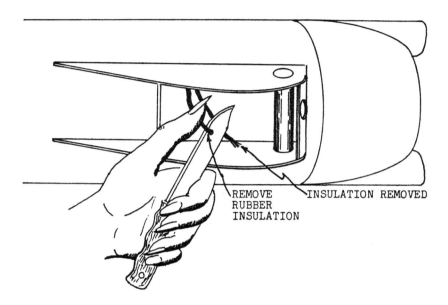

REMOVE
RUBBER
INSULATION

INSULATION REMOVED

FIG.10

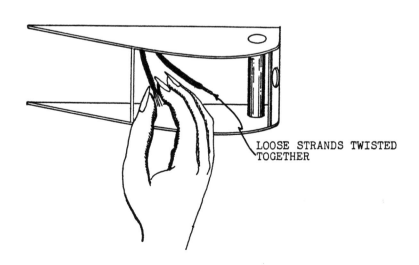

LOOSE STRANDS TWISTED
TOGETHER

12. Connect the bare wire ends of the food mixer to the bare wire ends of the new line cord. (*Figure 11*)

13. Screw an insulating wire nut onto each wire connection. (*Figure 12*)

14. Fasten the terminal cover plate in place to complete the repair.

SPECIAL NOTE: To prolong the life of food mixer line cords, never wrap the line cord tightly around the mixer body. When storing it always coil the line cord loosely by the side of the mixer.

<u>FIG.11</u>

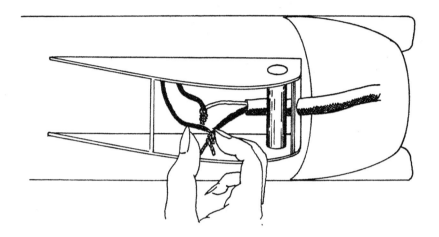

<u>FIG.12</u>

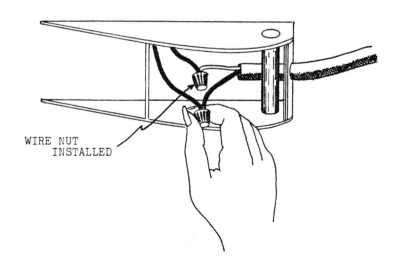

WIRE NUT
INSTALLED

Problem Solver #42

APPLIANCE: Food Mixer (Stand Type)

PROBLEM: **Mixer runs too slow or too fast for speed setting.**

EXPLANATION: This problem is the result of a defective or maladjusted component in the speed governing mechanism of mixers which feature continuous (no click) type speed controls.

TOOLS AND MATERIALS NEEDED:

(a) a flatblade screwdriver (medium size)

(b) two pairs of universal pliers

(c) a small can of light motor oil (sewing machine type)

(d) a paring knife

SOLUTION: 1. Set the speed control knob to the "off" position and remove the line cord plug from the wall outlet.

2. Remove the escutcheon plate at the rear of the control knob by prying it off with the sharp edge of a paring knife. (*Figure 1*)

3. Hold the control knob in the "off" position with one hand and remove the knob fastening screw by turning it counter-clockwise. (*Figure 2*)

CAUTION: Take care not to drop the flat washer and spring washer located under the knob screw. (*Figure 2*)

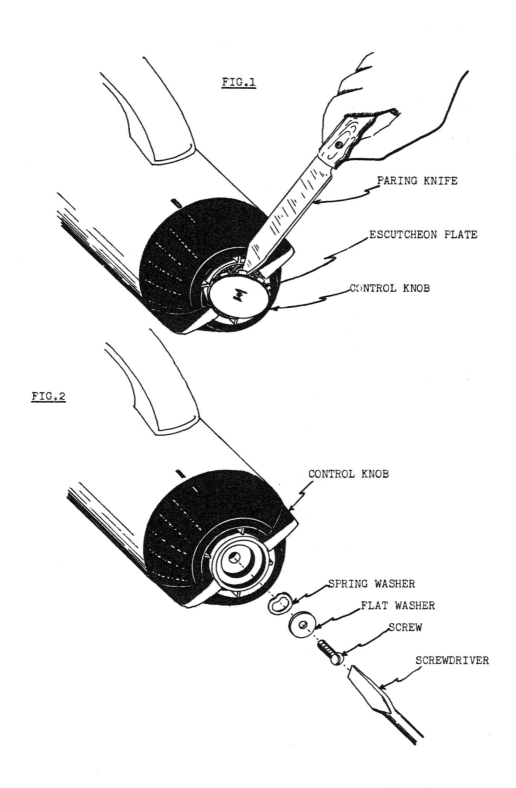

FIG.1

PARING KNIFE

ESCUTCHEON PLATE

CONTROL KNOB

FIG.2

CONTROL KNOB

SPRING WASHER

FLAT WASHER

SCREW

SCREWDRIVER

4. Remove the control knob by pulling it straight out. (*Figure 3*)

5. Grasp the thrust rod and remove it by pulling it straight out. (*Figure 3*)

   NOTE: The thrust rod is an adjustable link which synchronizes the knob setting with the motor speed. A close inspection of the rod will reveal that its construction consists of two sections. Both sections have threads and can be screwed together or apart. When the sections are screwed together to shorten the rod, the motor speed will be increased. When the sections are screwed apart to lengthen the rod, the motor speed will be decreased.

6. If the mixer runs too slow for the control knob setting, the length of the thrust rod must be shortened.

FIG.3

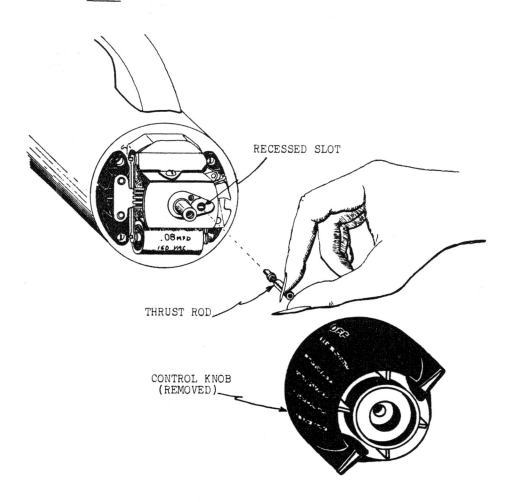

RECESSED SLOT

.08MFD
150 VAC

THRUST ROD

CONTROL KNOB
(REMOVED)

7. To shorten the length of the rod, grasp the front flat section of the rod with a pair of universal pliers. Grasp the round rear section with a second pair of universal pliers. Hold the front section steady and turn the rear section one full turn in a clockwise direction. (*Figure 4*)

   NOTE: A drop of motor oil placed on the threads will help to loosen stuck or stubborn threads.

8. Reassemble the mixer and test for correct speeds for knob settings. If the mixer speed is still too slow for the knob setting, repeat the adjustment of the thread rod (one full turn clockwise at a time) until mixer speed corresponds to control knob settings.

   CAUTION: When replacing the thrust rod, make certain that the flat portion of the front section is aligned and fully seated in the recessed slot. (*Figure 3*)

9. If the mixer runs too fast for the control knob setting, the thrust rod must be lengthened.

10. To lengthen the thrust rod, remove the rod as described in steps 1 to 5 above, grasp the rod with two pairs of universal pliers and turn the round rear section one full turn counter-clockwise. (*Figure 4*)

11. Reassemble the mixer and test for correct mixer speeds for control knob settings.

12. Repeat the adjustment if necessary.

FIG.4

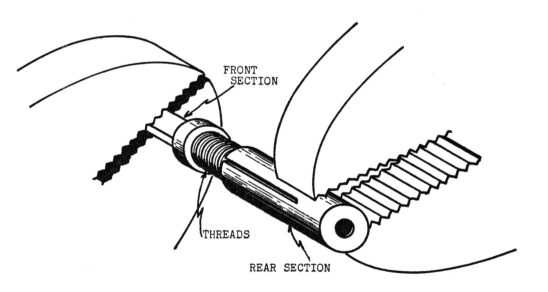

FRONT
SECTION

THREADS

REAR SECTION

Problem Solver #43

APPLIANCE: Food Mixer (Stand Type with Continuous Speed Control)

PROBLEM: **Mixer runs at full speed regardless of speed setting.**

EXPLANATION: The speed of this type mixer should vary continuously as the speed control knob is turned to different settings. If the mixer runs at its maximum speed regardless of the setting of the speed control knob, a small electrical component called a "capacitor" may have become defective.

TOOLS AND MATERIALS NEEDED:

    (a) a flatblade screwdriver (medium size)

    (b) a paring knife

SOLUTION: 1. Set the speed control knob to the "off" position and remove the line cord plug from the wall outlet.

    2. Remove the escutcheon plate at the rear of the speed control knob by prying it off with the sharp edge of a paring knife. (*Figure 1*)

    3. Hold the speed control knob in the "off" position with one hand, then remove the knob fastening screw by turning it counter-clockwise. (*Figure 2*)

    CAUTION: Take care not to drop the flat washer and spring washer located under the knob screw. (*Figure 2*)

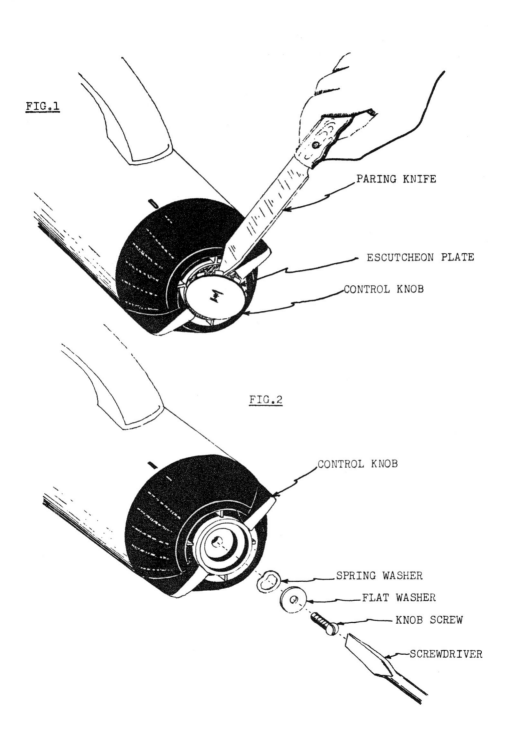

FIG.1

PARING KNIFE

ESCUTCHEON PLATE

CONTROL KNOB

FIG.2

CONTROL KNOB

SPRING WASHER

FLAT WASHER

KNOB SCREW

SCREWDRIVER

4. Remove the speed control knob by pulling it straight out. (*Figure 3*)

   CAUTION: Be sure thrust rod is not accidentally dropped. (*Figure 3*)

5. Locate the tubular-shaped "capacitor." (*Figure 3*)

   NOTE: The capacitor is one of the electrical components of the speed control mechanism. It is usually identified by markings which indicate its electrical size such as: .08MFD - 160 VAC. The defects of this type of component are not visible since they occur internally. The best method used to check this component, therefore, is by the process of elimination. This requires that it be replaced with a new one.

6. To insure correct purchase of a new replacement capacitor, take the original capacitor along with you to the local appliance service or parts store for comparison. If the capacitor is not available locally, it may be ordered by mail directly from the manufacturer's parts division. Be sure to include the model number of the mixer and all of the identifying data printed on the capacitor in your order request.

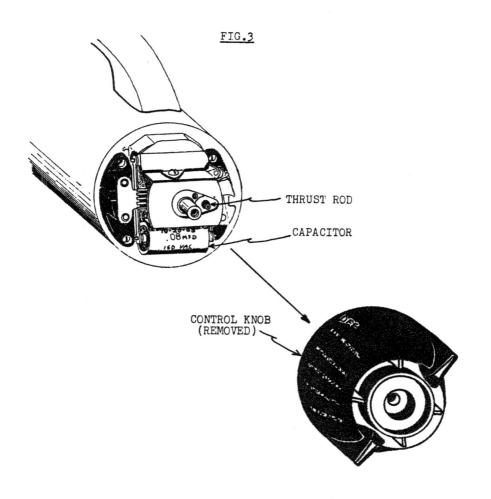

FIG.3

THRUST ROD

CAPACITOR

CONTROL KNOB
(REMOVED)

7. To remove the capacitor, press the flatblade edge of a screwdriver against the left electrical terminal until it clears the brass nipple of the capacitor. (*Figure 4*)

8. Grasp the capacitor with your other hand. Pull it down and to the left until the brass nipple on the right of the capacitor clears the right terminal. (*Figure 5*)

9. To install the new replacement capacitor, reverse steps 6 and 7.

10. Replace the speed control knob and test mixer operation.

    CAUTION: Make certain that the thrust rod is in its proper location before replacing the speed control knob. (*Figure 3*)

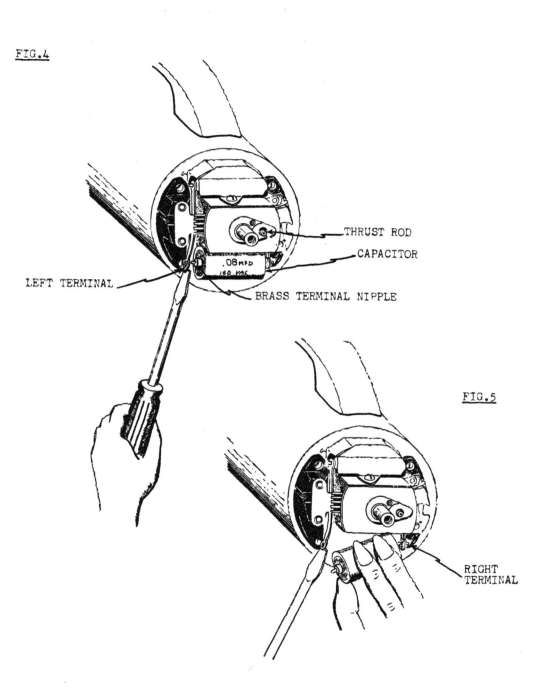

FIG.4

THRUST ROD

CAPACITOR

LEFT TERMINAL

.08 MFD
180 KDC

BRASS TERMINAL NIPPLE

FIG.5

RIGHT TERMINAL

Problem Solver #44

APPLIANCE: Food Blenders

PROBLEM: Motor hums but blades do not turn.

EXPLANATION: An audible humming sound produced by the motor with no visible movement of the blender blades is a symptom of a "stuck" component. More often it is the blade assembly of the blender which becomes stuck. This is a serious condition that must be attended to at once to avoid permanent damage to the motor.

TOOLS AND MATERIALS NEEDED:

(a)   a pair of universal pliers

(b)   a bread (or meat) cutting board

(c)   a jar of vaseline (petroleum jelly)

(d)   a package of pipe cleaners

(e)   an abrasive type cleaning pad (used to scour pots)

(f)   dishwashing detergent (soap)

SOLUTION:

1. Shut the blender off *immediately* and remove the line cord plug from the wall outlet.

2. Remove the jar from the blender and empty its contents.

3. Test for stuck blades by trying to turn them with the tip of a pencil. (*Figure 1*)

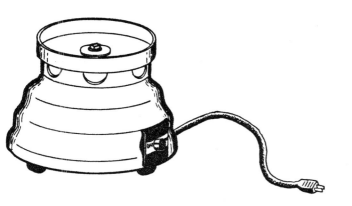

FIG.1

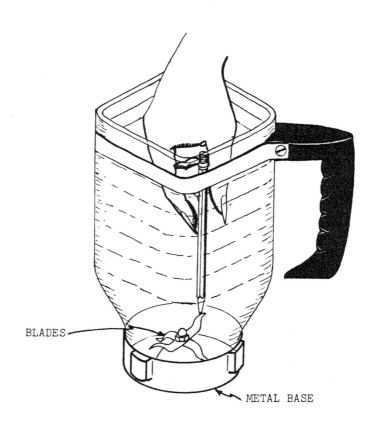

BLADES

METAL BASE

4. If blades do not turn freely when prodded with a pencil, the blade assembly is stuck and must be disassembled and examined to determine whether repair or replacement is required.

   NOTE: Disassembling instructions and servicing procedures for three different manufactured blenders are given in the steps that follow. These models represent the variety of blenders most often found in use today.

5. To take apart the blade assembly of the blender illustrated in *Figure 1*, unscrew the metal base from the jar and lift the blade assembly out. (*Figure 2*)

FIG.2

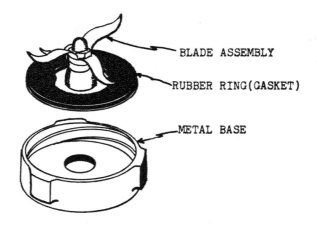

BLADE ASSEMBLY

RUBBER RING(GASKET)

METAL BASE

NOTE: Two versions of this type blender are manufactured. One employs a cap nut to fasten the blades
to the assembly. (*Figure 3*) The other type permanently rivets the blades to the assembly.

6. Examine the top center portion of the blade
   assembly. If the blades are fastened with a cap nut
   (*Figure 3*), the blade assembly can be taken apart
   and serviced. If the blades are permanently riveted
   as shown in *Figure 4*, the blade assembly cannot be
   serviced and must be replaced as a unit.

7. To service the blade assembly shown in *Figure 3*,
   bend the two lock tabs (used to prevent the cap
   nut from loosening) away from the nut with the
   flatblade of a screwdriver. (*Figure 5*)

CAUTION: Do not bend the lock tabs more than is
necessary to allow the cap nut to be turned. Over-
bending can cause them to break.

FIG.3

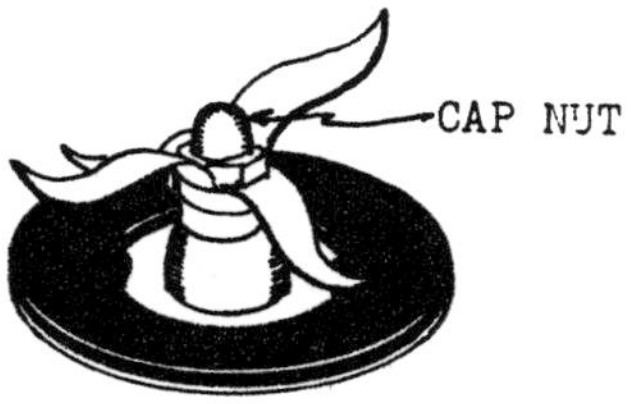
CAP NUT

FIG.4

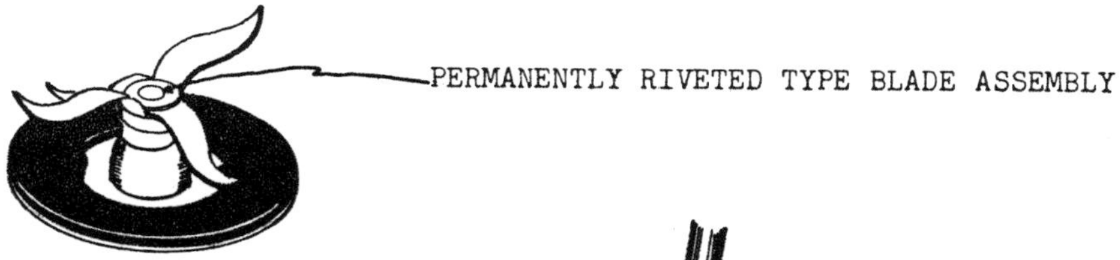
PERMANENTLY RIVETED TYPE BLADE ASSEMBLY

FIG.5

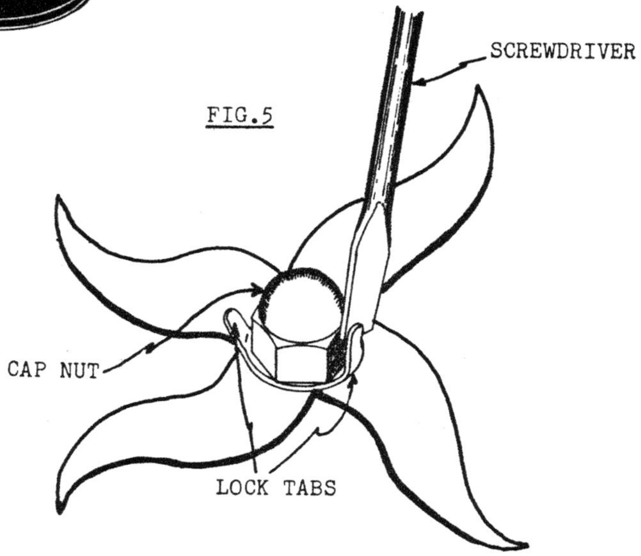
SCREWDRIVER
CAP NUT
LOCK TABS

8. Grasp the assembly by the blades and remove the cap nut by turning it counter-clockwise with a pair of pliers. (*Figure 6*)

   CAUTION: The blades of some model blenders have sharp edges. If so, wrap the end of a dish towel over the blades before grasping them to avoid injury to hand.

9. Lift off the lock tab washer, cap washer, and blades. (*Figure 7*)

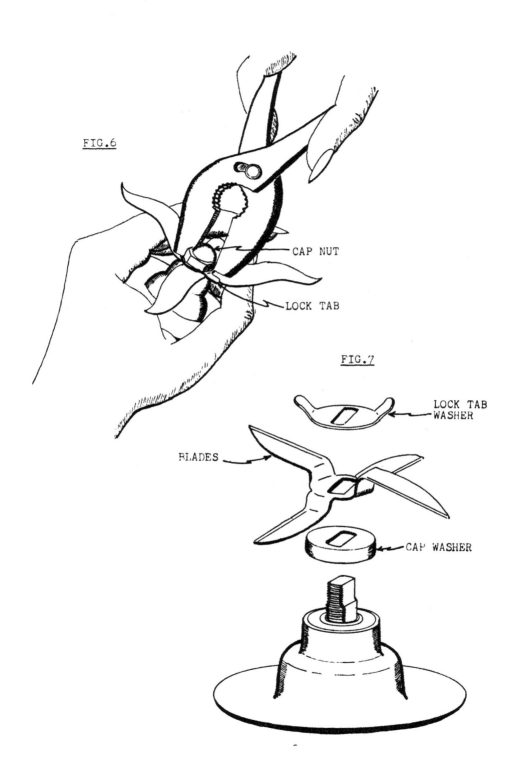

FIG.6

CAP NUT

LOCK TAB

FIG.7

LOCK TAB
WASHER

BLADES

CAP WASHER

10. Turn the remaining blade assembly upside down and tap the protruding drive shaft end against the surface of a hardwood bread board or meat cutting board until the drive shaft is removed from the blade assembly housing. (*Figure 8*)

    CAUTION: Spacer washers on the drive shaft need not be removed. Take care, however, not to lose them. (*Figure 9*)

11. Clean the drive shaft with an abrasive type cleanser or pad to remove rust, food residue, etc.

12. Clean the inner recess of the blade assembly housing with a folded pipe cleaner that has been dipped into a dishwashing detergent (soap). (*Figure 10*)

13. Rinse all parts well under hot tap water and allow to dry thoroughly.

14. Lubricate the drive shaft of the blade assembly by coating it liberally with vaseline (petroleum jelly), to complete the servicing.

FIG.8

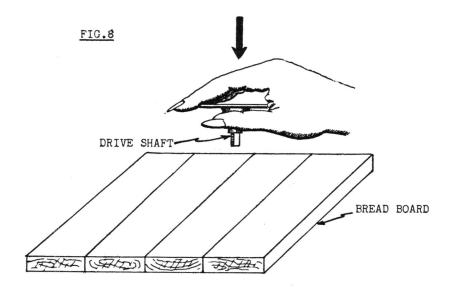

DRIVE SHAFT

BREAD BOARD

FIG.9

FIG.10

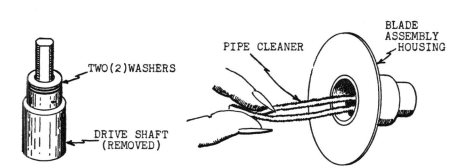

TWO(2)WASHERS

DRIVE SHAFT
(REMOVED)

PIPE CLEANER

BLADE
ASSEMBLY
HOUSING

15. To reconstruct the blade assembly, insert the drive shaft fully into the blade assembly housing. Place the cap washer and lock tab washer on the drive shaft. (*Figure 7*)

16. Screw the cap nut onto the drive shaft (clockwise) manually, then tighten it securely with a pair of pliers. Make certain that the flat sides of the cap nut are aligned with the two lock tabs. (*Figure 5*)

17. Bend the lock tabs firmly against the cap nut with a pair of pliers. (*Figure 11*) This will prevent the cap nut from loosening and complete the reassembly for this type blender.

    CAUTION: Be sure to replace the rubber ring (gasket) in its correct position atop the blade assembly (*Figure 2*) before screwing the metal base to the jar.

<u>FIG.11</u>

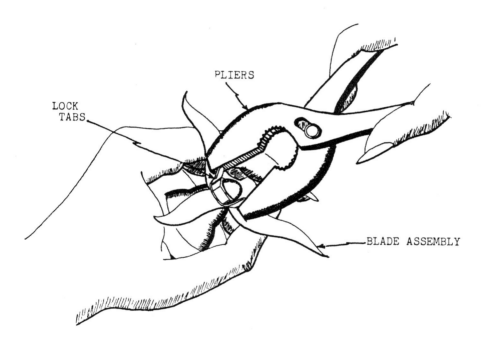

PLIERS

LOCK
TABS

BLADE ASSEMBLY

18. To take apart the blade assembly for the blender illustrated in *Figure 12,* place the jar on its side and remove the large nut located on the bottom of the jar by turning it counter-clockwise with a pair of pliers. (*Figure 13*)

SPECIAL NOTE: Blenders that do not have detachable jar bases are older models. The disadvantage of the one-piece jar design is the difficulty encountered in gaining access to the lower jar area and blade assembly whenever cleaning and/or maintenance becomes necessary.

FIG.12

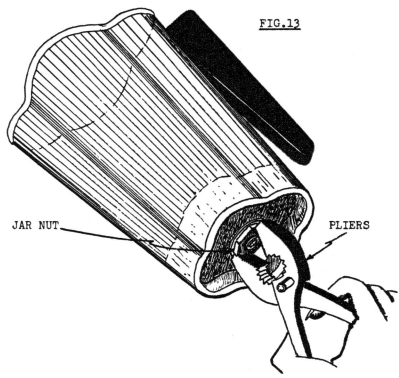

FIG.13

JAR NUT

PLIERS

19. Reach into the jar, grasp the blades and pull the blade assembly out of the jar. (*Figure 14*)

20. Hold the blades of the assembly securely and re-move the cap nut, turning it counter-clockwise with a pair of pliers. (*Figure 15*)

   CAUTION: If blades are sharp, wrap them with a dish cloth or towel to avoid injuring fingers.

21. Lift the blades off the assembly.

   NOTE: Blades should be inspected at this time to assess their condition. If blades are found to be chipped, bent, or otherwise defective, they should be replaced. Replacement blades are normally avail-able for purchase from local appliance repair shops. If not they may be ordered directly by mail from the manufacturer's parts supply division. Be sure to specify the exact model number (located on the base plate of the blender).

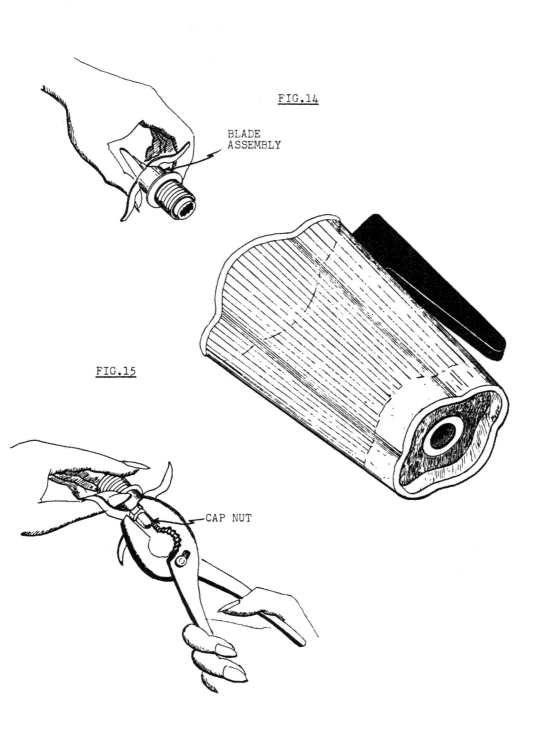

FIG.14

BLADE
ASSEMBLY

FIG.15

CAP NUT

22. Turn the remaining portion of the assembly upside down and tap the drive shaft end against a meat or bread board (*Figure 16*) until the drive shaft and bearing cap are removed. (*Figure 17*)

23. Clean the drive shaft with an abrasive type cleaning pad to remove all traces of rust, food residue, etc.

24. Clean the inside of the bearing housing and bearing cap with a folded pipe cleaner that has been dipped in dishwashing detergent (soap).

25. Rinse the bearing cap, bearing holder, and drive shaft well under hot tap water and allow to dry thoroughly.

26. Lubricate the entire length of the drive shaft by coating it liberally with vaseline (petroleum jelly).

FIG.16

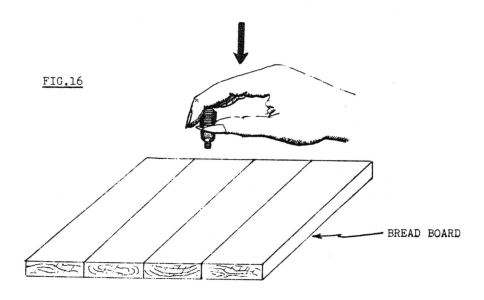

BREAD BOARD

FIG.17

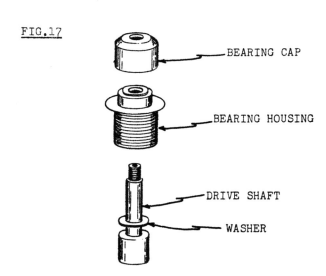

BEARING CAP

BEARING HOUSING

DRIVE SHAFT

WASHER

27. Reassemble the blade assembly and replace it in the jar by reversing the order in which it was taken apart. (Steps 18 to 22)

NOTE: Two steel washers and two rubber washers (gaskets) are located above and below the bottom of the jar to prevent liquid leakage. (*Figure 18*) These may come loose when the blade assembly is removed, or they may adhere to the jar and remain in place. Make certain that they are in proper position before securing the blade assembly to the jar. If either of the rubber washers is broken, it should be replaced at this time.

SPECIAL NOTE: The blades must turn freely if the blender is to operate efficiently. Periodic testing and maintenance of the blade assembly can prevent expensive motor repairs. Clean the blades, therefore, after use to prevent food residue build-up. Blenders which do not feature detachable jar bases are best cleaned by allowing them to run with the jar half-filled with hot water and a small quantity of dishwashing detergent (soap).

FIG.18

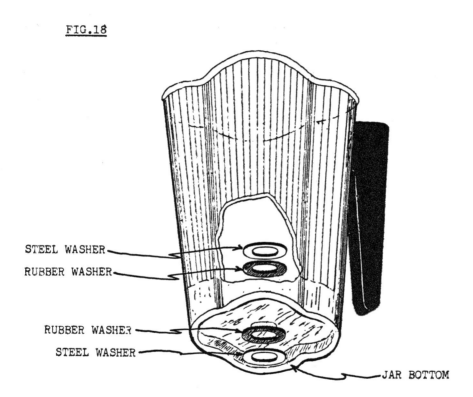

STEEL WASHER
RUBBER WASHER

RUBBER WASHER
STEEL WASHER

JAR BOTTOM

| **Problem Solver #45**

APPLIANCE: Food Blenders

PROBLEM: **Liquid leaks from bottom of jar.**

Liquid leaking from the jar even in small quantities can usually be detected by inspecting the area around the drive stud on top of the motor unit.

TOOLS AND MATERIALS NEEDED:

(a)   a pair of universal pliers

(b)   a butter knife

SOLUTION: NOTE: Two basic types of jars are used with blenders. One jar is constructed with a detachable metal base that can be unscrewed for cleaning. The other is constructed in one piece of glass or plastic.

1. For detachable base jars, check to see that the jar gasket used as a seal between the jar and the detachable metal base is correctly positioned on top of the blade assembly as shown in *Figure 1*.

2. Remove any food residue which may have accumulated on the gasket or blade assembly base. If the gasket is cracked or badly distorted, replace the jar gasket with a new one and retest the jar for leaks by operating the blender with water in the jar.

NOTE: Replacements for jar gaskets and/or other components, if required, may be purchased from local appliance repair shops which usually stock parts for blenders of different makes. If not available in local shops, replacement parts may be ordered from manufacturer's parts supply division. Be sure to include the model number of the blender which is listed on a name plate on the underside of the blender.

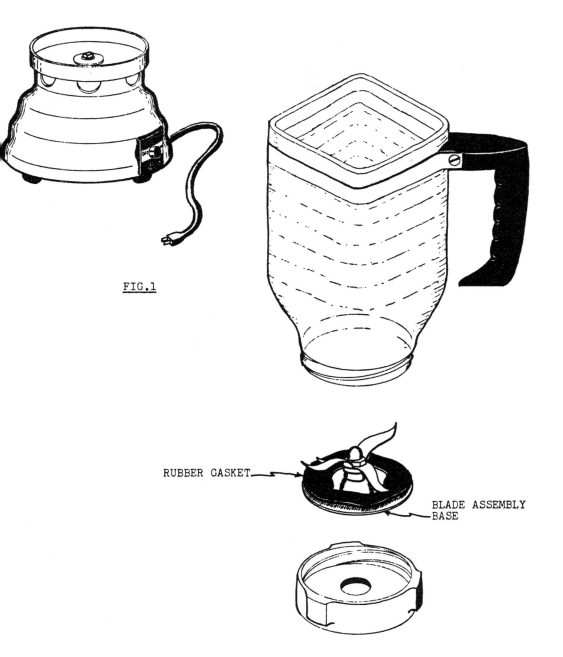

FIG.1

RUBBER GASKET

BLADE ASSEMBLY
BASE

3. If inspection of the gasket proves that it is in good condition and was correctly placed atop the blade assembly, proceed to examine the bottom edge of the jar for cracks and/or a chipped edge. (*Figure 2*) If jar edge is chipped or cracked, replace the jar.

4. If examination of jar and jar gasket proves that both are good, it means that liquid is leaking through a worn blade assembly bearing. This condition is corrected by replacing the entire blade assembly. (*Figure 3*)

    SPECIAL NOTE: Thorough routine cleaning (after each use) and periodic maintenance of the blade assembly can significantly prolong its life. Refer to Problem Solver #44 for complete cleaning and maintenance procedures.

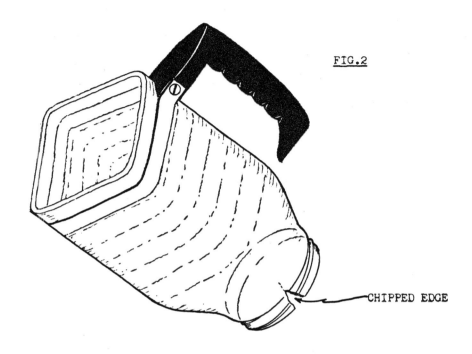

FIG.2

CHIPPED EDGE

FIG.3

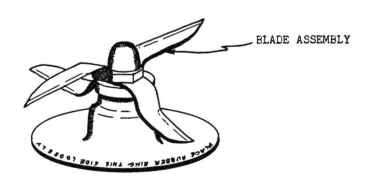

BLADE ASSEMBLY

PLACE RUBBER RING THIS SIDE LOOSELY

5. To check for a leak in the type blender that employs a one-piece jar as shown in *Figure 4,* remove the blade assembly.

6. To remove the blade assembly, grasp the bottom jar nut with a pair of pliers and remove it by turning it counter-clockwise. (*Figure 5*)

NOTE & CAUTION: Two types of jars, both similar in appearance, are used with this type of blender. The jar, depending upon its vintage, may be made of either plastic or glass. Avoid striking or subjecting glass type jars to excessive stress.

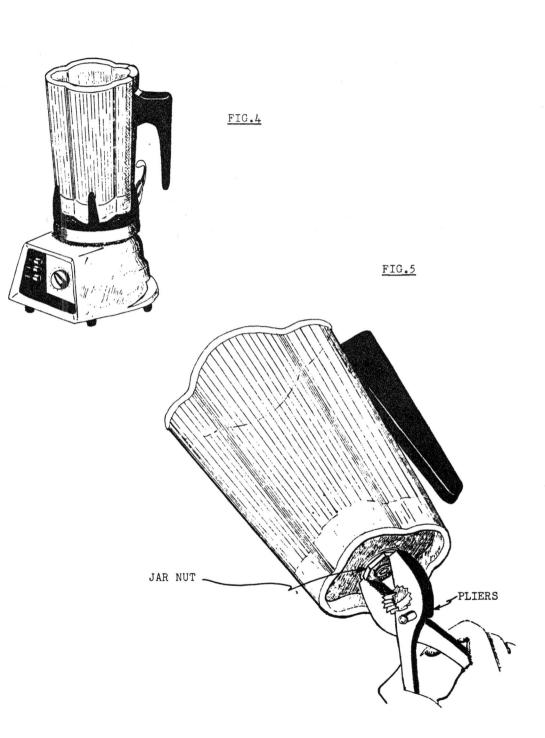

FIG.4

FIG.5

JAR NUT

PLIERS

7. Reach into the jar, grasp the blades and pull the blade assembly straight out. (*Figure 6*)

   CAUTION: Blades may be sharp. Wrap dish cloth or towel over blades before grasping them to avoid injury to fingers.

8. Remove the inner and outer steel washers from the jar. (*Figure 7*) Examine the two rubber washers (inner and outer) above and below the jar's bottom. (*Figure 7*)

   NOTE: The rubber washers may have become stuck to the glass jar. If so, they must be pried off with the front edge of a butter knife.

9. Examine the two rubber washers. If washers are brittle or cracked, replace them with new ones.

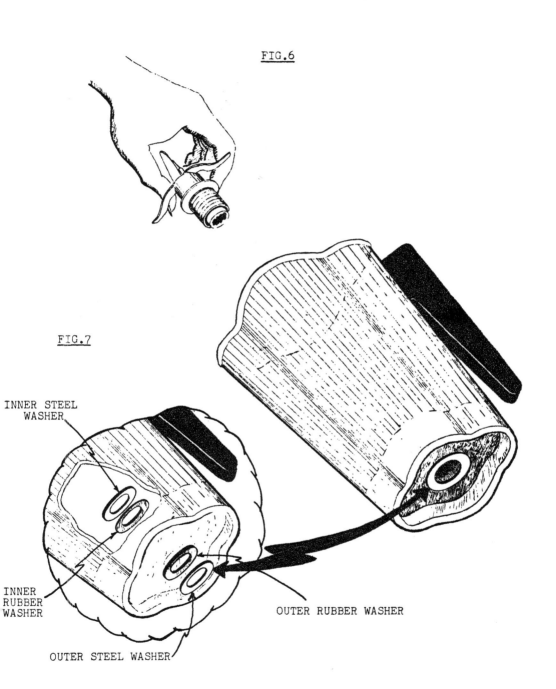

FIG.6

FIG.7

INNER STEEL
WASHER

INNER
RUBBER
WASHER

OUTER STEEL WASHER

OUTER RUBBER WASHER

10. Check the blade assembly at this time for wear. Hold the assembly firmly by the lower threaded area and push the cap nut from side to side. (*Figure 8*) If the top portion (blades and cap nut) of the assembly can be moved sideways, it means that the assembly is worn and will allow liquid to leak through it. Replace the entire blade assembly.

SPECIAL NOTE: Most food blenders are sturdily constructed and will, with normal use and reasonable care, give many years of satisfactory service. However, serious damage to the motor and/or blade assembly can result very quickly when this appliance is abused. The following suggestions will help prevent premature failure of this appliance.

1. Do not continue to attempt to blend substances which have caused the blender blades to slow excessively or stall. Should the blades stall while the blender is operating, shut it off immediately and adjust the substance being blended to avoid a reoccurrence.

2. Avoid placing whole ice cubes or other large hard substances into the blender. The impact of the blades against large hard substances can damage them. Crack ice cubes into pieces first.

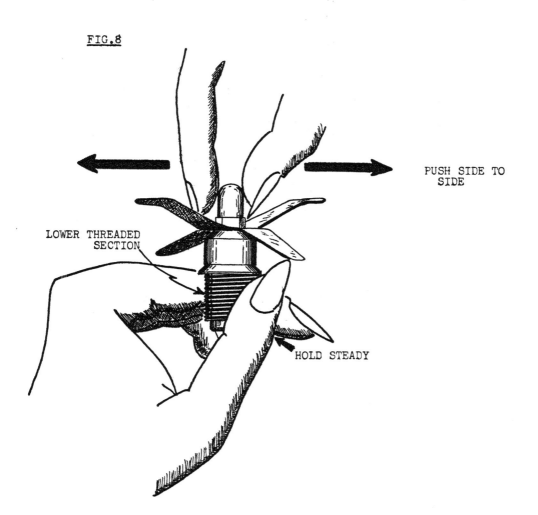

FIG.8

PUSH SIDE TO
SIDE

LOWER THREADED
SECTION

HOLD STEADY

Problem Solver #46

APPLIANCE: Food Blender

PROBLEM: **Blades stall intermittently during operation with loud grinding noise.**

EXPLANATION: This problem is most likely to occur when ice or other heavy food loads are being blended. It is caused by slippage in the coupling between the blade assembly and the motor drive. Invariably, the problem can be pinpointed to a worn component called the "drive stud."

TOOLS AND MATERIALS NEEDED:

(a) an 8 penny nail (a nail about 3 inches long)

(b) 2 pairs of universal pliers

SOLUTION: 1. Remove the line cord plug from the wall outlet.

NOTE: Two different makes of blenders have been chosen as examples of the most common types found in use. (*Figures 1 and 6*) The procedures described in this Problem Solver can be used to repair many other model blenders which have the same problem.

2. Inspect the drive stud for wear. (*Figure 2*) If drive stud is worn, replace it with a new one.

3. To remove the drive stud from the blender model shown in *Figure 1*, turn the motor unit down on its side and insert an 8 penny nail through one of the base plate ventilating holes until the nail passes between the blades of the ventilating fan. (*Figure 3*)

NOTE: Positioning the nail as described above will lock the motor shaft and prevent it from turning.

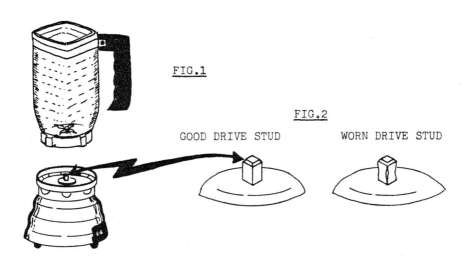

FIG.1

FIG.2

GOOD DRIVE STUD   WORN DRIVE STUD

FIG.3

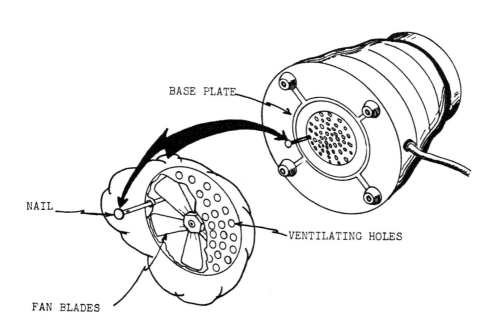

BASE PLATE

NAIL

VENTILATING HOLES

FAN BLADES

4. Grip the drive stud with a pair of pliers while continuing to hold the motor shaft locked with the nail and turn the drive stud counter-clockwise until it is removed. (*Figure 4*)

   CAUTION: Take care not to lose the slinger and steel washer which will come loose when the drive stud is removed. (*Figure 5*)

   NOTE: A drive stud replacement can be purchased from local appliance repair shops or ordered by mail from the manufacturer's parts division. Be sure to include the model number of the blender and refer to the part by name: "Drive Stud."

5. When replacing the drive stud, reinsert the nail between the ventilating fan blades to lock the motor shaft so that the drive stud can be securely tightened (clockwise).

FIG.4

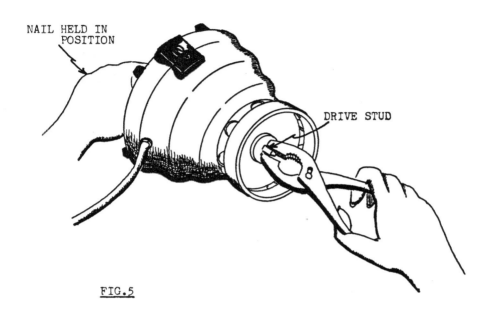

NAIL HELD IN
POSITION

DRIVE STUD

FIG.5

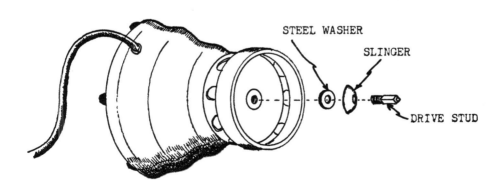

STEEL WASHER

SLINGER

DRIVE STUD

6. To remove the drive stud for the blender model illustrated in *Figure 6*, grip the slinger securely with a pair of pliers. Grip the drive stud with another pair of pliers. Hold the slinger steady and turn the drive stud counter-clockwise until it is removed. (*Figure 7*)

NOTE & CAUTION: The purpose of the slinger is to prevent liquids which may have leaked or over-flowed from the jar from spilling down into the motor of the blender where serious damage could result. Since it rotates with the motor, any liquid spillage that comes in contact with it is thrown out and away from the blender. As its name implies, it "slings" away liquid spillage. Take care not to misplace the slinger and steel washer which may come loose when the drive stud is removed. (*Figure 8*)

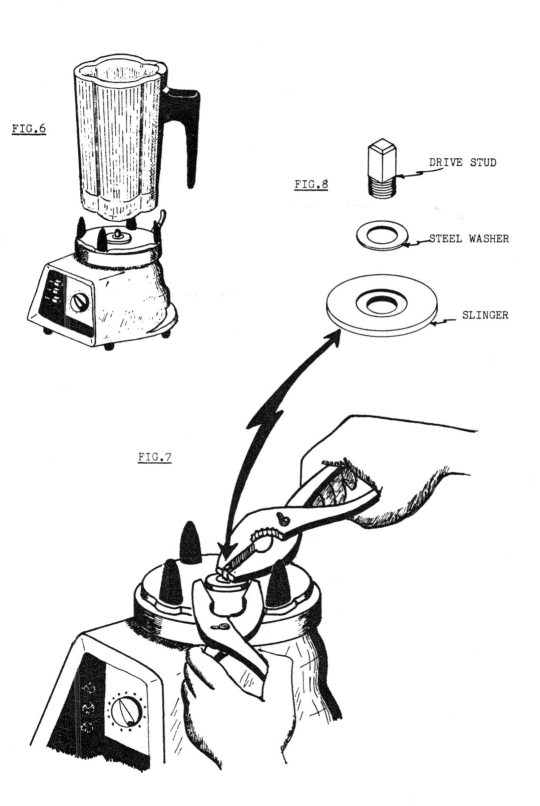

FIG.6

FIG.8

DRIVE STUD

STEEL WASHER

SLINGER

FIG.7

Problem Solver #47

APPLIANCE: Electric Fan (Table Top or Window Type)

PROBLEM: **Rattling noise during operation.**

EXPLANATION: A loose metal emblem, blade guard wire, or other component of the fan framework will often produce a loud annoying rattle.

TOOLS AND MATERIALS NEEDED:

(a)   a pair of universal pliers

(b)   a set of Allen wrenches (inexpensive sets are available from most local hardware stores)

(c)   a short length (one foot) of bailing wire

SOLUTION:

1. To locate the point from which the rattle is originating in a table top fan, first operate the fan until the noise is heard.

2. While the fan is still in operation, press a finger against the metal emblem (if used). (*Figure 1*) If the rattle stops when the emblem is held, it is probably loose and should be tightened.

   NOTE: Emblems (when used) are usually fastened to the blade guard with small metal tabs that fold over the blade guard wires. (*Figure 2*)

3. To tighten the emblem to the blade guard, switch off fan, remove the line cord from the wall outlet, and wait until fan blades come to a stop. Clamp the metal fastening tabs securely around the blade guard wires with a pair of pliers. (*Figure 2*)

4. To check for noise caused by the blade guard, press a finger against different points along the blade guard (especially where guard wires cross) until point is touched that stops the noise.

5. Switch off fan. Remove the line cord plug from the wall outlet, and wait until fan blades come to a stop. Carefully inspect guard wires where they cross (and are fastened) for broken welds. (*Figure 3*)

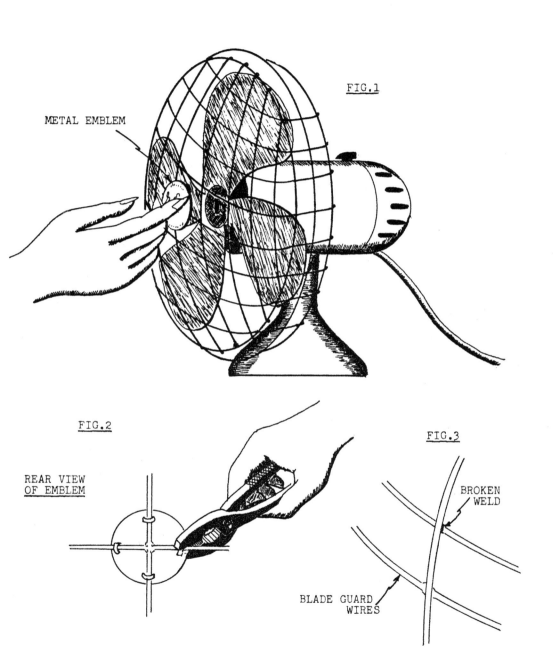

FIG.1

METAL EMBLEM

FIG.2

REAR VIEW
OF EMBLEM

FIG.3

BROKEN
WELD

BLADE GUARD
WIRES

6. To repair broken guard wire welds, wrap a piece of bailing wire across both guard wires to be fastened, and twist the bailing wire with a pair of pliers until the guard wires are held together securely. (*Figures 4 and 5*)

7. If examination proves that metal emblem and blade guard are secure, inspect the fan blades to see that:

    a. Blades do not come in contact with the blade guard.

    b. Fan blade is securely attached to the motor shaft.

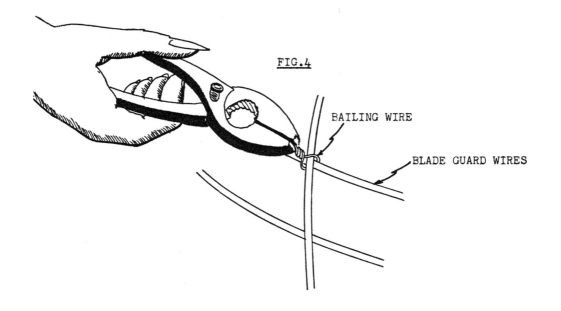

FIG.4

BAILING WIRE

BLADE GUARD WIRES

FIG.5

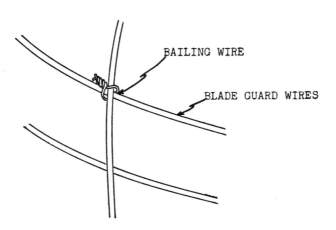

BAILING WIRE

BLADE GUARD WIRES

8. To check for noise caused by a fan blade striking the blade guard, disconnect the fan from the electric outlet, and slowly turn the fan blades by hand. When point of contact is reached it can be felt through the hand. Stop turning the fan blades when contact is felt and examine the blade and blade guard closely to locate the exact point of contact. (*Figures 6 and 7*)

SPECIAL NOTE: Contact between the fan blades and blade guard is often the result of a bent blade guard wire(s). Care should be exercised when handling or storing a fan to avoid striking or otherwise distorting the blade guard. Special precautions should be taken to position a fan securely to prevent it from falling when in use.

FIG.6

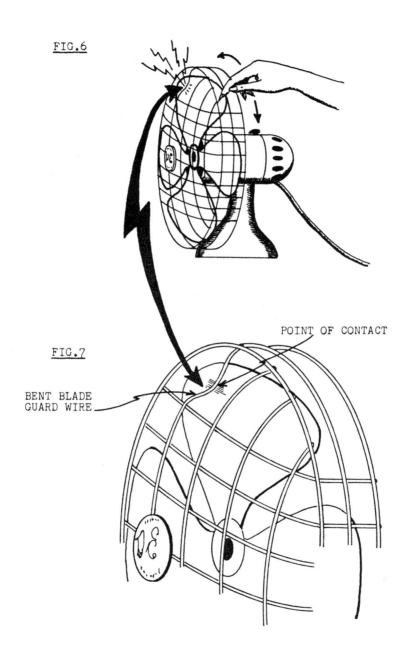

POINT OF CONTACT

FIG.7

BENT BLADE
GUARD WIRE

9. Bent blade guard wires may be re-formed by adjusting them manually until blade clearance is obtained.

10. If fan blade is loose on the motor shaft, tighten the set screw located on the fan blade hub. (*Figure 8*)

    NOTE: Fan blades are usually secured to the motor shaft with a screw having a recessed head called an Allen head. An Allen wrench of appropriate size is needed to tighten this type of screw.

11. To tighten the Allen set screw, reach through the back of the blade guard, insert the Allen wrench into the screw head and turn it clockwise. (*Figure 9*)

12. To locate the point from which the rattling noise is originating in a window fan, repeat the procedure outlined in steps 2 through 10 above.

    NOTE: Because of the difference in construction and location of window fans, they may produce rattling noises that are caused by components other than the fan blades and fan blade guard. Other sources of noise are the expandable side panels of the window fan and the window itself.

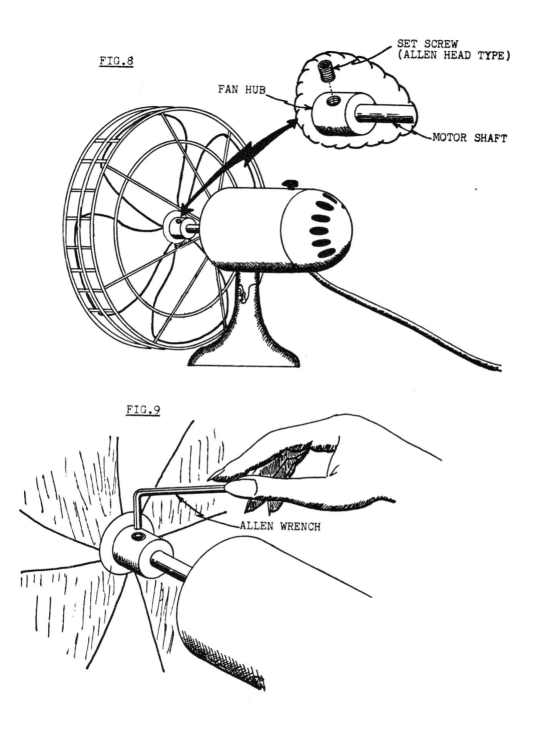

FIG.8

SET SCREW
(ALLEN HEAD TYPE)

FAN HUB

MOTOR SHAFT

FIG.9

ALLEN WRENCH

13. To locate window rattles, press along window sashes until noise stops. Insert a small wood or rubber wedge between window sash and window frame to stop the rattle. (*Figure 10*)

14. To locate rattles originating from the expandable side panels of a window fan, press against both panels while the fan is in operation until a point is reached where pressure stops the rattle. (*Figure 11*)

15. To stop the rattle insert a small wood or rubber wedge between the expandable panel and the stationary fan frame. (*Figure 12*)

NOTE: Hand pressure against individual window panes will disclose loose glass panels. These should be properly re-puttied to make them secure and weather tight.

FIG.10

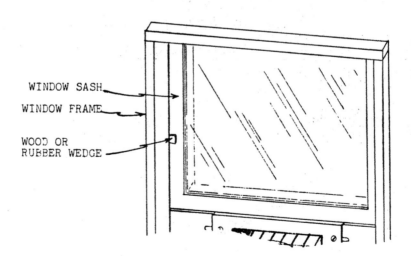

WINDOW SASH

WINDOW FRAME

WOOD OR
RUBBER WEDGE

FIG.11

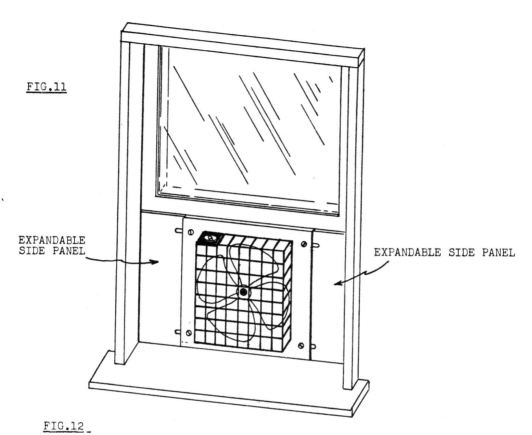

EXPANDABLE
SIDE PANEL

EXPANDABLE SIDE PANEL

FIG.12

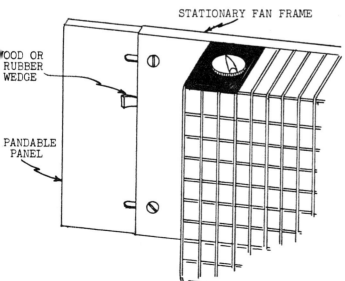

STATIONARY FAN FRAME

WOOD OR
RUBBER
WEDGE

EXPANDABLE
PANEL

Problem Solver #48

APPLIANCE: Electric Fan (Table Top and Window Type)

PROBLEM: **Excessive vibration.**

EXPLANATION: Any degree of vibration that can be noticed when a fan operates is excessive. In almost all cases, vibration is caused by an unbalanced fan blade. Fan blades can become unbalanced when fans are dropped or whenever blades are struck with sufficient force to bend them.

TOOLS AND MATERIALS NEEDED: None

SOLUTION:
1. Disconnect fan plug from wall outlet. Wait until fan blades come to a stop.

2. Check the fan blade guard for distortion. Straighten bent blade guard wires by bending them back into correct shape manually. (*Figure 1*)

3. Reach through the fan blade guard and turn the fan blades slowly by hand. Using a single reference point on the front portion of the blade guard, check to see that each blade is the same distance from that point. (*Figure 2*)

   NOTE: Fan blades that are closer or farther away from the reference point must be bent into alignment with all other blades.

FIG.1

DISTORTED FAN BLADE
GUARD WIRE

FAN BLADE
GUARD

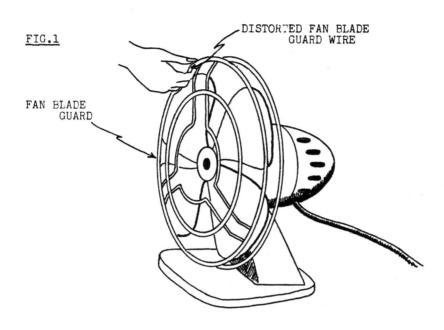

FIG.2

REFERENCE
POINT:
FRONT PORTION
OF BLADE GUARD

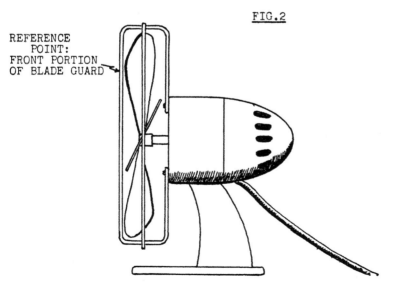

4. To align bent fan blades, reach through the blade guard and carefully bend blade into position by hand. (*Figure 3*)

5. Check to see that all blades are equally distanced from any reference point on the rear position of the blade guard. (*Figure 4*)

6. Connect fan to electric wall outlet after each adjustment and check fan vibration. Repeat steps 4 and 5, if necessary, until there is no excessive vibration.

NOTE: The procedures outlined above are usually all that is necessary to correct fan blades that are only slightly unbalanced. Blades that have been severely damaged and show visible evidence of cracks, tears, and/or deep nicks should be replaced. Replacement of fan blades should be performed by a qualified appliance repair technician.

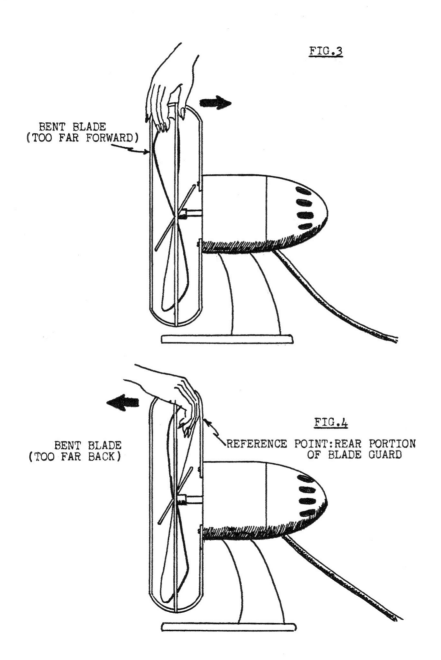

FIG.3

BENT BLADE
(TOO FAR FORWARD)

FIG.4

BENT BLADE
(TOO FAR BACK)

REFERENCE POINT:REAR PORTION
OF BLADE GUARD

Problem Solver #49

APPLIANCE: Electric Fan (Table Top Type or Window Type)

PROBLEM: **Fan will not start unless blades are turned by hand.**

EXPLANATION: Fans that need a starting push to get them going gener-
                 ally need lubrication. In most cases, two or three drops
                 of oil placed in appropriate locations will make the fan
                 work properly.

TOOLS AND MATERIALS NEEDED:

    (a) a small dispensing can of motor oil (about 2 oz. of type SAE #20)

    (b) a flatblade screwdriver (medium size)

    (c) a small dispensing can of penetrating oil (rust dissolver)

SOLUTION:

1. Disconnect fan plug from wall outlet. Wait un'il fan blades come to a stop.

2. Test to see that the fan blades turn freely. Spin the blades by hand and observe how they come to a stop. Blades should *slow* to a stop. If they stop abruptly or if any opposition can be felt when the blades are spun, the motor bearings should be lubricated.

   NOTE: Small inexpensive table top fans are not equipped with external oil holes (ports) to direct lubricating oil to the motor bearings. Fans that do not provide oil ports are usually advertised as having "self-lubricating" motor bearings. Normally, the self-lubricating qualities of these bearings enable the parts to maintain a low degree of friction, thus allowing a fan to start and run properly. During periods of idleness, however, moisture and other corrosive elements in the air can cause the motor shaft to rust and therefore require additional lubricating oil.

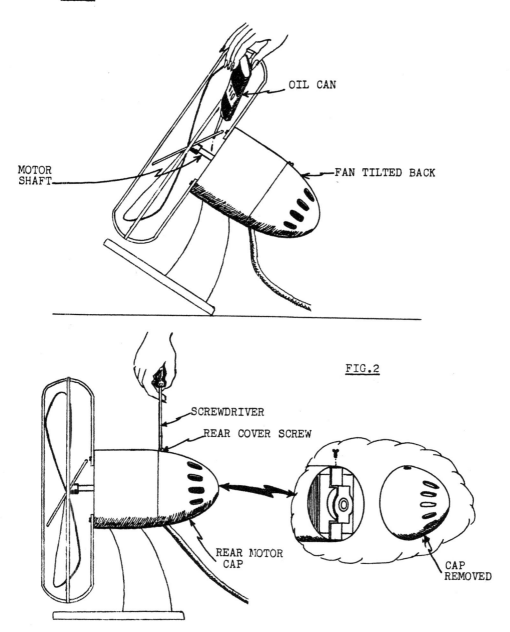

FIG.1

OIL CAN

MOTOR
SHAFT

FAN TILTED BACK

FIG.2

SCREWDRIVER

REAR COVER SCREW

REAR MOTOR
CAP

CAP
REMOVED

3. To lubricate the front bearing of a table top type fan shown in *Figure 1*, tilt the fan back and place three drops of oil on the motor shaft. Keep the fan tilted back for several minutes to allow the oil to run down the shaft and into the motor bearing.

4. Spin the fan blades once or twice by hand so that the oil is distributed thoroughly into the bearing.

5. To lubricate the rear bearing, access to the bearing is necessary.

6. First take off the rear motor cap. Remove the screw (on some models more than one screw may be used) that fastens the cap to the motor by turning it counter-clockwise with a screwdriver. Lift the cap off the motor. (*Figure 2*)

7. Tilt the fan forward and place three drops of oil between the motor shaft and rear bearing. (*Figure 3*)

8. Spin the fan blades once or twice by hand while the fan is still tilted forward.

   CAUTION: Do not over-oil (two or three drops is sufficient; otherwise oil will spill into other parts of motor). Wipe excess oil off with rag.

9. Replace the motor cap securely and operate the fan for about five minutes.

10. Re-test the fan blades to see that they turn freely. (Step 2)

   NOTE: Window type fans usually employ larger motors than do table top models, and they come equipped with oil ports; the accessible openings of small diameter tubes that lead directly to the motor bearings.

FIG.3

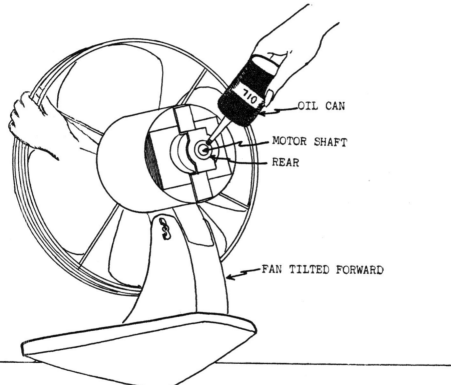

OIL CAN

MOTOR SHAFT

REAR

FAN TILTED FORWARD

11. Test window type fan blades for ability to turn. (Step 2) If the fan sticks, proceed as follows.

12. First make sure that dust or other foreign matter has not clogged the front and rear oil ports. Clear both oil ports by inserting a straightened paper clip or hairpin fully into each oil port. (*Figure 4*)

13. Place three drops of oil into each oil port and operate the fan for about five minutes. (*Figure 5*)

SPECIAL NOTE: In some severe cases, it may not be possible to free the fan motor shaft by the normal lubricating methods described above. If such a case is encountered, a special penetrating (rust loosening) type oil should be applied to the motor shaft bearings and allowed to soak in overnight. Then, the steps outlined above should be followed before applying the regular motor oil. To insure efficient trouble-free operation of fans, lubricate fan motor bearings (one or two drops of oil) at least once a month when the fan is used continuously, and at least once every six months during idle or intermittent use.

WINDOW FAN

FIG.4

PAPER CLIP

REAR OIL PORT

FRONT OIL
PORT

FIG.5

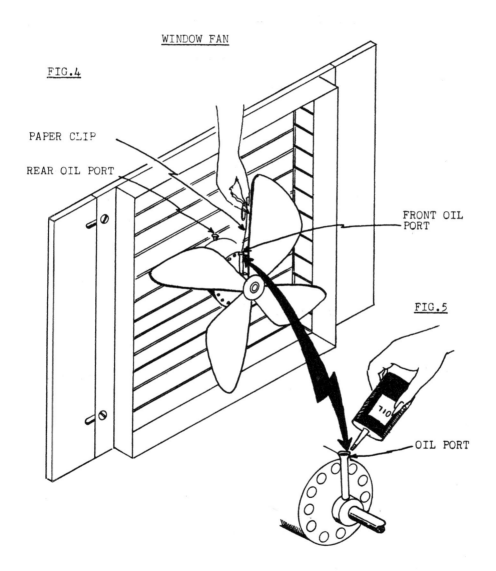

OIL PORT

Problem Solver #50

APPLIANCE: Electric Table Top Fan (Oscillating Type)

PROBLEM: **Fan will not oscillate.**

EXPLANATION: The back-and-forth motion of an oscillating type fan depends upon a series of parts that link the rotating shaft of the motor to the fan motor swivel. The oscillating action can be disrupted or stopped completely by even minor defects in the oscillating mechanism.

TOOLS AND MATERIALS NEEDED:

(a) a small dispensing can of lubricating motor oil (SAE #20)

(b) a flatblade screwdriver (medium size)

(c) a pair of universal pliers

SOLUTION:

1. As a precaution, make certain that the oscillator control knob is fully tightened to start the fan oscillating. (*Figure 1*)

2. If the fan fails to oscillate or oscillates intermittently even when the control knob is in its correct position, the components of the oscillating mechanism must be checked to pinpoint the problem.

3. Remove the fan plug from the electric outlet and wait until the fan blades come to a stop.

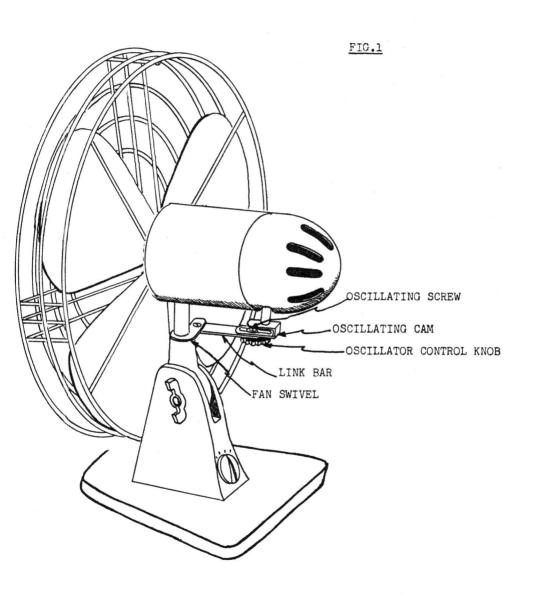

FIG.1

OSCILLATING SCREW

OSCILLATING CAM

OSCILLATOR CONTROL KNOB

LINK BAR

FAN SWIVEL

4. Remove the oscillator control knob. Place a screwdriver in the slot of the oscillating screw. Keep the screw from turning with the screwdriver, and unscrew the control knob until it is removed. (*Figure 2*)

CAUTION: Place the oscillating screw and washers safely aside to avoid losing them. (*Figure 3*)

SPECIAL NOTE: Although many types of oscillating mechanisms have been used in different makes and models of oscillating fans, the type used in this Problem Solver is of ordinary design and often used by many manufacturers. Moreover, the steps describe servicing procedures that are basic and that may be applied to other types of oscillating fans as well.

FIG.2

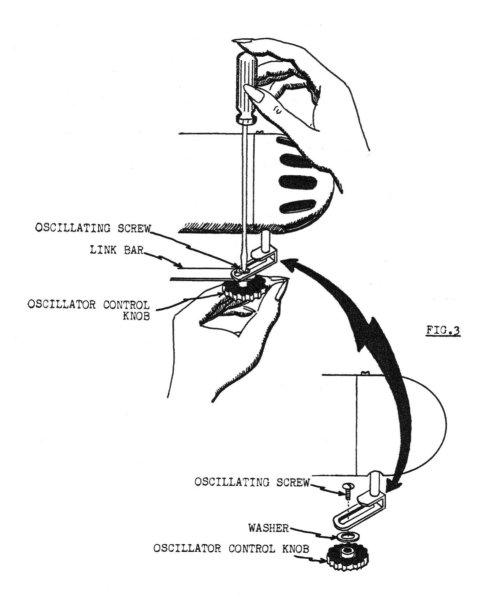

OSCILLATING SCREW

LINK BAR

OSCILLATOR CONTROL
KNOB

FIG.3

OSCILLATING SCREW

WASHER

OSCILLATOR CONTROL KNOB

5. Move the link bar away from the oscillating cam so that no contact can be made between them. (*Figure 4*)

6. Grasp the fan motor and swing it back and forth manually. The fan motor should swing freely. If it is difficult to move (stuck), lubricate the fan motor swivel by tilting the fan on its side and forcing lubricating oil into the swivel joint. (*Figure 5*)

7. If the test proves that the motor swivel is free, proceed to check the oscillating cam.

8. Plug the fan into the wall outlet and allow it to operate. Watch to see if the oscillating cam rotates. (*Figure 4*) If the oscillating cam does not rotate, the problem lies within the gear section of the mechanism. Further testing and service should be performed by a qualified appliance technician only.

9. If the oscillating cam does rotate, the problem is probably caused by a bent link bar or worn link bar pivots.

FIG.4

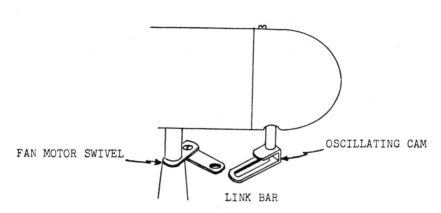

FAN MOTOR SWIVEL

OSCILLATING CAM

LINK BAR

FIG.5

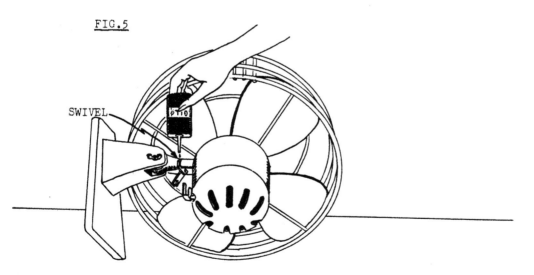

SWIVEL

10. Examine the link bar. If link bar is bent, straighten it with a pair of pliers. (*Figure 6*)

11. Test the link bar for worn pivots. Grasp the link bar end and move it back and forth. (*Figure 7*) If the pivot screw tilts or excessive motion can be felt, tighten the pivot screw until excess motion is eliminated.

    NOTE: On some fans a rivet is used instead of a pivot screw. Loose, bent or broken rivet type pivots must be replaced by a qualified appliance technician. Some economy model fans employ construction techniques that truly defy repairs. For such fans, it is more practical to either forego the use of its oscillating feature and use it as a stationary fan or purchase a new one.

FIG.6

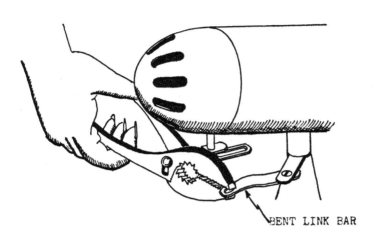

BENT LINK BAR

FIG.7

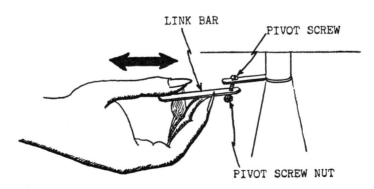

LINK BAR

PIVOT SCREW

PIVOT SCREW NUT

12. To tighten a loose pivot screw, hold the bottom nut with a pair of pliers and turn the pivot screw clockwise with a screwdriver. (*Figure 8*)

    NOTE: It should not be possible to over-tighten the pivot screw to a point which would prevent the link bar from swiveling. If the link bar does become locked when the pivot screw is tightened, the pivot screw is worn and must be replaced. Special individual parts such as the pivot screw may or may not be made available for replacement. Often these small parts are supplied as part of a complete replacement assembly, which might include the link bar and other components. It is sound practice to replace as many corresponding parts as required whenever any portion of the oscillating linkage is found to be worn.

13. Reassemble cam bar to oscillator cam by replacing the cam screw, washer, and control. (*Figures 2 and 3*)

14. Place a drop of lubricating oil on each pivot end of the link bar and on the oscillating cam to complete the work.

    SPECIAL NOTE: Periodic lubrication of the fan swivel and the oscillating linkage pivots will minimize parts wear and oscillator failure.

FIG.8

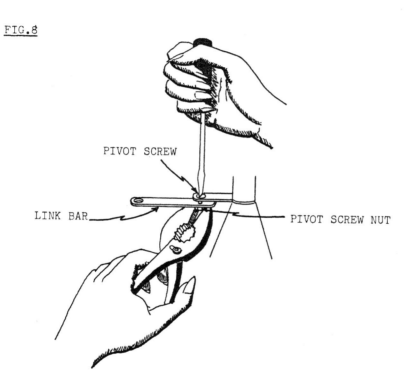

PIVOT SCREW

LINK BAR

PIVOT SCREW NUT

Problem Solver #51

APPLIANCE: Hair Dryer (Hat Box Type)

PROBLEM: **Air turns cool after short period of operation.**

EXPLANATION: Anything that prevents the full flow of air through the dryer can cause the heat producing element to overheat. A safety switch in most dryers is used to sense the excessive heat and automatically shut the heating element off before it can be damaged.

TOOLS AND MATERIALS NEEDED:

    (a)   a flatblade screwdriver (medium size)

    (b)   a phillips screwdriver (medium size)

    (c)   a one-inch paint brush

    (d)   a pair of tweezers

SOLUTION:

1. Check the air intake grille to see that it is not blocked. Do not place anything over the air intake grille that could prevent the intake of air. (*Figure 1*)

2. Make certain that the plastic cap provides enough outlet for the discharged air to escape when it is placed over hair.

3. Examine the hose to see that it is not obstructed or collapsed.

   NOTE: Hoses that have collapsed cannot be repaired and must be replaced.

4. To clean a clogged hose or replace a collapsed hose with a new one, the hose must be disconnected from dryer.

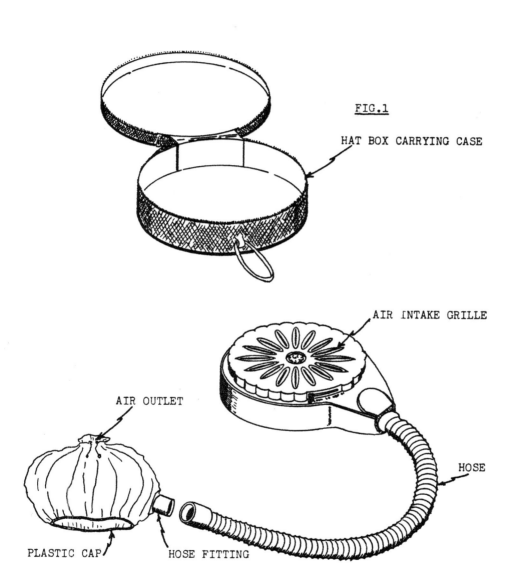

FIG.1

HAT BOX CARRYING CASE

AIR INTAKE GRILLE

AIR OUTLET

HOSE

PLASTIC CAP

HOSE FITTING

5. To disconnect the hose, remove the dryer housing screws with a screwdriver. (*Figure 2*)

   NOTE: Screwdriver needed may be either flatblade or phillips type depending upon the type of screws used.

6. Lift the top half of the dryer housing up and lift hose end up and out of lower half of housing. (*Figure 3*)

   NOTE: New replacement hoses can be purchased for most model hair dryers at local appliance repair shops. If not available locally, they may be ordered directly from nearest manufacturer's parts supply division.

7. If hose and plastic cap assembly are in good order, the motor-blower assembly located inside the dryer housing should be examined.

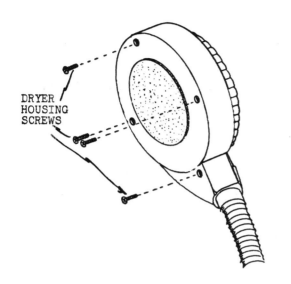

FIG.2

DRYER
HOUSING
SCREWS

FIG.3

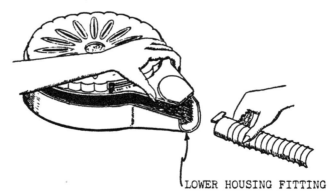

LOWER HOUSING FITTING

8. To gain access to the motor-blower assembly, set the control knob to the "off" position. Then remove it by pulling it straight out. (*Figure 4*)

9. Lift top half of housing up (after housing screws have been removed, *Figure 2*) to remove it. (*Figure 5*)

10. Remove accumulation of dust, hair, etc., on the motor with a clean soft paint brush. Pick off hair which may have become entwined around the motor shaft with a pair of tweezers. (*Figure 6*)

   SPECIAL NOTE: A great deal of dust, lint, and other matter is drawn into hair dryers during normal use. Good preventive maintenance should include a thorough cleaning of the internal motor-blower assembly at least once every six months.

FIG.4

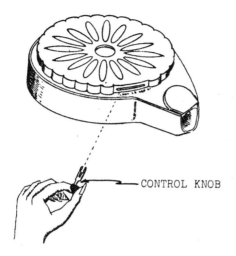

CONTROL KNOB

FIG.5

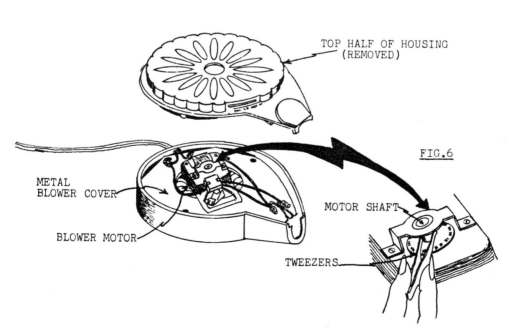

TOP HALF OF HOUSING
(REMOVED)

FIG.6

METAL
BLOWER COVER

BLOWER MOTOR

MOTOR SHAFT

TWEEZERS

11. Lift motor-blower assembly out of bottom half of dryer housing and brush clean the blower impeller and lower housing. (*Figure 7*)

12. Make certain that blower impeller can turn freely when spun by hand.

13. To reassemble dryer, place motor-blower assembly carefully into the lower half of the dryer housing. (*Figure 5*) Place the hose end into the lower housing fitting. (*Figure 3*) Position the top half of the dryer housing in place and replace the control knob by pushing it firmly into its holder (over the "off" position). (*Figure 4*)

14. Replace the dryer housing screws to complete the work. (*Figure 2*)

FIG.7   BLOWER ASSEMBLY

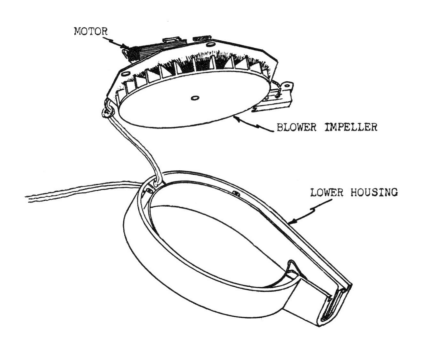

MOTOR

BLOWER IMPELLER

LOWER HOUSING

Problem Solver #52

APPLIANCE: Hair Dryer (Hand Held Type)

PROBLEM: **Dryer blows cool air only.**

EXPLANATION: The absence of any heated air points to a burned-out heating element in the hair dryer.

TOOLS AND MATERIALS NEEDED:

(a)   a flatblade screwdriver (medium size)

(b)   a phillips screwdriver (small size)

(c)   a pair of heavy-duty scissors (poultry shears)

(d)   a sharp paring knife

(e)   two porcelain wire nuts (#2)

SOLUTION:

1. To inspect the heating element, remove the line cord plug from the wall outlet before performing any work on the dryer.

   NOTE: In hand held dryers such as the type illustrated in *Figure 1*, the heating element is located directly behind the grille in the front of the nozzle. The dryer case must be disassembled to gain access to the heating element.

2. To disassemble the dryer case, remove the grille screws by turning them counter-clockwise with a screwdriver. (*Figure 2*)

FIG.1

NOZZLE

GRILLE

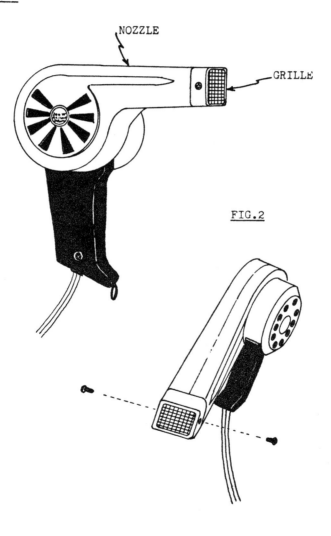

FIG.2

3. Pull the grille off and carefully separate the case halves to expose the heating element. (*Figure 3*)

4. Slide the insulating sleeve off and examine the heating element wire. If the insulated wire connected to it is broken off, the heating element must be replaced. (*Figure 4*)

   NOTE: Heating elements for dryers made by leading manufacturers can usually be purchased from a local appliance repair shop. Replacement heating elements for less familiar makes of dryers will probably have to be ordered directly from the manufacturer's parts supply division.

5. To remove the burned-out heating element, cut the remaining lead wires as close to the heating element as possible with either a diagonal wire-cutting pliers (if available) or a pair of heavy-duty kitchen shears (such as poultry shears).

6. Lift the element out of its recessed mount and set it aside to be used for comparison with the replacement heating element.

7. To install the replacement heating element, first prepare the two lead wires that are to be connected to the heating element wires by cutting through the insulation (about one-half inch up from the wire ends) with a sharp paring knife. (*Figure 5*)

   CAUTION: Take care not to cut into the copper wire.

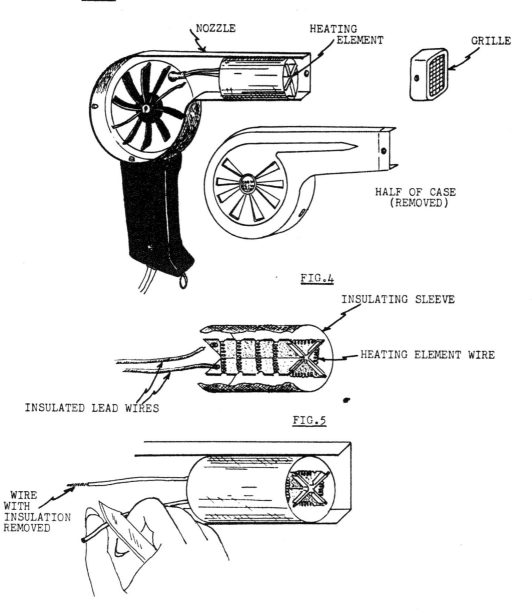

FIG.3

NOZZLE HEATING ELEMENT GRILLE

HALF OF CASE (REMOVED)

FIG.4

INSULATING SLEEVE

HEATING ELEMENT WIRE

INSULATED LEAD WIRES

FIG.5

WIRE WITH INSULATION REMOVED

8. Pull each piece of cut insulation off the wire ends.

9. Place the replacement heating element into position in the dryer nozzle and connect the bare ends of the dryer wires to the bare ends of the element wires by twisting them together clockwise. (*Figure 6*)

10. Insulate each wire connection with a porcelain wire nut. Push the wire nut over the connection and turn it clockwise until it threads itself onto the wire connection securely. (*Figure 7*)

    CAUTION: Make sure that the insulated connection wires are clear of the heating element.

11. Reassemble both halves of the case making sure that the connecting wires are not pinched between them.

12. Push the grille over the front nozzle and replace the grille screws to complete the repair.

<u>FIG.6</u>

WIRES TWISTED TOGETHER

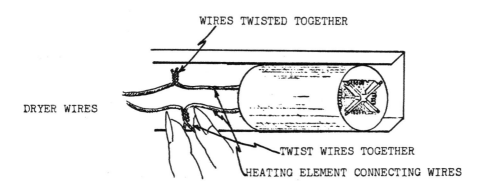

DRYER WIRES

TWIST WIRES TOGETHER

HEATING ELEMENT CONNECTING WIRES

<u>FIG.7</u>

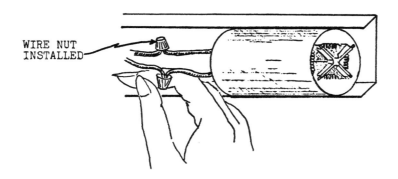

WIRE NUT
INSTALLED

Problem Solver #53

APPLIANCE: Hair Dryer (Portable)

PROBLEM: **Excessive noise during operation.**

EXPLANATION: In the construction of hair dryers, very little space is allowed between the fan impeller blades and the impeller housing. A severe shock to the dryer, if it were dropped or otherwise abusively handled, could cause the impeller housing to be moved out of proper alignment with the impeller blades. This would cause the impeller to strike a portion of the housing and thus produce an objectionable noise.

TOOLS AND MATERIALS NEEDED:

(a)   a phillips screwdriver (medium size)

(b)   a paring knife

(c)   a pair of universal pliers

(d)   a small squeeze bottle of white resin type (all purpose) glue

SOLUTION:
1. Remove the dryer line cord plug from the wall outlet.

2. Remove the screws used to fasten the top cover to the lower half of the dryer case by turning them counter-clockwise with a phillips screwdriver. (*Figure 1*)

   NOTE: It is a common practice for manufacturers to cover case screws with decorative escutcheons or name plates. These name plates must often be removed to reveal the location of case screws.

3. Remove the name plate by carefully prying up one corner of the plate with a paring knife. (*Figure 2*)

FIG.1

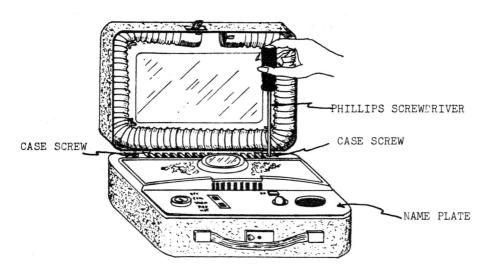

PHILLIPS SCREWDRIVER

CASE SCREW

CASE SCREW

NAME PLATE

FIG.2

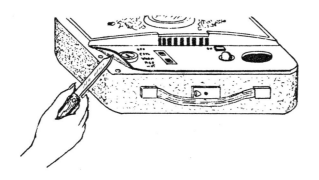

4. Grasp the loosened corner of the plate and remove the plate completely by pulling it up slowly by hand. (*Figure 3*)

   CAUTION: Take care not to bend the name plate too sharply to avoid permanent creases.

5. Remove additional case screws located under name plate.

6. Remove the switch control knob by pulling it straight up and out. (*Figure 4*)

   NOTE: Loose or broken switch control knobs can often be mended. If the control knob needs repair, refer to Section II, General Repair Procedures, "Plastic Parts" for complete details.

FIG.3

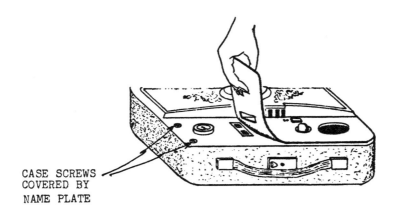

CASE SCREWS
COVERED BY
NAME PLATE

FIG.4

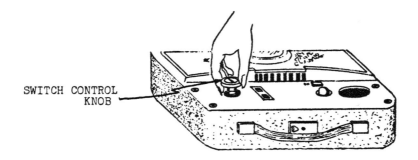

SWITCH CONTROL
KNOB

7. Lift the top of the case up and off the lower case section. (*Figure 5*)

8. Examine impeller housing screws for looseness Make sure impeller housing is in correct position, then tighten hexagon head screws with a pair of pliers. (*Figure 6*)

   NOTE: If the plastic impeller housing is found to be cracked it can be repaired. Refer to Section 2, General Repair Procedures, for complete instructions on how to repair plastic components.

9. Operate the dryer to test for correct alignment of impeller blade and impeller housing. If impeller blade continues to strike housing, loosen housing screws with pliers and readjust housing position until impeller clears housing.

10. To reassemble the dryer, place the top portion of the case onto the lower section. (*Figure 5*)

11. Position the switch control knob so that the flat side of the knob shaft matches the flat side of the switch shaft and press the knob firmly onto the switch shaft. (*Figure 4*)

12. Replace all the case fastening screws.

13. Carefully smooth the name plate so that it will lie flat atop the case. Coat the lower side of the name plate with glue and allow the glue to become tacky before pressing the name plate onto the case.

FIG.5

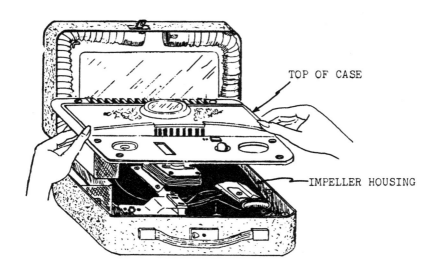

TOP OF CASE

IMPELLER HOUSING

FIG.6

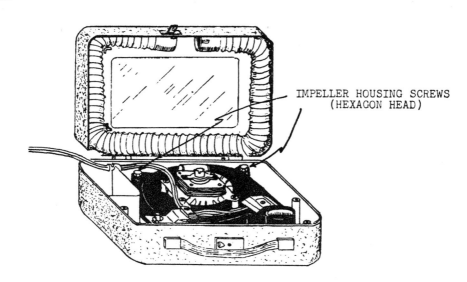

IMPELLER HOUSING SCREWS
(HEXAGON HEAD)

Problem Solver #54

APPLIANCE: Electric Can Opener

PROBLEM: **Cuts can intermittently.**

EXPLANATION: The ability of a can opener to cut evenly and continuously depends mostly upon the condition of the cutter wheel. A dull or stuck cutter wheel can cause skip cutting and in severe cases can cause the can to be dropped from the opener during operation.

TOOLS AND MATERIALS NEEDED:

(a) a screwdriver (medium size) (flatblade or phillips as required)

(b) a can of scouring cleanser (abrasive type)

(c) a piece of cloth

(d) a paring knife

(e) a jar of petroleum jelly

SOLUTION: NOTE: Make sure that the operating lever is fully depressed when starting the opener to allow the cutter wheel to pierce the can. (*Figure 1*) Failure to do so can lead to the mistaken assumption that the can opener is malfunctioning.

1. Observe the cutter wheel when can opener is cutting a can. The cutter wheel must turn along with the can. If the cutter wheel is stuck it must be removed, cleaned, and lubricated.

2. Remove the can from the opener and disconnect the line cord plug from the wall outlet.

    CAUTION: Do not attempt to turn the cutter wheel by hand to see if it is stuck. Cutter wheels can be sharp enough to cut your fingers.

3. Remove the cutter wheel by turning the cutter wheel screw completely out counter-clockwise with a flatblade screwdriver. (*Figure 2*)

FIG.1

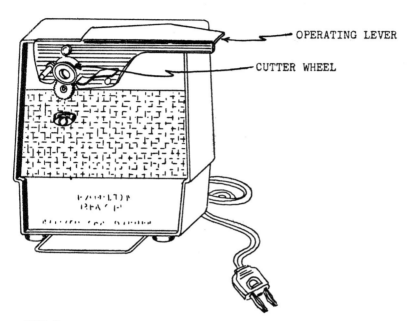

OPERATING LEVER

CUTTER WHEEL

FIG.2

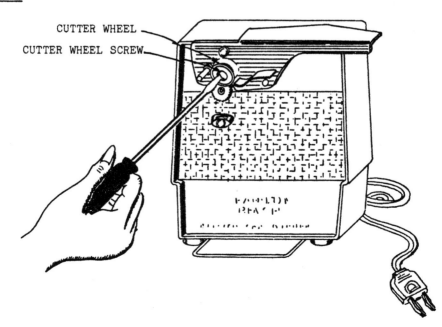

CUTTER WHEEL

CUTTER WHEEL SCREW

4. Take note which side of the cutter wheel faces out (front face is usually cone shaped) so that wheel can be correctly replaced later. (*Figures 3 and 4*)

5. Pull the cutter wheel straight out to remove it. Remove the cutter wheel spring located directly behind the cutter wheel. (*Figure 3*)

   CAUTION: Use care when grasping the cutter wheel to avoid cutting fingers. If wheel is stuck, pry it off with the flatblade of a screwdriver.

6. Examine the cutter wheel for sharpness. (*Figure 4*) If wheel appears dull and/or chipped it must be replaced.

   NOTE: Cutter wheel replacements are available from local appliance repair shops and parts suppliers.

7. If the cutter wheel is sharp, clean the wheel to remove rust and accumulation of hardened food residue.

8. To clean the wheel thoroughly, pour enough abrasive type cleanser onto a dampened cloth to form a paste. Scour both sides of the cutter wheel until food residue and rust are removed.

FIG.3

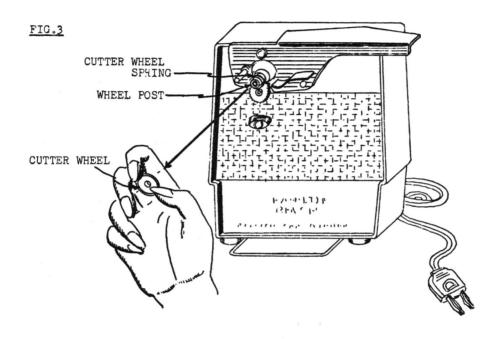

CUTTER WHEEL
SPRING

WHEEL POST

CUTTER WHEEL

FIG.4

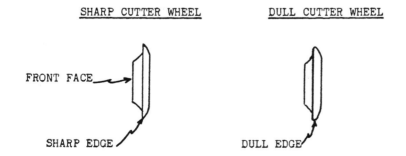

SHARP CUTTER WHEEL   DULL CUTTER WHEEL

FRONT FACE

SHARP EDGE   DULL EDGE

9. Scrape the inside hole of the cutter wheel with the point of a paring knife to remove rust and food residue hardened there and rinse it under warm tap water. (*Figure 5*)

10. Scrape away rust and food residue from cutter wheel screw with paring knife. (*Figure 6*) Be especially thorough under the head of the screw. Rinse it under warm tap water.

11. Scrape food residue from the cutter wheel spring with paring knife and rinse it clean under warm tap water.

12. Clean the cutter wheel post.

13. Allow the wheel, wheel screw, wheel spring, and wheel post to dry, then coat each with a very light film of petroleum jelly.

14. Place the cutter wheel spring over the wheel post; replace the cutter wheel and fasten it with the wheel screw. Turn the screw clockwise until tight.

NOTE: Make certain that the cutter wheel is faced correctly. (*Figures 3 and 4*)

SPECIAL NOTE: The cutter wheel should be cleaned periodically by brushing it with soap and water and residue, the growth of bacteria, and insure more efficient operation.

FIG.5

FIG.5

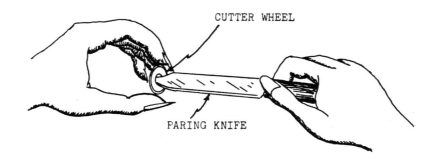

CUTTER WHEEL

PARING KNIFE

FIG.6

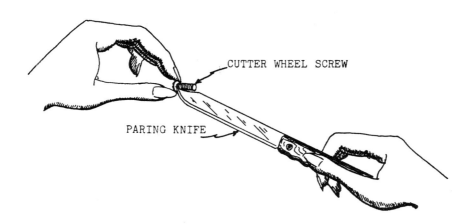

CUTTER WHEEL SCREW

PARING KNIFE

Problem Solver #55

APPLIANCE: Electric Can Opener

PROBLEM: **Can opener does not operate.**

EXPLANATION: If you find that the wall outlet has power (check by plug-
                  ging in another appliance) the most likely fault is the
                  can opener switch. The contact points of can opener
                  switches often become bent out of position or dirty
                  through normal use and must be adjusted and/or
                  cleaned to restore operation.

TOOLS AND MATERIALS NEEDED:

(a) a phillips screwdriver

(b) a pair of universal pliers

(c) a pair of tweezers

(d) a fingernail emery board

SOLUTION: 1. Disconnect the line cord plug from the wall outlet.

                 2. Remove the case screws by turning them counter-
                     clockwise with a phillips screwdriver. (*Figure 1*)

FIG.1   <u>REAR VIEW OF CAN OPENER</u>

OPERATING LEVER(RAISED)

SWITCH
BUTTON

CASE SCREWS

PHILLIPS
SCREWDRIVER

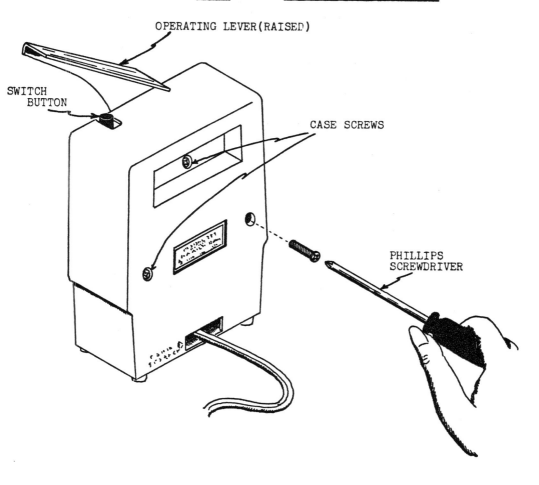

3. Grasp the operating lever with one hand and the case with the other and pull the case away from the can opener assembly. (*Figure 2*)

4. Remove the switch cover plate screw by turning it counter-clockwise with a pair of pliers. (*Figure 3*)

5. Lift the switch cover plate off to expose the switch contacts. (*Figure 4*)

6. Lower the operating lever onto the switch button and depress it as far as it will go. Check to see that the upper movable switch contact touches the lower stationary contact when the button is depressed with the operating lever. (*Figure 5*)

7. If the upper contact point does not touch the lower contact, bend the lower contact point upward with a pair of tweezers to shorten the gap between both contact points. (*Figure 6*)

8. Check to see that contact is made *only* when the operating lever depresses the switch button.

   NOTE: If the lower contact is bent too far upward, contact between the points will be continuous and the can opener will not shut "off."

9. Clean the contact points carefully (where they touch) by rubbing both points very lightly with the "fine" side of an emery board. (*Figure 7*)

10. Reassemble the switch cover plate and can opener case to complete the repair.

FIG.2

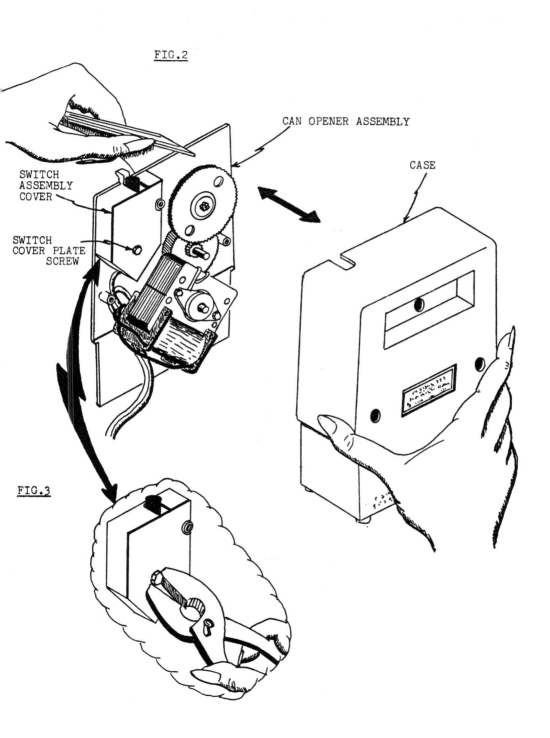

CAN OPENER ASSEMBLY

CASE

SWITCH
ASSEMBLY
COVER

SWITCH
COVER PLATE
SCREW

FIG.3

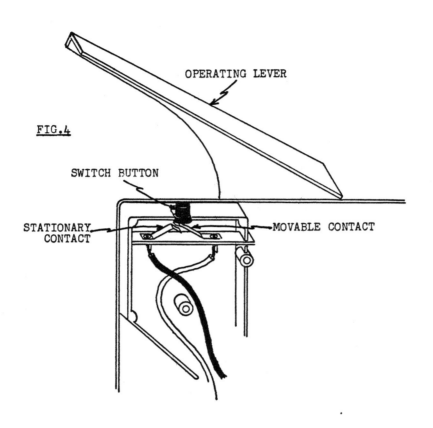

OPERATING LEVER

FIG.4

SWITCH BUTTON

STATIONARY CONTACT

MOVABLE CONTACT

FIG.5

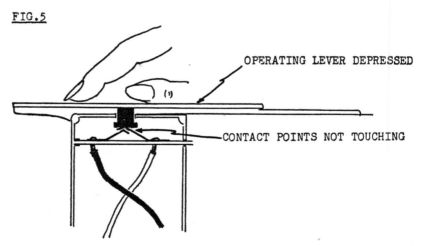

OPERATING LEVER DEPRESSED

CONTACT POINTS NOT TOUCHING

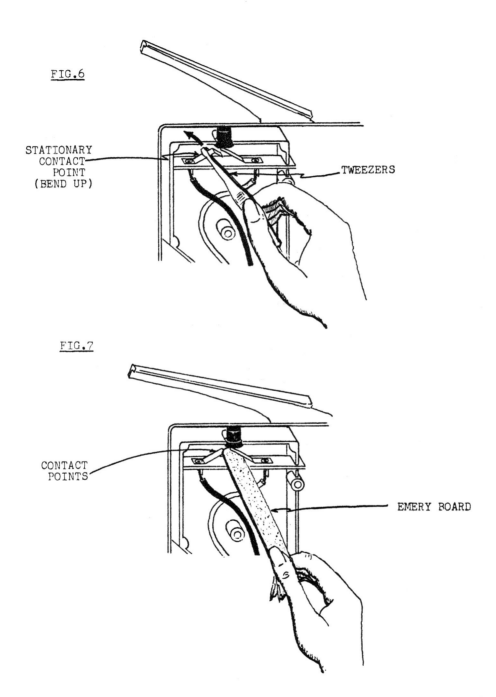

FIG.6

STATIONARY
CONTACT
POINT
(BEND UP)

TWEEZERS

FIG.7

CONTACT
POINTS

EMERY BOARD

Problem Solver #56

APPLIANCE: Rotisserie (Vertical Spit Type)

PROBLEM: **Heating element glows red but spit does not turn.**

The spit which rotates the roast or poultry in this type of broiler is coupled and driven by a small electric motor. If the spit does not engage the motor drive securely, it will not turn.

TOOLS AND MATERIALS NEEDED:

(a)   a paper clip

SOLUTION: SPECIAL NOTE: Make certain that roasts, poultry, etc., are trimmed to proper size. Oversize meats with protruding portions may contact the heating element or cover and prevent the spit from turning.

1. Unplug the broiler and allow it to cool to room temperature.

2. Grasp the turntable tray and attempt to turn it (either direction). (*Figure 1*) If turntable spins freely, it is not engaged with the drive shaft. (*Figure 2*)

FIG.1

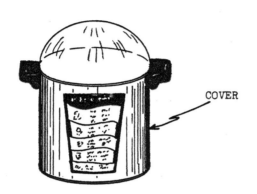

COVER

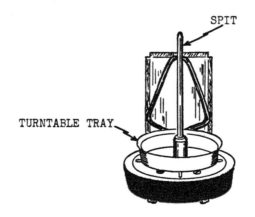

SPIT

TURNTABLE TRAY

3. Remove the turntable tray (*Figure 2*) and inspect the recessed slot in the bottom of the turntable which engages the drive shaft. (*Figure 3*) Check to see that food particles and/or other substances have not clogged it.

4. If slot is clogged, clear the slot with a paper clip bent open as shown in *Figure 4*.

5. Replace the turntable trap atop the drive shaft and test to see that they are engaged.

   NOTE: When properly engaged, the turntable tray will not spin freely when pushed by hand. If the turntable engages the drive shaft, but does not rotate when the rotisserie is operated, the problem is caused by a more serious defect of the gears or motor, and should be brought to a qualified service technician for further testing and repairs.

FIG.2

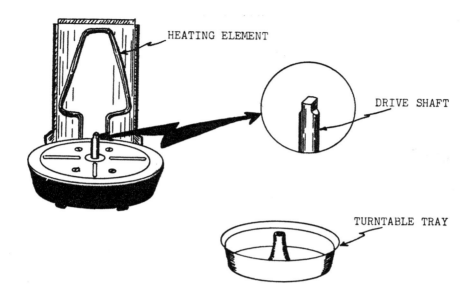

HEATING ELEMENT

DRIVE SHAFT

TURNTABLE TRAY

FIG.3

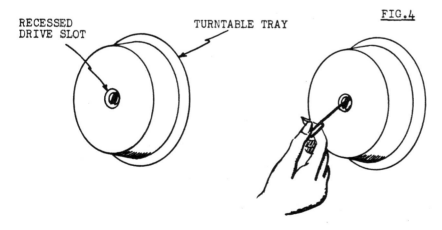

RECESSED
DRIVE SLOT

TURNTABLE TRAY

FIG.4

Problem Solver #57

APPLIANCE: Lady's Electric Shaver

PROBLEM: **Razor pinches.**

EXPLANATION: An electric razor will "pinch" when it catches skin between broken teeth. It will also "pull" rather than cut hair when the cutter head is dull.

TOOLS AND MATERIALS NEEDED:

(a) a tube of toothpaste

(b) toilet water (or men's after shave lotion)

SOLUTION:

1. Inspect the head (comb and cutter assembly) for broken teeth. (*Figure 1*)

2. If teeth are broken, replace the entire head. Remove the head as you would normally to clean it thoroughly.

   NOTE: Replacement heads may be purchased from local factory authorized service shops.

3. If the shaver head has no broken teeth, hone the head to restore its sharpness.

4. To hone the head, rub a small quantity of toothpaste into the head (*Figure 2*) and operate the razor for about two minutes.

5. Remove the head (as for cleaning) and rinse it under hot water to remove the toothpaste.

6. Wipe the head with a finger moistened with toilet water (or men's after shave lotion) and test the razor for improved cutting ability.

7. If necessary, repeat steps 4, 5, and 6 until the razor cuts cleanly without pinching.

FIG.1

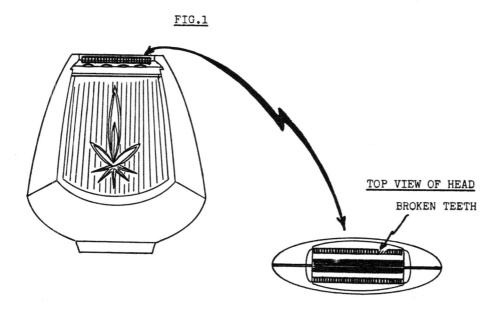

TOP VIEW OF HEAD

BROKEN TEETH

FIG.2

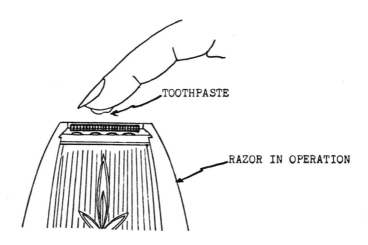

TOOTHPASTE

RAZOR IN OPERATION

Problem Solver #58

APPLIANCE: Lady's Electric Shaver

PROBLEM: **Razor runs too slow (may pinch).**

EXPLANATION: Brush cleaning alone does not remove accumulations
                    of hair and other solid particles in the cutting head
                    of an electric razor. These solid particles build to excess
                    and reduce the speed of the razor by preventing the free
                    movement of the cutting head.

TOOLS AND MATERIALS NEEDED:

(a) cleaning brush (supplied with razor)

(b) a small saucer or ashtray

(c) a bottle of toilet water or men's after shave lotion

SOLUTION:
1. Brush the cutting head clean with razor brush as is usually done before or after each use.

2. Remove the cutting head and brush clean area below the cutting head. (*Figures 1 and 2*)

   NOTE: Procedures for routine cleaning may vary slightly for different make razors. Follow manufacturer's instructions. The cleaning procedure described in the steps that follow will wash and lubricate the cutting head and should be applied periodically (every two months) to prevent the cutting head from becoming clogged.

3. Replace the cutting head. (*Figure 3*)

4. Pour about ¼ inch of toilet water or men's after shave lotion into a small saucer or ashtray. (*Figure 4*)

5. Start the razor and immerse the cutting head in the toilet water. (*Figure 4*) Remove the razor after a minute or so and allow excess toilet water to drip off.

   NOTE: Do not wipe the head dry.

6. Allow razor to air dry for a few minutes before using.

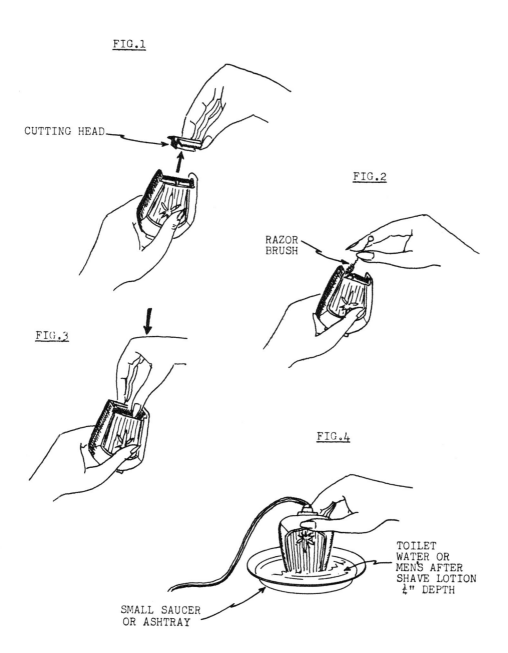

FIG.1

CUTTING HEAD

FIG.2

RAZOR BRUSH

FIG.3

FIG.4

TOILET
WATER OR
MEN'S AFTER
SHAVE LOTION
$\frac{1}{4}$" DEPTH

SMALL SAUCER
OR ASHTRAY

Section II

General Repair Procedures

#59 Fuses and Circuit Breakers

How To: Locate and replace a blown fuse.

Explanation: Fuses are safety devices. Their purpose is to protect electrical equipment (appliances) and the electrical house wires from damage. When a fuse blows, it is an indication that the demand for electric power has exceeded the safe carrying capacity of the electric supply line. A fuse contains a short metal link through which all of the electric power in a supply line must flow. The metal link is designed to melt apart when the electric power flowing through it is excessive and generates more heat than the metal fuse link can withstand. The types of fuses most commonly found in home use are constructed with a screw base and are called plug fuses. There are three common varieties of plug fuses: (1) standard base; (2) standard base, time delay; and (3) tamperproof (fusestat). (*Figure 1*) Time delay fuses are designed to withstand short periods of excessive electric power draw without blowing. This feature is especially useful in house circuits that supply motor-driven appliances (washing machines, refrigerators, clothes dryers, etc.). The ordinary standard base and tamperproof base fuses are generally adequate for use with heating appliances.

Tools and Materials Needed:

      (a) a replacement fuse (same electrical rating—amperes—and type as original)

      (b) a flashlight

Steps:

      1. When fuse is suspected of having blown, turn off all switches (appliances, lights, etc.) that have stopped operating.

      2. Locate fuse box that contains the house fuses. (*Figure 2*)

FIG.1   PLUG TYPE FUSES

STANDARD BASE   STANDARD BASE   TAMPER PROOF
                 (TIME DELAY)

FIG.2   TYPICAL FUSE BOX

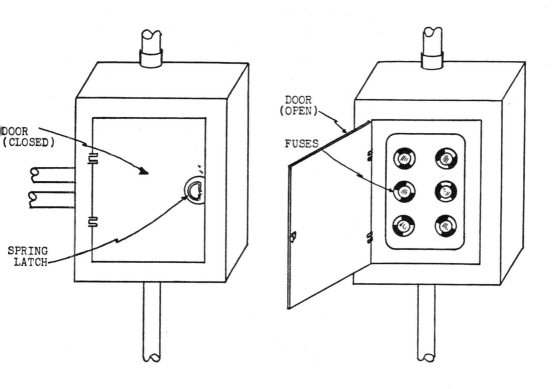

3. Examine the small window of each fuse in the fuse box. Use a flashlight to aid visibility. The window of a blown fuse (or fuses) will usually appear blackened or clouded.

NOTE: Some electric lines use two fuses for protection.

4. Remove the suspect fuse by unscrewing it (counter-clockwise) from its socket.

5. Examine fuse to identify its electrical size and type. Its electrical size (in amperes, or amps) is usually printed on the metal edge surrounding its window and on the small metal contact tip on its base. (*Figure 3*)

NOTE: It is always wise to anticipate the possibility of a fuse blowing and to keep an assortment of replacement fuses available near the fuse box.

6. Select a replacement fuse that is identical to the blown fuse and screw the new fuse (or fuses) into the fuse socket.

NOTE AND CAUTION: Standard base plug fuses are made available in sizes of 5 amps, 10 amps, 15 amps, 20 amps, 25 amps, and 30 amps. Since the screw bases of these fuses are identical, they may accidentally be interchanged. Extreme precautions should be taken to avoid replacing a blown fuse with one which has a higher amp rating. Tamperproof plug fuses are also available in the amps sizes listed above. Their screw base construction, however, does not permit different size fuses to be interchanged since different sized screw bases are provided for each electrical size.

7. After fuses have been replaced, turn on appliances, lights, and other electrical apparatus that had gone dead.

NOTE: If circuit fuse blows again when appliance or other electrical apparatus is turned on, it indicates that the electrical overload is still present and must be disconnected from the power line. In most instances, the faulty appliance or other electrical apparatus can be identified by elimination. This will require a systematic trial of each appliance. If, however, the defective apparatus cannot be isolated after a reasonable effort has been made, a licensed electrician should be called to correct the condition.

FIG.3

FUSE SIZE(IN AMPERES)

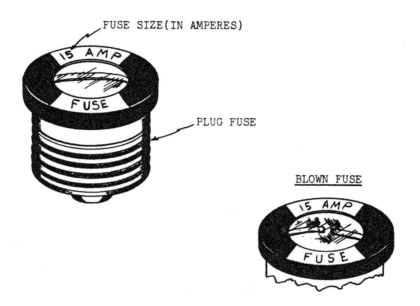

PLUG FUSE

BLOWN FUSE

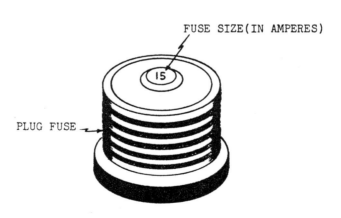

FUSE SIZE(IN AMPERES)

PLUG FUSE

#60 Male Plugs

How To: Replace a two-prong male plug.

EXPLANATION: Many types of male plugs are on the market; however, most are not suitable for use on heat-producing appliances. The type of plug recommended is generally referred to as a "heavy-duty male plug" and is shown in the illustrations.

TOOLS AND MATERIALS NEEDED:

(a) a heavy-duty two-prong male plug (available at any electrical hardware store)

(b) a sharp paring knife

(c) a flatblade screwdriver (medium size)

STEPS:

1. Remove the defective plug by cutting the line cord about one-half inch before the plug; then discard it. This will eliminate any weakened, frayed, or oxidized wire that might interfere with the operation of the new plug. (*Figure 1*)

2. Remove about three inches of outer insulation (when encountered) by slitting it lengthwise with a sharp knife. (*Figure 2*)

   CAUTION: Take care not to cut through the inner wire insulation.

3. Remove about one inch of the inner rubber insulation from each wire end. (*Figure 3*)

   CAUTION: Avoid cutting any of the fine wire strands.

FIG.1

CUT OFF PLUG

FIG.2

REMOVE OUTER INSULATION

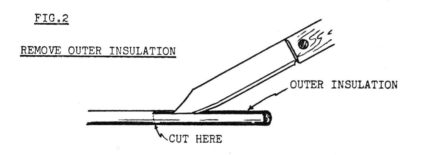

OUTER INSULATION

CUT HERE

FIG.3

REMOVE INNER INSULATION

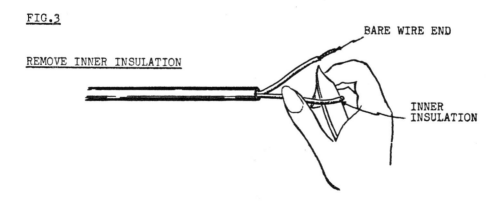

BARE WIRE END

INNER
INSULATION

4. Feed the wire ends of the remaining prepared line cord through the replacement male plug and tie an "Underwriter's knot" as shown in steps a, b, and c of *Figure 4*.

5. Twist the loose strands of each wire end together tightly. (*Figure 5*)

   CAUTION: Carefully straighten the wire strands before attempting to twist them together to prevent wire strands from puncturing fingers.

6. Pull the Underwriter's knot down into the cavity of the plug.

7. Loosen both terminal screws of the plug, but do not force them beyond their stop points. (*Figure 5*)

8. Bring each line cord wire end around the back of each prong, and wrap the bare wire portion of each end around and under the plug terminal screws in a clockwise direction. (*Figure 6*)

   NOTE: Avoid getting insulation caught under the terminal screws.

9. Cut off any excess wire that protrudes from under the terminal screw heads and tighten the screws with a screwdriver.

   NOTE: Make certain that there are no loose strands of wire that can touch both of the plug prongs and cause a short circuit

10. Slide the fiber cover plate over the prongs. (*Figure 6*)

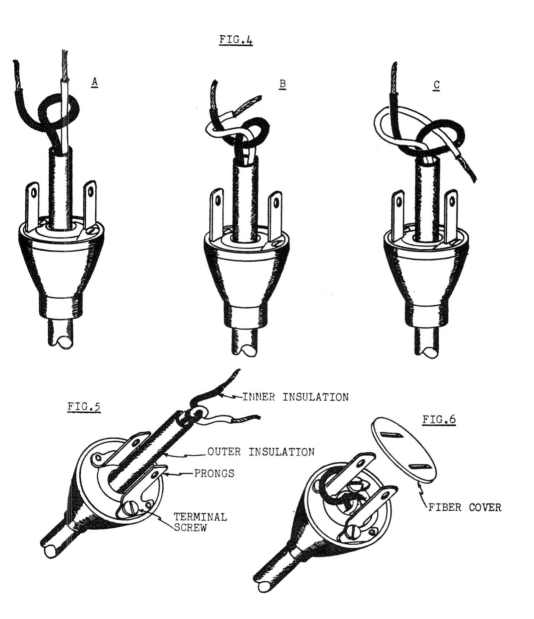

FIG.4

A

B

C

FIG.5

INNER INSULATION

OUTER INSULATION

PRONGS

TERMINAL
SCREW

FIG.6

FIBER COVER

#61 Female Plugs

How To: Replace a female appliance plug.

EXPLANATION: Female appliance plugs are used to provide a convenient method of disconnecting the line cord from the appliance. Female appliance plugs vary in size, and some have as many as three cavities. The female plug shown in the illustration is the type commonly used for coffee makers, waffle bakers, and other appliances and is, therefore, more often encountered. Moreover, the steps used to replace this female plug can be applied to all other varieties of this plug.

TOOLS AND MATERIALS NEEDED:

(a) a sharp paring knife

(b) a female appliance plug
(available at any electrical hardware store)

(c) a flatblade screwdriver (medium size)

STEPS: 1. Cut the defective plug off by cutting the line cord about one-half inch in front of the plug with a sharp paring knife. (*Figure 1*)

2. Take old plug to electrical hardware store and match new replacement plug to it.

3. Remove the screws that fasten the two halves of the new plug together. (*Figure 3*)

CAUTION: Take care not to drop the two nuts. (*Figure 6*)

4. Remove about three-quarters of an inch of insulation from the line cord wire ends with a sharp knife. (*Figure 2*)

CAUTION: Do not cut off any strands from wire ends.

5. Twist wire strands together tightly and form each wire end into a hook. (*Figure 3*)

FIG.1

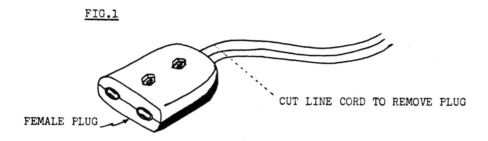

FEMALE PLUG

CUT LINE CORD TO REMOVE PLUG

FIG.2

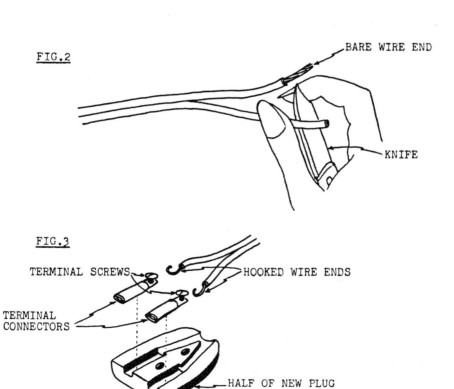

BARE WIRE END

KNIFE

FIG.3

TERMINAL SCREWS

HOOKED WIRE ENDS

TERMINAL
CONNECTORS

HALF OF NEW PLUG

6. Loosen (do not remove) the two terminal screws located in terminal connectors. (*Figure 3*) Place the hooked wire ends under the terminal screws in a clockwise direction and tighten terminal screws securely. (*Figure 4*)

CAUTION: Do not overtighten terminal screws. Wire ends may be broken.

7. Place terminal connections into cavities in the plug body. (*Figure 5*)

8. Put other half of plug body in place and put plug body together with nuts and fastening screws. (*Figure 6*)

CAUTION: Make certain line cord wire ends do not touch each other. Check to be sure that wire is routed in plug groove and does not obstruct assembly.

#62 Terminals and Wire Connectors

How To: Connect a wire end to a terminal.

EXPLANATION: In an electrical circuit, any point to which a wire end is connected is called a terminal. Terminals provide a convenient means of connecting electrical parts to their respective wires. In appliances, the most common types of terminals used are the "terminal screw" and the "male terminal spade." Since each terminal secures wire differently, the preparation of the wire ends will depend upon the type of terminal used.

FIG.4

HOOKED WIRE ENDS OF LINE CORD
INSTALLED ON TERMINAL
CONNECTORS

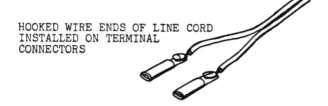

FIG.5

TERMINAL CONNECTORS
INSTALLED IN HALF
OF NEW PLUG

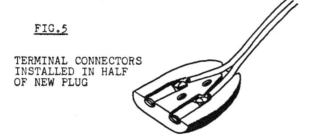

FIG.6

NUTS

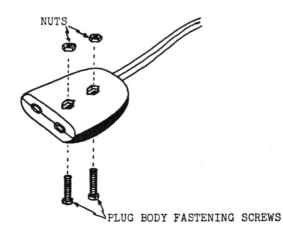

PLUG BODY FASTENING SCREWS

Tools and Materials Needed:

> (a) a flatblade screwdriver (medium size)
>
> (b) a sharp paring knife
>
> (c) a solderless wire connector (size and type as required) purchased at electrical hardware store
>
> (d) a crimping tool (for solderless wire connectors), available at local electrical hardware store
>
> (e) a pair of long-nose pliers
>
> (f) an emery board

Steps:

1. Prepare the wire end for connection to terminal screw.

   > NOTE: A wire may be connected to a terminal screw in one of two ways. In the first, the bare wire end is formed into a hook. The hooked wire end is then placed under the head of the terminal screw. In the second, an appropriate type of solderless terminal connector is first attached to the wire end. The terminal connector is then placed under the terminal screw.

2. To prepare the hooked wire type of connection, first remove about one-half inch of wire covering (insulation) from the wire end. (*Figure 1*) Use a sharp paring knife to cut through the insulation and pull the cut insulation off the wire end. (*Figure 2*)

   > CAUTION: When cutting insulation, make certain that copper wire is not nicked or otherwise damaged by knife.

3. If the wire uncovered is solid (one single thick strand of copper), simply form the bare end into a hook with the tip of a pair of long-nose pliers. (*Figure 3*)

FIG.1

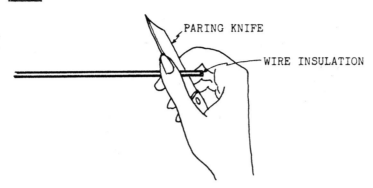

PARING KNIFE

WIRE INSULATION

FIG.2

SOLID BARE WIRE

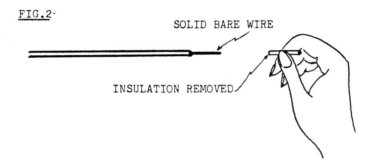

INSULATION REMOVED

FIG.3

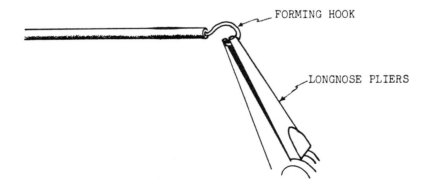

FORMING HOOK

LONGNOSE PLIERS

4. If the wire uncovered is stranded (many strands of fine wire) (*Figure 4*), twist the strands together tightly with fingers (*Figure 5*); then form it into a hook with the tip of the long-nose pliers. (*Figure 6*)

5. Place the bare wire hook under the loosened terminal screw, with the hook end facing the direction in which the screw tightens (clockwise). Tighten the terminal screw securely with a screwdriver. (*Figures 7 and 8*)

CAUTION: Do not overtighten terminal screw.

CAUTION: Make sure that none of the wire insulation (covering) gets under the terminal screw to prevent good contact.

CAUTION: Only *one* hooked wire end should be placed under any one terminal screw. If more than one wire is to be connected to a single terminal screw, the wire ends must first be prepared with an appropriate solderless terminal connector. (*Figure 9*) The steps that follow describe the procedures for installing solderless terminal connectors on wire ends for use under terminal screws.

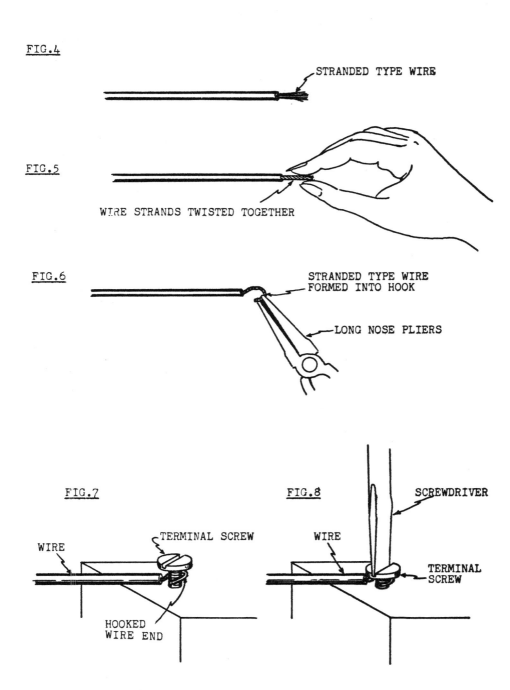

FIG.4

STRANDED TYPE WIRE

FIG.5

WIRE STRANDS TWISTED TOGETHER

FIG.6

STRANDED TYPE WIRE
FORMED INTO HOOK

LONG NOSE PLIERS

FIG.7

TERMINAL SCREW

WIRE

HOOKED
WIRE END

FIG.8

SCREWDRIVER

WIRE

TERMINAL
SCREW

6. Remove about one-half inch of insulation from the wire end. Insert the bare wire end into the wire connector as far as insulation permits. (*Figure 10*)

7. Fasten the wire connector to the wire by placing it halfway into the appropriate size jaw opening of the crimping tool and squeezing the tool handles together hard. (*Figure 11*)

NOTE: Solderless terminal connectors are made available in many sizes and types. Three important specifications are to be considered when selecting solderless terminal connectors for use with terminal screws. They are: the size (thickness) of the wire on which it is to be installed; the size (thickness) of the terminal screw body onto which it will connect; and the necessary shape of the terminal connector (spade- or ring-shaped). (*Figure 9*) It is always best to take the old (original) terminal connector along with you to the hardware store so that it can be matched with the one to be purchased.

8. When the male terminal spade is used instead of a terminal screw, the wire end must be prepared with a solderless female terminal connector, which may be purchased in any electrical hardware store.

FIG.9   SOLDERLESS TERMINAL CONNECTORS USED WITH TERMINAL SCREWS

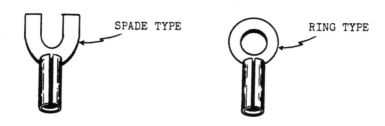

SPADE TYPE   RING TYPE

FIG.10

WIRE   BARE WIRE END

FIG.11

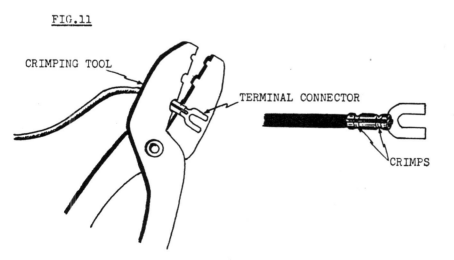

CRIMPING TOOL

TERMINAL CONNECTOR

CRIMPS

9. To prepare the wire end and to install a female terminal connector, refer to steps 6 and 7 for the necessary procedures.

10. Clean the male terminal spade of any dust or dirt by sanding it lightly with an emery board. (*Figure 12*)

11. Connect the female terminal to the male terminal by pushing it on. (*Figure 13*)

#63 Splicing Wires

How To: Join wires with solderless wire connectors.

Explanation: In electrical terms the joining of two or more electric wires is commonly referred to as "splicing." When properly made, a splice produces a wire connection that is a good mechanical bond (wires do not come apart) and a good electrical bond (does not obstruct the flow of electricity). The two splicing techniques described in the following steps can be adapted to cover practically all repair situations that require the joining of wires.

Tools and Materials Needed:

(a) a sharp paring knife

(b) a solderless sleeve connector
(size to correspond with size of the wires to be spliced)

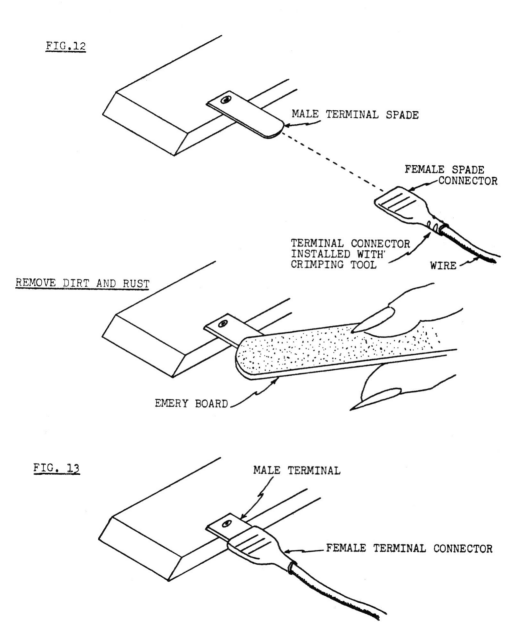

FIG.12

MALE TERMINAL SPADE

FEMALE SPADE
CONNECTOR

TERMINAL CONNECTOR
INSTALLED WITH
CRIMPING TOOL

WIRE

REMOVE DIRT AND RUST

EMERY BOARD

FIG. 13

MALE TERMINAL

FEMALE TERMINAL CONNECTOR

(c) a length of "spaghetti" insulation (pre-formed, sleeve-shaped insulating material available in various diameters and lengths from electrical hardware, electronics, or radio-TV repair stores)

(d) a crimping tool

(e) a wire nut, available from local electrical hardware store (size is determined by the size and number of wires being joined)

(f) a small piece of fine sandpaper (1" square)

(g) a pair of pliers

STEPS:

1. Select the type of splice which would best meet your repair need. (*Figures 1 and 2*)

   NOTE: The splice shown in *Figure 1* employs a solderless sleeve connector and is used whenever space and the routing of the wires in the appliance demand a continuous, non-bulky splice. The splice shown in *Figure 2* uses a wire nut (simple to install) and can be used whenever space is not a problem or the insulating protection afforded by the wire nut is needed.

2. To complete the splice shown in *Figure 1*, remove a length of insulation (from each wire end) equal to the length of the solderless sleeve connector to be used. Cut the insulation with a sharp paring knife and pull it from the wire ends. (*Figure 3*)

3. Clean the wire ends carefully by wiping them gently with fine sandpaper.

4. Next, cut a piece of spaghetti insulation twice the length of the solderless sleeve connector. Slip the spaghetti insulation onto one of the wires to be spliced. (*Figure 4*)

5. Slip both wire ends (from opposite directions) into the sleeve connector. (*Figure 5*)

FIG.1

SPLICING SLEEVE WITH SPAGHETTI INSULATION
COVERING IN PLACE

FIG.2

WIRE NUT

FIG.3

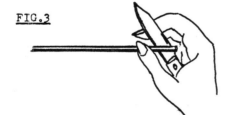

INSULATION BEING REMOVED

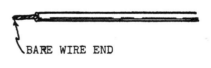

BARE WIRE END

FIG.4

SPAGHETTI INSULATION

BARE WIRE ENDS

FIG.5

SLEEVE CONNECTOR (SPLICING SLEEVE)

6. Fasten the sleeve connector to the wires by placing a crimp in the center of the sleeve connector with the crimping tool. (*Figure 6*)

7. Slide the spaghetti insulation into place over the sleeve connector to complete the splice. (*Figure 1*)

8. To complete the splice shown in *Figure 2*, remove about one-half inch of insulation from each wire end with a paring knife. (*Figure 3*)

9. Clean the wire ends with sandpaper. (*Figure 4*)

10. Cross the wire ends (*Figure 7*) and twist wires together with fingers. (*Figure 8*) Complete the twist to the end of the wires with a pair of pliers. (*Figure 9*)

11. Press wire nut onto wire ends and turn nut clockwise until wire nut is securely attached.

    CAUTION: Make certain that the wire nut covers all of twisted wire ends. If not, length of twisted wire ends must be shortened.

    SPECIAL NOTE: Wire nuts are made from plastic or porcelain. Plastic wire nuts can be used in situations in which they will not be subjected to extreme heat. Porcelain wire nuts should be used whenever they are to be exposed to high temperatures.

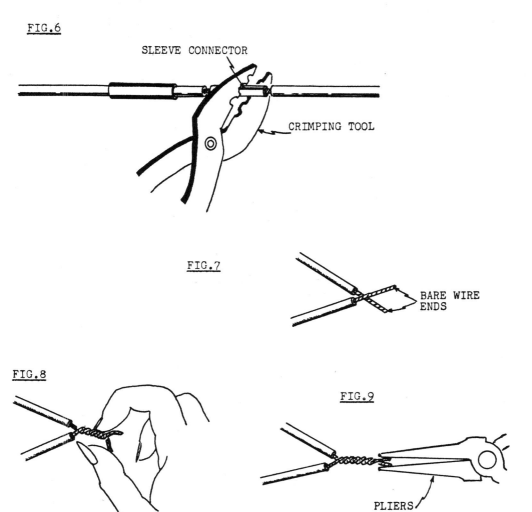

FIG.6

SLEEVE CONNECTOR

CRIMPING TOOL

FIG.7

BARE WIRE ENDS

FIG.8

FIG.9

PLIERS

#64 Insulating Wires

How To: Insulate wire.

Explanation: The material (insulation) used to cover electrical wires acts as a barrier to the flow of electricity. Different materials are used to cover wire. In addition to their electrical insulating qualities, these materials must be capable of withstanding the extreme conditions to which they may be exposed in appliances. These conditions include the presence of oil or grease, high degree of heat, and the presence of excessive moisture. Therefore, whenever it becomes necessary to replace wire insulation, the material used must have the same qualities as that of the original covering.

Tools and Materials Needed:

(a) a pair of scissors

(b) a roll of ½" wide electrical insulating tape (electrical friction tape, electrical plastic tape, or fiberglass tape) selected according to the specific application.

Steps: 1. Determine the type of insulating material required.

NOTE: Electrical friction tape (cloth), electrical plastic tape, and fiberglass tape are three common types of insulating material that are readily available from any electrical hardware store. Moreover, they are easily applied and can fulfill the need for practically every wire repair that requires insulation. Friction tape is a cloth material that contains a black tar-like substance. It can be used for a general repair work as long as it is not exposed to extreme heat or moisture. Plastic tape is a strong elastic type material that is extremely useful whenever a high degree of electrical insulating quality (without bulk) is required. It is also a very effective insulator against moisture. However, it should not be used when it is likely to be exposed to heat. Fiberglass tape, because of its non-inflammable, heatproof characteristics, should be used whenever insulation is required in a condition of extreme heat. All of the insulating tapes discussed above are applied in the same manner and are described in the steps that follow.

2. Begin at a point on the wire about one inch from the bare section to be insulated. (*Figure 1*)

FIG.1

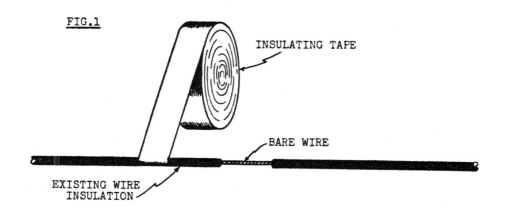

INSULATING TAPE

BARE WIRE

EXISTING WIRE
INSULATION

FIG.2

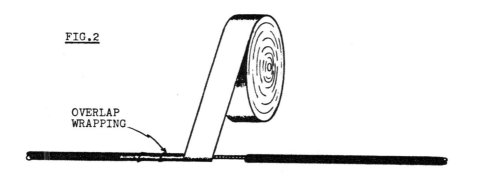

OVERLAP
WRAPPING

FIG.3

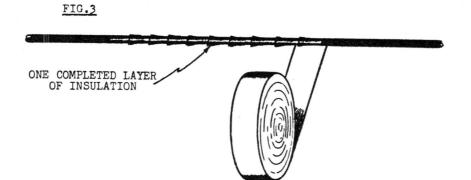

ONE COMPLETED LAYER
OF INSULATION

3. Hold the tape at an angle to the wire and wrap tape around wire. (*Figure 1*)

4. Overlap each turn one-half the width of the tape. (*Figure 2*)

5. Continue wrapping tape for at least one inch past the bare wire section to complete one layer of insulation. (*Figure 3*)

   NOTE: Two layers of insulating tape are generally used for added security, whenever the additional bulk thus created does not interfere with the routing (placement) of the wires.

6. Begin wrapping second layer of insulation from the point at which the first layer ended. (*Figure 4*)

7. Continue wrapping (overlap one-half the width of the tape each turn) back to where the first layer began and cut tape with scissors to complete the second layer. (*Figure 5*)

#65 Mending Heating Elements

How To: Mend broken heating element wire.

EXPLANATION: The practice of mending broken (parted) heating element wire is only a temporary measure. It is intended to restore the operation of an appliance for an emergency need, or when a new replacement element is not available from supply sources. When properly mended, however, the life of heating elements can be extended for many years. Rejoining broken (parted) heating element wire requires the use of fastening devices that can withstand the intense operating heat produced by the element wire. Three methods have proven to be the most effective means of mending element wire. They include the use of a mending sleeve, a nut and bolt, or a blind rivet. The most effective method of the three is the use of the blind rivet because of its tremendous

FIG.4

START OF SECOND LAYER

FIG.5

TWO LAYERS OF INSULATION COMPLETED

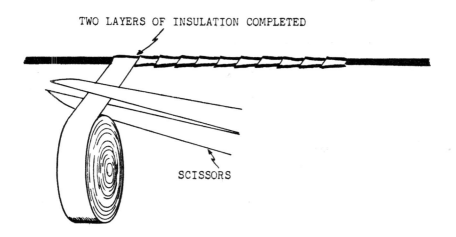

SCISSORS

holding power and the fact that it will not become loose. Otherwise, the selection of the type of fastener to be used will depend upon availability and/or the relative ease or difficulty of installation. The steps below describe the procedures for employing each of the three fasteners.

TOOLS AND MATERIALS NEEDED:

All materials and tools listed are available from local electrical hardware stores.

Repair Method Employing Mending Sleeve

(a) a solderless sleeve wire connector

(b) a pair of pliers

Repair Method Employing Nut and Bolt

(a) a #6-32 brass nut and bolt

(b) a pair of long-nose pliers

(c) a flatblade screwdriver (medium size)

Repair Method Employing Blind Rivet

(a) a 1/8″ diameter × 3/16″ grip length steel blind rivet

(b) a back-up washer (1/8″ hole) for use with rivet

(c) a blind riveting tool

STEPS:

1. To rejoin broken element wire with a solderless sleeve connector, straighten approximately one-fourth inch of both wire ends with long-nose pliers. (*Figure 1*)

2. Insert the wire ends into the solderless sleeve connector. (*Figure 2*)

3. Crush the wire connector with a pair of pliers to complete the mend. (*Figure 3*)

4. To rejoin broken element wire with a brass nut and bolt, form both wire ends into loops. (*Figure 4*)

<u>FIG.1</u>

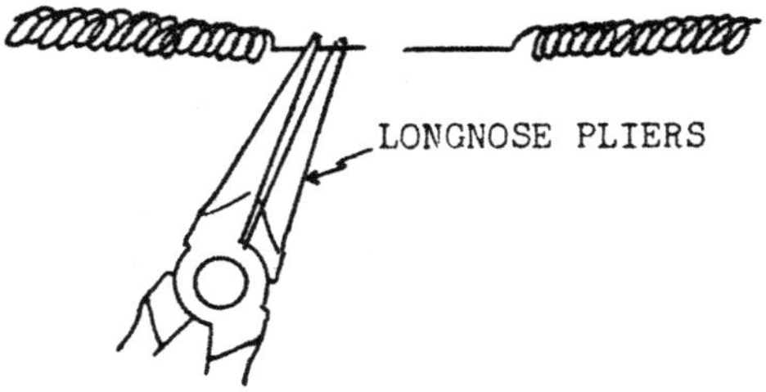

LONGNOSE PLIERS

<u>FIG.2</u>

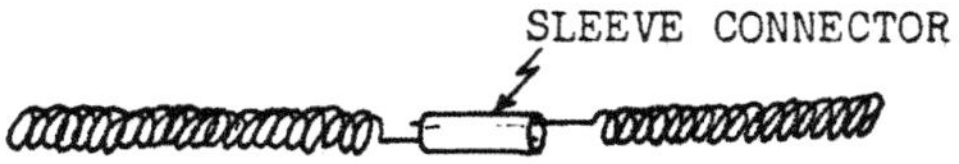

SLEEVE CONNECTOR

<u>FIG.3</u>

<u>FIG.4</u>

5. Insert bolt through wire loops and thread on the nut. (*Figure 5*)

6. Tighten the nut and bolt securely with a screwdriver and pliers to complete the mend. (*Figure 6*)

7. To rejoin broken heating element wire with a blind rivet, form both ends into loops. (*Figure 4*)

8. Insert rivet mandrel into rivet tool nosepiece. (*Figure 7*)

9. Insert the rivet through the wire loops and place back-up washer on bottom of rivet. (*Figure 8*)

10. Fasten the rivet with the riveting tool. Squeeze the handles of the tool firmly until the rivet mandrel is snapped free of rivet. (*Figure 9*)

11. This completes the mend. (*Figure 10*)

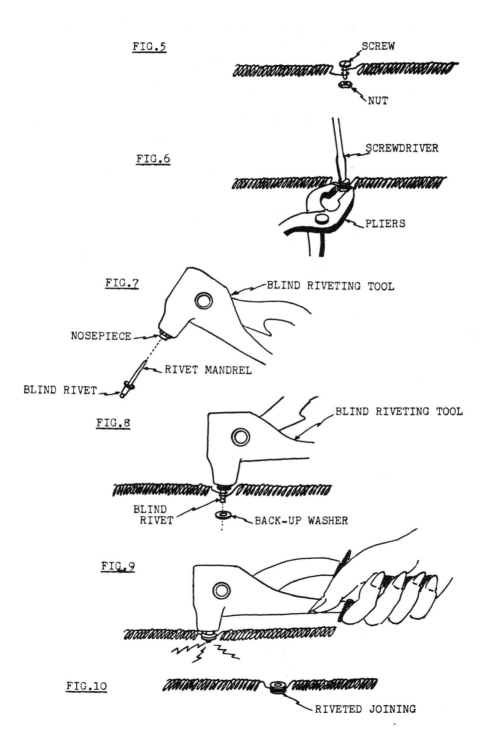

FIG.5

SCREW

NUT

FIG.6

SCREWDRIVER

PLIERS

FIG.7

BLIND RIVETING TOOL

NOSEPIECE

RIVET MANDREL

BLIND RIVET

FIG.8

BLIND RIVETING TOOL

BLIND RIVET

BACK-UP WASHER

FIG.9

FIG.10

RIVETED JOINING

#66 Connecting Heating Elements

How To: Connect heating element wire to a terminal screw.

Explanation: In many appliances, the heating element wires are connected (terminate) directly to a terminal screw. Inspection of an element wire that fails to heat will often disclose that the end of the element wire has burned or broken away from a terminal screw. A good heating element terminal connection must be electrically secure (good conductor of electricity), and it must also prevent the intense operating heat of the element wire from reaching and destroying the terminal screw. The steps below describe a method of reconnecting heating element wire to a terminal screw that satisfies both requirements.

Tools and Materials Needed:

(a) a pair of long-nose pliers

(b) a pair of universal pliers

Steps: 1. Remove the terminal nut by unscrewing it from the terminal screw with the universal pliers. (*Figure 1*)

2. Remove the two metal washers. Make certain that the broken piece of heating element wire located between the metal washers is also removed. (*Figure 2*)

3. Inspect the metal washers and terminal nut. If terminal nut and washers appear badly overheated (blackened or charred), replace them with new ones.

4. Straighten approximately two inches of the element wire end with the long-nose pliers. (*Figure 3*)

FIG.1

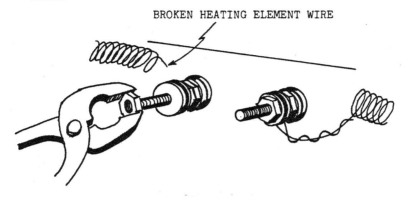

BROKEN HEATING ELEMENT WIRE

FIG.2

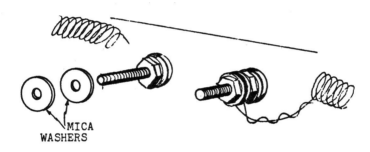

MICA
WASHERS

FIG.3

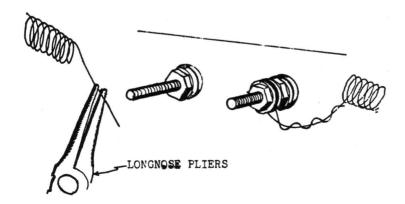

LONGNOSE PLIERS

5. Replace one metal washer on the terminal screw.

6. Wrap the element wire one turn around the terminal screw, allowing at least one inch of the wire to extend out from the screw. (*Figure 4*)

7. Insert the second metal washer onto the terminal screw. (*Figure 5*)

8. Replace the terminal nut and tighten it securely with the universal pliers. (*Figure 6*)

    CAUTION: Do not overtighten terminal nut. Element wire may be crushed and damaged.

9. Twist the end of the element wire extending out from the terminal screw back over the element wire (*Figure 5*) to complete the terminal connection.

#67 Plastic Knobs

How To: Mend a broken plastic appliance control knob.

EXPLANATION: Appliance control knobs crack most often at a point where they grip the metal shafts of switches.

TOOLS AND MATERIALS NEEDED:

(a) a small tube of plastic cement
(available at hardware stores and children's hobby shops)

(b) a spool of nylon sewing thread

<u>FIG.4</u>

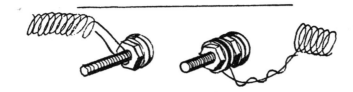

<u>FIG.5</u>

TWIST WIRE BACK

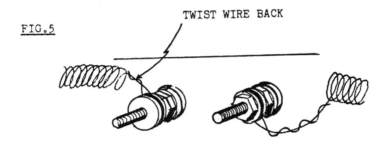

<u>FIG.6</u>

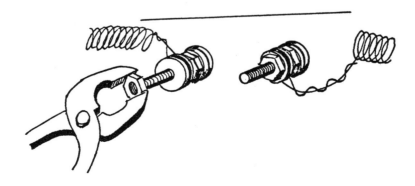

STEPS:

1. Locate small piece of control knob which has been broken off. (*Figure 1*)

2. Carefully apply plastic cement from tube along the edges of the break. (*Figure 2*)

3. Replace the broken piece onto the knob and hold the piece firmly in place until the cement begins to dry (about one minute). (*Figure 3*)

4. Wrap the shaft section of the knob with nylon thread. (*Figure 4*) Make certain thread is pulled tight after each turn. Wind thread as close together as possible.

5. Coat the wound thread with plastic cement. Allow cement to dry thoroughly (about two hours) to complete the mend.

#68 Plastic Parts

How To: Mend cracked or broken plastic appliance parts.

EXPLANATION: The use of plastic materials in the construction of modern appliances is quite extensive. In general, plastic materials have many advantages over some of the metal materials they have replaced. One important advantage is that plastics are good insulators, and when made into appliance parts that are to be handled by the user, they greatly reduce the possibility of electric shock. In normal use, plastic appliance parts can endure as well as most of the previously used metals. Under abnormal conditions, however, such as when an appliance is dropped or struck, plastic components can be cracked or pieces can be broken off.

TOOLS AND MATERIALS NEEDED:

(a) a tube of plastic cement

(b) an epoxy cement kit (transparent)

(c) a small roll of masking tape (¾" wide)

FIG.1

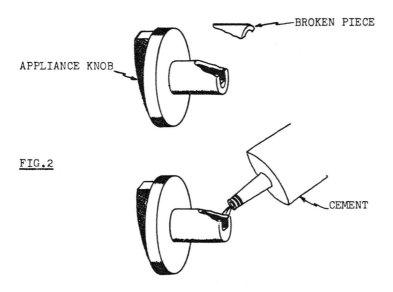

BROKEN PIECE

APPLIANCE KNOB

FIG.2

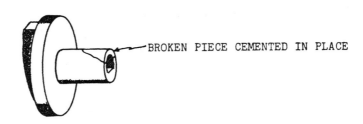

CEMENT

FIG.3

BROKEN PIECE CEMENTED IN PLACE

FIG.4

NYLON THREAD WRAPPING

(d) a sheet of fine (#00) sandpaper

(e) a handful of fine steel wool

(f) a tube of toothpaste

(g) a number of wooden toothpicks

STEPS:

1. Determine the type of cement to be used for the plastic repair.

   NOTE: Many types of plastic materials are used for the construction of appliance components. For mending purposes, however, we shall only determine how the particular type of plastic to be mended will respond to the two commonly used types of cement. For some plastics, plastic cement acts as a solvent and rejoins cracked or broken pieces by actually welding them together. There are other types of plastic materials, however, that are not affected by plastic cement. For these it is best to use an epoxy cement.

2. To pretest the effectiveness of plastic cement, apply a small drop of the cement with a toothpick on a portion of the plastic part that cannot normally be seen.

3. Stir the drop of cement with a toothpick. If the plastic surface is softened (gummy) by the cement, it indicates that the plastic cement will work well. If the plastic remains hard, the epoxy cement will have to be used instead.

4. To mend plastic with plastic cement, first make sure that the pieces to be joined are clean. Wash plastic parts with soap and water to remove any oil or grease. Dry thoroughly.

5. Apply plastic cement sparingly along cracked edges of both broken pieces. (*Figure 1*)

6. Press pieces together firmly and hold them together steadily until cement starts to harden (about one minute).

7. Place a strip of masking tape across (at right angles to) the cemented crack. (*Figure 2*) Pull masking tape taut so that it holds the pieces firmly in place.

FIG.1

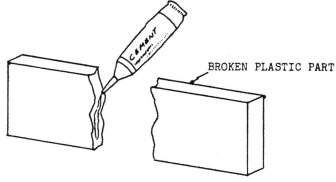

BROKEN PLASTIC PART

FIG.2

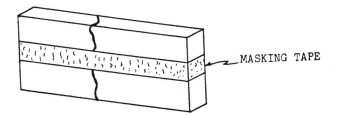

MASKING TAPE

8. Allow plastic cement to dry completely (about two hours). Then remove masking tape. (*Figure 3*)

9. Inspect the mend. If mended crack mars the appearance of the appliance, it may be refinished to improve its appearance.

    NOTE: Besides restoring the finish of mended plastic parts, it may also be desirable at times to remove scratches that accumulate through normal use on the surface of plastic parts and to restore their original luster. This may be accomplished by following steps 10 through 13 as outlined in this section.

10. For mended cracks and deep scratches, first smooth the area by rubbing it *lightly* with a piece of fine sandpaper. (*Figure 4*)

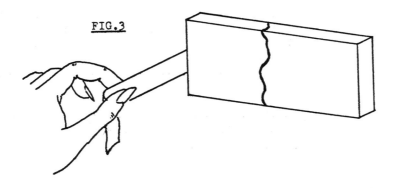

FIG.3

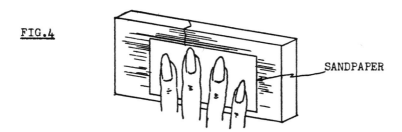

FIG.4

SANDPAPER

11. After all deep scratches have been removed with sandpaper, form a pad with fine steel wool and rub area with steel wool until all fine scratches left by sandpaper are removed. Area should now take on a smooth but hazy appearance. (*Figure 5*)

12. Thoroughly dampen a piece of soft cloth with water. Fold the cloth into a tight pad. (*Figure 6*) Squeeze about one inch of toothpaste onto the cloth and polish plastic area (rub back and forth in straight, even strokes) until luster is obtained.

13. Wipe toothpaste off with soft, clean dry cloth and inspect degree of luster obtained. If it is unsatisfactory, repeat polishing with more toothpaste until finish is satisfactorily restored.

14. To mend plastic components with epoxy cement, first clean plastic with soap and water to remove all dirt, oil, or grease.

15. Prepare an adequate quantity of epoxy cement for the repair at hand. (*Figure 7*)

    NOTE: Epoxy cement is supplied in kits containing two ingredients. These ingredients must be mixed in equal quantities just prior to use. Once the two ingredients are mixed, the hardening process begins.

    CAUTION: Use care and avoid unnecessary contact with epoxy ingredients when working with them. Always follow manufacturer's precautions and instructions.

16. After epoxy cement has been prepared, complete the application of the cement and refinishing of plastic surface (if needed) as outlined in steps 5, 6, and 7. However, be sure to allow epoxy cement 24 hours to set (cure) before removing masking tape or trying to restore plastic finish.

FIG.5

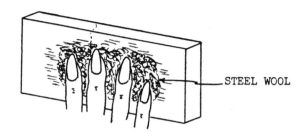

STEEL WOOL

FIG.6

 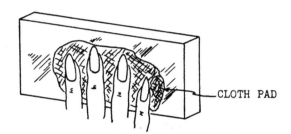

CLOTH PAD

FIG.7

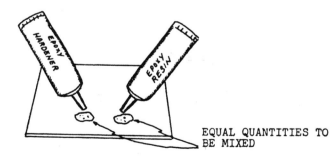

EQUAL QUANTITIES TO
BE MIXED

<u>GLOSSARY</u>

<u>SMALL FLATBLADE SCREWDRIVER</u>

<u>PHILLIPS TYPE</u>

<u>MEDIUM FLATBLADE SCREWDRIVER</u>

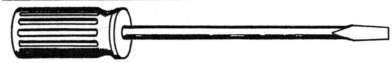

<u>LARGE FLATBLADE SCREWDRIVER</u>

<u>LONG NOSE PLIERS</u>

<u>DIAGONAL CUTTING PLIERS</u>

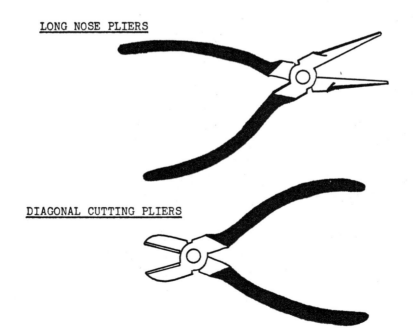

GLOSSARY

UNIVERSAL PLIERS

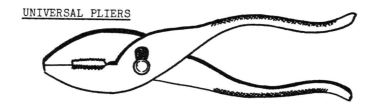

CRIMPING TOOL

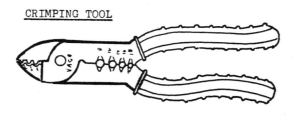

BLIND RIVETING TOOL

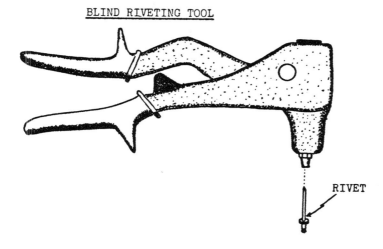

RIVET

ABOUT THE AUTHOR

Michael Squeglia is a teacher of appliance repair at the secondary level of the New York City public school system. He organized the first course of study in this field for the New York City Board of Education. Working with industry, he developed innovative curricula in manpower programs designed to train appliance technicians.

Mr. Squeglia acquired his practical knowledge in 1947 when he began work as a radio-TV-appliance technician and later as an operator of his own service shop in the New York metropolitan area.

He is the author of numerous other books including *Automatic Washers*, *Room Air Conditioners*, *Electric Dryers and Dishwashers*, each prepared for the National Appliance Radio TV Dealers Association (N.A.R.D.A.).